FICHTE IN BERLIN

McGill-Queen's Philosophy of Religion Series
Series editors: Garth Green and George Di Giovanni

The McGill-Queen's Philosophy of Religion Series is dedicated to studies at the interface of philosophy and religion, primarily but not exclusively in the context of the Western traditions of philosophy and theology – whether the studies are historical or systematic in character, whether their motivating interests originate on the side of philosophy or of religion, and whatever their philosophical idioms or religious commitments. The goal is to clarify the nature of a philosophy of religion, and at the same time to promote it as a discipline by illustrating its relevance to philosophy, religious studies, and theology. These are the fields of study from which the series draws its main audience, among professionals as well as students. The series publishes in English and also invites translations of primary texts or important secondary sources. These publications are usually single-authored, without excluding the possibility of significant edited volumes.

1 Fichte in Berlin
  The 1804 Wissenschaftslehre
  Matthew Nini

FICHTE IN BERLIN

THE 1804 WISSENSCHAFTSLEHRE

MATTHEW NINI

McGill-Queen's University Press
Montreal & Kingston ◆ London ◆ Chicago

ISBN 978-0-2280-2131-5 (cloth)
ISBN 978-0-2280-2132-2 (paper)
ISBN 978-0-2280-2152-0 (ePDF)
ISBN 978-0-2280-2153-7 (ePUB)

Legal deposit second quarter 2024
Bibliothèque nationale du Québec

Printed in Canada on acid-free paper that is 100% ancient forest free (100% post-consumer recycled), processed chlorine free

This book has been published with the help of a grant from the Canadian Federation for the Humanities and Social Sciences, through the Awards to Scholarly Publications Program, using funds provided by the Social Sciences and Humanities Research Council of Canada.

Funded by the Government of Canada | Financé par le gouvernement du Canada | Canada | Canada Council for the Arts | Conseil des arts du Canada

We acknowledge the support of the Canada Council for the Arts.
Nous remercions le Conseil des arts du Canada de son soutien.

McGill-Queen's University Press in Montreal is on land which long served as a site of meeting and exchange amongst Indigenous Peoples, including the Haudenosaunee and Anishinabeg nations. In Kingston it is situated on the territory of the Haudenosaunee and Anishinaabek. We acknowledge and thank the diverse Indigenous Peoples whose footsteps have marked these territories on which peoples of the world now gather.

LIBRARY AND ARCHIVES CANADA CATALOGUING IN PUBLICATION
Title: Fichte in Berlin : the 1804 Wissenschaftslehre / Matthew Nini.
Other titles: 1804 Wissenschaftslehre
Names: Nini, Matthew, author.
Description: Series statement: McGill-Queen's philosophy of religion series ; 1 | Includes bibliographical references and index.
Identifiers: Canadiana (print) 20230595421 | Canadiana (ebook) 2023059543X | ISBN 9780228021322 (paper) | ISBN 9780228021315 (cloth) | ISBN 9780228021537 (EPUB) | ISBN 9780228021520 (ePDF)
Subjects: LCSH: Fichte, Johann Gottlieb, 1762-1814—Criticism and interpretation. | LCSH: Idealism, German. | LCSH: Philosophy, German—19th century.
Classification: LCC B2848 .N56 2024 | DDC 193—dc23

CONTENTS

PREFACE

This book is a study of a particular period in the life and work of the philosopher Johann Gottlieb Fichte (1762–1814). It attempts a close reading of the major texts that Fichte produced in Berlin between 1804 and 1806 and argues that these texts constitute a whole. The centrepiece of this period is the second set of lectures on the *Wissenschaftslehre* from 1804, a difficult text whose argument I have attempted to reconstruct in detail. "*Wissenschaftslehre*" is not just the name that Fichte gives to the theoretical part of his philosophy. The word also designates an intellectual exercise aimed at achieving an insight, one that grounds a certain manner of living in the world as a knowing subject. Fichte's goal as a philosopher was to have his students achieve this insight, allowing them to think for themselves and become philosophers in their own right. If Fichte produced some seventeen versions of his *Wissenschaftslehre* over the course of twenty years, it was because different audiences with different concerns required different conditions in order for the foundational insight to be achieved. This does not mean that Fichte did not struggle with the articulation of individual versions, or that their clarity and effectiveness remain consistent. What is essential is the insight, and this remains. *Reconstruction* is an essential part of achieving insight. One does what Fichte does until one starts to perform the exercise for oneself. In this spirit, I do not consider this book to be just a historical account. Its self-aware reconstruction of Fichte's argument is, like every serious book on Fichte, an original and personal rendition of the exercise that is *Wissenschaftslehre*. I have chosen to do this with a lesser-known (though no less robust) version of the *Wissenschaftslehre* that emphasizes the role of performing the *Wissenschaftslehre* as an integral part of the completion of the content of the *Wissenschaftslehre* itself. This book is therefore my attempt to facilitate the reader's own philosophical insight. The book's success can only be measured by whether or not it has helped the reader perform the philosophical exercise that is herein presented in its historical context.

My work would not have been possible were it not for my teachers at McGill, Garth Green, George di Giovanni, and Torrance Kirby, as well as my host in Freiburg, Philipp Schwab. I wrote this book during my *Wanderjahre*. My guides and hosts all deserve genuine thanks: Josefine Wickenbrock in Freiburg; Maren Coors in Hildesheim; Mirna Marić in Zagreb; Veronika Zikmundová and Robert Kanócz in Prague; Vesna Topić in Belgrade and then Sarajevo; Christophe Guillet and Duncan McDonald in Montreal; Hadi Fakhoury and Sean McGrath, whose friendship transcends geography. Finally, I would like to thank Isabelle Lindsay, who made the index and whose help was indispensable during the editorial process.

This book reworks material that has previously appeared elsewhere. Chapter 1 borrows from "The System Must Construct Itself. Manifestation and Autopoiesis in Fichte's 1804 Wissenschaftslehre," in *Perspectives on the Self – Reflexivity in the Humanities*, eds. Vojtěch Kolman and Tereza Matějčková (Berlin: De Gruyter, 2022), 61–79. Chapter 5 relies in part on "Bildung as Standpoint: Philosophy of Religion as Philosophy of Culture in Fichte's Middle Period," in *Annali online della Didattica e della Formazione Docente*, 12 (2020), 327–41. I thank the editors for allowing me to do so.

Freiburg-im-Breisgau,
Summer 2023

ABBREVIATIONS

1804/2 *The Science of Knowing: J.G. Fichte's 1804 Lectures on the Wissenschaftslehre.* Translated by Walter E. Wright. Albany: SUNY, 2005.

AA *Immanuel Kants gesammelte Schriften (Akademieausgabe).* 22 vols to date. Berlin: de Gruyter, 1902–.

CPJ Kant, Immanuel. *Critique of the Power of Judgment.* Edited by Paul Guyer. Translated by Paul Guyer and Eric Matthews. Cambridge: Cambridge University Press, 2000.

CPR Kant, Immanuel. *Critique of Pure Reason.* Edited and translated by Paul Guyer and Allen W. Wood. Cambridge: Cambridge University Press, 1998.

DM Ivaldo, Marco. "The Doctrine of Manifestation in Fichte's Principien (1805)." Translated by Garth Green. *Laval Philosophique et Théologique* 72 (2016): 35–64.

EPW Fichte, Johann Gottlieb. *Early Philosophical Writings.* Edited and translated by Daniel Breazeale. Ithaca: Cornell University Press, 1988.

ES Gueroult, Martial. *L'évolution et la structure de la doctrine de la science chez Fichte.* 2 vols. Paris: Belles Lettres, 1930.

FEW Fichte, Johann Gottlieb. *Foundation of the Entire Wissenschaftslehre and Related Writings (1794–95).* Edited and translated by Daniel Breazeale. Oxford: Oxford University Press, 2021.

FiG *J.G. Fichte im Gespräch. Berichte der Zeitgenossen.* Edited by Erich Fuchs, in cooperation with Reinhard Lauth and Walter Schieche. 8 vols. Stuttgart-Bad Cannstatt: Frommann-Holzboog, 1978–2012.

FNR Fichte, Johann Gottlieb. *Foundations of Natural Right.* Edited by Frederick Neuhouser. Translated by Michael Baur. Cambridge: Cambridge University Press, 2000.

FTP Fichte, Johann Gottlieb. *Foundations of Transcendental Philosophy (Wissenschaftslehre) Nova Methodo*. Edited and translated Daniel Breazeale. Ithaca: Cornell University Press, 1992.

GA *J.G. Fichte-Gesamtausgabe der Bayerischen Akademie der Wissenschaften*. Edited by Erich Fuchs, Reinhard Lauth, and Hans Gliwitzky. Stuttgart-Bad Cannstatt: Frommann-Holzboog, 1964–.

IWL Fichte, Johann Gottlieb. *Introductions to the Wissenschaftslehre and Other Writings*. Edited and translated by Daniel Breazeale. Indianapolis: Hackett, 1994.

MPW Jacobi, Friedrich Heinrich. *The Main Philosophical Writings and the Novel Allwill*. Edited and translated by George di Giovanni. Montreal and Kingston: McGill-Queen's University Press, 1994.

PR *The Philosophical Rupture between Fichte and Schelling: Selected Texts and Correspondence (1800–1802)*. Edited and translated by Michael G. Vater and David W. Wood. Albany: SUNY, 2012.

SE Fichte, Johann Gottlieb. *System of Ethics*. Edited and translated by Daniel Breazeale and Günter Zöller. Cambridge: Cambridge University Press, 2005.

SW *Johann Gottlieb Fichtes sämmtliche Werke*. Edited by I.H. Fichte. 8 vols. Berlin: Viet & Co., 1845–46; and *Johann Gottlieb Fichtes nachgelassene Werke*. 3 vols. Bonn: Adolphus-Marcus, 1834–35.

SWN Schiller, Friedrich. *Schillers Werke, Nationalausgabe*. Edited by Julius Petersen et al. 43 vols to date. Weimar: Hermann Böhlaus Nachfolger, 1943–.

FICHTE IN BERLIN

INTRODUCTION
On Fichte's Development up to 1804

J.G. Fichte's thought is inextricably linked to the word *Wissenschaftslehre*. This expression, which has entered the English language as a term of art ("Science of Knowing" and "Doctrine of Science" are older, inadequate attempts at translation), is the name given to Fichte's theoretical philosophy and the title of some seventeen works, either books or series of lectures, of which he is the author.[1] Superficially, these works, written over the course of twenty years, seem radically different from one another, addressing different issues, using different terms, and making different arguments. Fichte, however, maintained that his most important insights remained unchanged throughout his career, each work attempting to unfold the single idea that is *Wissenschaftslehre* (WL).

While at least outwardly problematic in regard to each new version of the WL, this assertion becomes particularly difficult to accept in regard to the evolution that Fichte's thought underwent at the turn of the century. The first versions of the WL, written in Jena – the 1794 *Foundation of the Entire Wissenschaftslehre*, the 1796–99 lectures on the *Wissenschaftslehre Nova Methodo*, and their companion texts – present a cohesive philosophical vision: the attempt at reconciling freedom and necessity in view of giving an account of human subjectivity. But from 1800 onwards, the WL changes radically in its presentation. In the interval, Fichte lost his professorship at Jena and moved to Berlin, where he had become a private lecturer and tutor. An accusation of atheism made in Jena and the ensuing controversy still haunted him. Moreover, major philosophical disputes with his contemporaries meant that he was forced to mount a defence of the perceived weaknesses in his thought. The new versions of the WL produced in Berlin change nearly all the terms with which Fichte's students were familiar: gone are the *I* and *not-I* [*Ich*, *nicht Ich*], the check [*Anstoß*], fact/act [*Tathandlung*] and summons [*Aufforderung*]. They are replaced by new series of terms that would not remain consistent. Moreover, what was once a rigorously transcendental philosophy now used terms like *light*, *life*, and *the absolute* to convey a religious philosophy modeled on the Gospel of John. Fichte, however, remained adamant: the WL was what it had always been.

This problem, that of the passage [Übergang] from Jena to Berlin, cannot be addressed merely by comparing different versions of Fichte's work. Rather, the answer is to be found in the nature of WL itself. The WL is an exercise, one born of an insight that would have occurred to Fichte some time in 1793[2] and that he subsequently would have tried to capture in writing. The first written version of the WL, the 1794 *Foundation*, was meant to be a manual for the use of Fichte's students, a recipe book to which they could refer as they tried to reproduce for themselves what they had seen the master perform in front of them. Fichte himself was less their teacher than their guide, whose task it was to create the conditions for students to have an insight of their own. Once this insight occurred, the students would be able to reproduce the transcendental form of Fichte's philosophy in their own terms, with each individual arriving at the truth by means of their own work and after their own fashion. As Fichte famously said, "the kind of philosophy one chooses depends on the kind of person one is."[3]

There is, then, a sense in which Fichte's own articulations of the WL are incommensurable. Each was produced under different circumstances and for different audiences. Fichte's task was to elevate the novice to a standpoint from which rigorous systematic thinking was possible, not adjudicate its content.[4] At the same time, the insight always leads to the unfolding of a series of thoughts that, in their relations to one another, achieve certainty. To use the terms Fichte adopted in 1804, the journeyman philosopher does not *construct* a radically new system; rather one *reconstructs* for oneself what is true. Put even more simply, one comes to feel at home in the truth. In the progression of Fichte's own work, there is a tension between the ephemerality of philosophy as thought performed, and philosophy as science of science, a rigorous foundation for inquiry into what is true. This tension exists in regard to the relationship between different versions of the WL, as well as the relationship that WL has with particular philosophical sciences Fichte sees as being derived from his "science of science." Thinking with Fichte means conferring primacy to the practical over the theoretical. Hence, if Fichte's body of work does not achieve systematic coherence, it does at least constitute a series of complementary viewpoints. Each version of the WL is what each other might have been; the relationship of WL with each particular subject matter derived from it is always one that knowledge that is *certain* manifests itself as *a certain kind* of knowing. Even Fichte's claims of systematicity (that his WL never changed and that only five particular sciences are necessarily derived from WL as science of science) are rehearsed in different ways at different moments. Hence, the strengths of one version cannot simply be transplanted to fill the lacunae of another; each WL is a whole unto itself. Seeing WL as an exercise whose performance is itself an integral element of its content means radically re-evaluating the question of its continuity or discontinuity after Jena. The WL is always the same; the WL is also something new each time it is performed. Having performed the WL for oneself in the past means that one can compare the articulated record to the ineffable insight from which it arose – a kind of progress is possible, as the history of the elaboration of WL will bear out. And it is precisely in addressing the question of the relationship between insight and articulation that the second version of the WL from 1804 proves to be one of the most robust versions.

When Fichte announced the publication of the first version of the WL, the *Foundation*, in October 1794, he wrote that what was about to appear was, as the title suggests, only the groundwork for a larger project. It was to be followed the next year by a full system, divided into theoretical and practical parts.[5] On Fichte's definition, philosophy is always radical philosophy – that is, it must provide for its own foundation. The foundational principles are not to be situated beyond the particular philosophical reflection to which it gives rise but always as a part of it, at its root, its *radix*. In 1794, concerned with human subjectivity and the relationship that it, as free, has to all the forms of necessity that exercise constraint over it, Fichte offers a disciplined account of the idea of a foundation. In this context, the foundation at which he arrives is that facts of consciousness are always accompanied by an awareness of the subject's act of knowing and that the relationship between these two elements is necessary: put simply, consciousness and self-consciousness are inseparable. As Fichte himself was aware, this approach is conditioned by human finitude – hence the particularization of the first principle through the term "*I*." But intellectual spontaneity (the idea that nothing external causes our thoughts but that we ourselves are responsible for them) is not exhausted by the mere concept of individual consciousness, and Fichte would change tack in the *Nova Methodo* lectures to address the problem of intersubjectivity. It is also possible to begin from the other end entirely, still using the main insight of WL – that is, that thinking and thinking-of-thinking are inseparable. This approach would imply presuming the unity of knowledge and then seek to trace back all of knowing's discernable forms in consciousness to their original unity. Such a style would be more theoretical and certainly less malleable than the foundationalist approach; but it provides a considerable advantage as well: that of offering a systematic logic from which one can deduce other forms of knowing. Instead of being a "foundation," this articulation of the WL would be a *philosophia prima*[6] or "first philosophy" in Aristotle's terms, a thinking-about-thinking that subsequently grounds thinking particular subject matters.

Historically, this change of tack occurs at the critical junction that is the Jena-Berlin transition, though not all at once. Fichte will require several attempts over the course of several years before he is able to produce a coherent, articulate, and complete version of a first philosophy, namely, the second set of lectures on the WL in 1804. At least in part, the revision that produced the 1804 lectures was the product of an internal requirement of the WL itself – the need to integrate the discursive expression of the WL into its own theoretical standpoint. Put otherwise, Fichte was trying to create conditions for his listeners that would lead each of them to arrive at an insight that occurs all at once. There is no way to facilitate this insight other than to use language. Yet the discursive process that is language necessarily moves one further away from the immediacy of the desired insight. The solution is to integrate discourse into the very exercise that is WL. The listener must be aware that the insight sought cannot be captured by language but that for the sake of the exercise required, one must treat it *as if* it could be attained in this way, ultimately integrating one's presuppositions into the insight as the latter's product, not its source. In sum, to ask "what is *Wissenschaftslehre*?" is to already be doing it. This approach offers the most robust form of exercise Fichte had yet put forward. The 1804/2 lectures are in this regard perhaps his most successful attempt at outlining a philosophical exercise, one whose conclusions will ultimately coincide with its execution in the pure spontaneity that unites being (what is experienced immediately) and knowing (discourse), called *esse in mero actu*, "being in mere act."

The 1804 lectures treat the absolute principle that is *esse in mero actu* in two parts. The first is a theory of truth that seeks to arrive at it – in other words, to produce the insight into it (in Fichte's German, to see into it, *einsehen*). There are any number of ways one can achieve this, and the lecturer gives a sketch that encompasses all the fundamentals of this in the first four lectures. Their difficulty, however, leads to another, more specific discursive approach: a dialectic between two philosophical positions, realism and idealism. These generalized positions, the product of historical controversy about the WL, each presume that some lesser form of agency actually exhausts spontaneity. Realism considers it to be being, while for idealism it is knowing. Neither is aware of its own presuppositions, and both will therefore reason toward a logical end that creates an aporia that only WL can solve.

The second part of the 1804/2 lectures is a theory of appearance. If the insight is ultimately that thinking and thinking-of-thinking constitute a necessary relationship, then the pure activity or spontaneity found at the end of the first part must be confronted with the possibility of real content. The second part therefore juxtaposes the absolute with the possibility of any object of thought at all. In Fichte's day, one would call this placeholder content "facts of consciousness." In contemporary parlance, a philosophy of the facts of consciousness is enveloped by phenomenology, and it is precisely this term that Fichte uses to describe the theory of appearances. The phenomenology will have to demonstrate that the pure spontaneity that is the absolute, *esse in mero actu*, is not derived from particular acts of knowing – if anything, it is the other way around. Particular acts of knowing are themselves the image of the absolute. That is to say, within a particular, contingent act of knowing, one finds a necessary relationship that is spontaneity itself.

The 1804/2 ends with the assertion that all forms of scientific enquiry – that is, wherever an a priori functions as a regulative principle for treating particular content – can be structurally derived from the WL. The four broadest sciences derived from the science of science that is WL are religion, ethics, right, and natural philosophy.[7] Yet Fichte will not consecrate individual treatises to each of these disciplines. Rather, in the period that succeeds the presentation of the 1804/2 WL, he will produce other work, often popular lectures directed towards a general public. In what follows, it will be argued that even if these works occasionally have a problematic relationship to Fichte's WL, from them one can derive a further refinement of the phenomenology begun in the second part of 1804/2. Fichte's theory of appearance suggests that subjectivity is itself the appearance of the absolute. Subsequent texts on the philosophy of history (in *The Characteristics of the Present Age*, 1804–05), the *Principles of the Doctrines of God, Morals, and Right* (1805), and the philosophy of religion (in *The Way Towards the Blessed Life*, 1806) will build on this. They will establish that subjective experience is free but follows a priori principles and exists in time; that the absolute structure that is spontaneity manifests itself freely in time – said otherwise, that individual moral progress is indeed possible and is the trajectory of free reason; and that the realization of this progress is a vocation cultivated through interiority. The progression is one of carving out a space of interiority for the subject whose free activity is reason and simultaneously understands itself to be acting in such a manner.

In addition to the WL's own internal development, external factors, both historical and conceptual, play a role in this evolution. The major shift in approach that occurs from 1799 to 1804 is occasioned first by a historical event, the atheism controversy.[8] While the accusations of atheism that led to Fichte losing his professorship in Jena and fleeing to Berlin constitute a political event, he saw things otherwise. Retrospectively, he framed the event as a philosophical one, involving the role of religion in his system. In his defence, the *Divine Governance* essay that represents Fichte's philosophical stance during the controversy is in fact his first attempt at articulating a philosophy of religion on the principles of the WL.[9] The accusations that would continue to haunt Fichte years after the controversy subsided would impact not only the religious rhetoric that found its way into his work but also cultivate a desire to establish a "doctrine of religion" separate from but closely allied to the WL and further still, allow for the term "God" to be used as a synonym for the ineffable absolute at the heart of the 1804/2 WL.

Philosophical debates played an even greater role in the evolution of Fichte's thought. In the wake of the atheism controversy, Fichte's contemporaries seized the opportunity to voice criticisms of the perceived shortcomings of the WL. Partly because of the language of *I* and *not-I* but also because of a number of still-implicit aspects of the WL as a whole, Fichte's readers often conflated intellectual spontaneity with individual subjectivity. Yet as Fichte would work out in the period between the atheism controversy and the 1804 WL, this criticism made the same mistake of which it accused the WL. Schelling will criticize Fichte's *I* in the name of an absolute principle, claiming that the WL can serve as a legitimate beginning to philosophy but cannot arrive at the absolute principle that relates indifferently to both being and knowing. Jacobi, on the other hand, asserts that God, the unity of being and knowing, is absolutely in-itself and cannot be expressed, meaning that the WL cannot speak of God, and can only achieve systematicity by positing as absolute an idol of its own fabrication. In both instances, Fichte's interlocutor has been thinking according to a maxim of which he is not aware. For Schelling, this maxim is realism, the idea that we have immediate access to an absolute, such that being takes precedence over consciousness. For Jacobi, the maxim is idealism, the idea that what is in-itself is inaccessible. Consciousness is not consciousness-*of* being but merely consciousness in-and-for-itself, giving precedence to thought. But Fichte does not mean to caricature Jacobi as an idealist, nor Schelling as a realist. If anything, they were the opposite: Jacobi, the champion of lived faith as opposed to abstract philosophy, was an anti-idealist; for his part, Schelling had goals that, far from naïve realism, were close to those of the WL. The point is that both find themselves caught in a struggle that dissolves when one achieves a higher standpoint.

Yet Fichte will also learn something from both Jacobi and Schelling, incorporating elements of their thought into the new articulation of the WL. Indeed, the strengths and weaknesses of both are intimately related, and in reworking the WL, Fichte would not resort to simple refutation: both Schelling's and Jacobi's positions could be corrected using the WL itself, allowing for their insights to be incorporated into its new expression.

It is WL that propels the realism-idealism dialectic forward, and WL will itself be the highest point and resolution of the conflict.

Fichte admired Jacobi, and the use of feeling in the WL had always been closely allied to Jacobi's use of the term. Now, Fichte's new expression of the WL as first philosophy will accept Jacobi's stance but turn it on its head: Jacobi accepts a truth in-itself, but one that remains inaccessible by means of philosophy. Fichte will reply that the problem at hand is not arriving at what is true in-itself by means of philosophical construction but rather realizing that if we can do philosophy at all, it is because we proceed from this truth – we do not do philosophy; rather, we are ourselves the philosophical expression of reason. It is the truth that speaks us. This is a direct consequence of the cooperation of consciousness and self-consciousness, which do not exist outside each other but rather arise together in a single act: their relationship, in Fichte's terms, is genetic, sharing a common internal root, rather than an external cause.[10]

It is precisely this last point that will become clear to Fichte in the protracted debate with Schelling between 1800 and 1802. Through the bitter dispute with his former disciple, Fichte becomes aware that the unity of consciousness and self-consciousness, of knowing and knowing-of-knowing, cannot lie in one or the other. Discourse (thinking) and the truth it expresses (being) come apart when examined in judgment but are aboriginally united. This is the more abstract, logical expression of what we earlier called Fichte's integration of language into the WL. Schelling had already expressed something similar with the idea of indifference. Yet according to Fichte, Schelling's expression of the indifferent absolute does not live up to its own standards, still positing this absolute as external to being and thought. Yet this would mean that either it is a self-enclosed external being, validating Jacobi's criticisms, or is *prima facie* consciousness's own ground, its own activity, meaning that it is ultimately thinking. Again, Fichte's solution will be to claim that to be truly indifferent, the absolute must be found in the internal relationship between being and thinking. Another point learned from Schelling is what Fichte will come to call *attention*, a way of attending to our own inner activity that lets us see the relationship between thinking and awareness-of-thinking. What Schelling had called intellectual intuition, the subjective side of the Schellingian system, does not produce objects but rather incites one to realize that one is engaged in a certain kind of thinking about being. Fichte brings this a step further by insisting on its reversal: I do not "think" the absolute; rather, through becoming aware of a mental state of affairs, I realize that I dwell within it, and my thoughts are the product of this unity in activity.[11]

From 1800 onward, Fichte's conceptual challenge is to show that the corrective to both Jacobi's and Schelling's philosophies arises naturally from the WL itself. After a number of false starts, Fichte would offer a coherent account of this in 1804. The key lies in the evolution of one of the central concepts of the Jena WL, the *Tathandlung*. The insight at the heart of all versions of the WL is that thought is an activity that always belongs to an I, to self-consciousness, and that in the activity of thinking, recognition of the I will emerge. The *Ich* is therefore the foundational principle, but only when properly understood. As Fichte will write at the beginning of the 1794 *Foundation*, the foundational principle or *Grundsatz* is an activity to be performed rather than the object of a proof, emerging in its activity. It must therefore always have some objective content: when one engages in the activity that is objective knowing "out there," something else arises, concomitant with the object.[12] Yet this foundational principle cannot lead us to some fact apart from the consciousness in which it is present: the I does not posit some (objectified) principle outside of itself. Rather, it "posits itself through its own activity."[13] Crucial to the proper understanding of this foundational principle is that its constructive activity – the discursive side of it that generates objects in consciousness via judgment – is in fact the same activity that manifests itself as oblique self-recognition. Fichte reconciles these two aspects by means of the neologism *Tathandlung*, or fact/act.

Leading up to 1804, as he thought through the dilemma of the real and the ideal suggested by Schelling and Jacobi, it occurred to Fichte that the solution was to think his old concept of *Tathandlung* in terms of a unified, ineffable, and dynamic absolute. If the fact/act that is *Tathandlung* expresses a self-positing by dynamically linking statement and performance, the same could be done for the real and ideal: the absolute, above real and ideal, relates to the particular as an original to an image [*Bild*]. They have a shared origin, a genetic root, in the activity of image-making, otherwise called phenomenology [*Phänomenologie*]. Writes Fichte in 1804:

> Now, from the time it first arose, the WL has taught that the primary error of all previous systems has been that they began with something factical [*von Tatsachen auszugehen*] and posited the absolute therein. The WL, on the other hand, attests to another foundation, a fact that is *act* [*Tathandlung*], which in these lectures I have called *Genesis*, using a Greek term that is more readily understood than the German. Hence from the time it first arose, the WL ... has never admitted that the "I" as *found* and *perceived* is its principle. As something found, it is never a pure I, but always the individual person of each of us[.] Thus the WL has always testified that it recognizes the I as pure only as *produced*, and that, as a science, it never places the I at the pinnacle of its deductions, because the productive process will always stand higher than what is produced. This production of the I, and with it the whole of consciousness, is now our task.[14]

Tathandlung has now morphed into genesis. Moreover, Fichte has clarified that the first principle of WL has never been the I, or merely subjective spontaneity, but rather the process that produces this knowing I, *Tathandlung*/genesis.[15] Ultimately, genesis will imply that nothing really exists outside the absolute. The images that it "generates" are in fact constitutive of the absolute: particular subjects, free agents in the world, are themselves the necessary appearing of the absolute.

How can that which is entirely contained within itself produce an external world?[16] The answer is that the absolute's activity of imaging is contained within itself, a twofold movement of leaving in appearance and returning in knowing that constitutes a single outward movement that fashions an image [*Abbilden*]. To use the most frequent metaphor of 1804, it is *in* the ineffable light that is the absolute that what *is* appears.[17] In the end, consciousness, that for which the world *is*, is itself what is made manifest. Consciousness is the absolute's appearance.

This theory of appearing is the product of the transcendental argument structure found in the 1804/2 WL, emerging from the fullest form of the constant foundation of the WL, the fivefold synthesis. Explaining the fivefold synthesis and exploring how Fichte puts it to use is the chief theoretical task of this book. More activity than theory, the only way to give an account of it is to perform it. For now, a brief overview of what the fivefold synthesis is will have to suffice. Its initial version is the product of the first half of the 1804/2 text, its "theory of truth" (lectures 1–15) and prompts a phenomenological investigation into the absolute as one life. Near the end of this investigation, in 1804/2's twenty-sixth lecture, Fichte offers the definitive version of his fivefold synthesis:

1. Seeing sees into another, life.
2. But in so doing, it negates itself. Life is in fact the ground of seeing (reversal).
3. Seeing is part of life, life's own inwardness (life through seeing, seeing through life).
4. The terms therefore constitute a single movement, an externalization generated by the "throughness" of both terms (genetic version of seeing into life).
5. The genetic seeing into life is itself reversible; this externalization is internal to life; facticity belongs to genesis (reconstruction).[18]

Here, seeing stands in for knowing as a single activity that unifies two otherwise heterogeneous aspects: my knowledge of particulars, and my awareness, when knowing them, that I am in fact the knower engaged in this activity. That of which the knower is aware [*Einsehen; ich sehe ein*] is the very dynamism of intellectual activity itself. This is the heart of the exercise that is WL, my insight into knowing's self-positing. Through this awareness, I see that my spontaneous knowing is not the ground of the pure activity but rather the other way around: seeing is the form of life. Yet instead of describing it as a check [*Anstoß*], as he would have in the earlier WL, Fichte here considers it to be the activity that is life, always made incarnate in a particular living being. To live is to do so in the realm of the particular and finite, yet as image of an ineffable pure activity. The particular I is not the image of some universal I but rather the face of the hidden absolute, its features coming to light in the actions of particular consciousness. Life's dynamism and the activity of living things is therefore one single movement that is internal to the absolute.

These arguments can only be made lucid through a close reading of the text of the 1804/2 WL. Fichte intended for its hearers (and later, its readers as well) to engage in a transformative exercise that would first facilitate an insight and then serve as a guide to the elaboration of a personal philosophical position. It is only after we have been through the exercise that the fivefold synthesis and its consequent *Bildlehre*/phenomenology can become clear. Part 1 of this book is therefore dedicated to closely examining the 1804/2. Its two chapters treat the two parts of the text: chapter 1 examines the theory of truth contained in lectures 1–15; chapter 2 examines the theory of appearance contained in lectures 16–28.

Herein, I have tried to suggest that construing WL as a *philosophia prima* necessarily evokes a phenomenology: thinking-of-thinking must move downward to accommodate the possibility of thinking about something in particular. This is necessitated by the very structure of the WL, which sees experience as a constitutive element. Yet the series of popular lectures that follow the exposition of the WL in the years 1804 to 1806 do not offer a catalogue of the ways in which one can think about experience. Indeed, Fichte does not offer four treatises on the four ways of analyzing one's own experience of the world that, together with WL, constitute the fivefold expression of "science" [*Wissenschaft*]. Instead, Fichte seeks to secure the link between thinking-of-thinking and the possibility of thinking about what is external. The reasons for this approach can only be found in the WL itself. If the external appearance of images belongs to the absolute's appearing to itself, then what is external – objects of experience – are in some sense internal to the pure activity that is the absolute, *esse in mero actu*. The question, then, is how particular sciences can be the science-of some particular delimitation of experience *and* ultimately an expression of science-of-science. Since experience is always particular, one can build on this question by asking: how does *my* particular experience of the world belong to the absolute's appearance? Or better still: how is my subjective activity an expression of WL?

Fichte believes he can answer both questions through the development of a phenomenology as extension of the WL. The passage from science-of-science to particular sciences is also the passage from intellectual spontaneity in its broadest sense to *my agency*, the subjective experience of an individual. The world that Fichte wishes to describe is our world, the one in which my experiences really occur. Fichte not only seeks to elaborate a WL which allows me to describe the logical structures of my action in the world, but a philosophy that allows me to feel at home in that world. To that end, the passage to particular sciences and those sciences themselves will describe standpoints that allow one to grasp the world in a fully human manner: they are forms of discourse subjectively adapted to one's experiences. Completing his phenomenology, Fichte seeks to provide insight into what it means to be a knowing subject in the world; reintroducing the notion of feeling, Fichte will account for fundamental aspects of subjective existence such as the experience of time, the practical concept of freedom, our sense of having a vocation, and our capacity for interiority.

It is precisely this cultivation of subjectivity necessitated by a phenomenology that the three chapters of the second part of this book will address. The *Characteristics of the Present Age* (1804–05) establishes that time is the field in which subjectivity engages in free action. The *Principles of the Doctrines of God, Morals, and Right* (1805) analyzes the concept of appearance, arguing that free subjectivity active in time is always determined but also called to a higher form of self-realization – that is, the free use of Reason in view of the betterment of humanity. The *Way towards the Blessed Life* is at once a doctrine [*Lehre*] of religion and the lynchpin moment in a phenomenology according to the WL – if WL is genetic, finding its sources within and not in some external thing, so too with a phenomenology; self-realization is to be found through an inward journey. As highest particular science, religion is a type of discourse about a specific object. But this object, which the *Blessed Life* calls God, is the same as the WL – the absolute truth internal to all other forms of discourse. Religion embodies its own kind of discourse, one that arrives at the same goals as the WL but by means of feeling rather than dialectic; religion is discourse about the subjectively felt sense of truth contained in any kind of discourse, the science of the personal dimension of discourse – said otherwise, of how one can speak with conviction.

Taken together, the first philosophy that is WL and the extended phenomenology constituted by explorations of time, appearance, and religion provide a portrait of Fichte's thought during this, his middle period. This is not to say that it provides a complete philosophical system; rather, the works both scientific and popular that were given in Berlin are dependent on and elaborated out of the version of the WL that was intended for the same audience, the 1804/2. One of the main goals of this book, then, is to demonstrate that this context, Berlin from 1804 to 1806, sees Fichte thinking in a certain register, one defined by the concerns of the 1804/2 WL.

More important, this book is meant to help readers perform the exercise that is WL for themselves. Like any commentary on Fichte's work, this text can only convey the author's unique way of thinking through the exercise. The measure of success of such works is whether or not they allow readers to arrive at their own insight. As Fichte says, "our living thinking and insight … can't be shown on a blackboard[.]"[19]

PART ONE
The 1804 *Wissenschaftslehre*

PREFATORY REMARKS: "BRINGING THE WISSENSCHAFTSLEHRE TO UTTER CLARITY"

In the summer of 1803, Fichte wrote to Schiller that he was "still completely occupied with the *Wissenschaftslehre*; not in order to find it, or to improve it, but rather, to bring it to utter clarity."[1] Since arriving in Berlin four summers earlier, in July 1799, Fichte had not ceased to work on the WL, preparing a far more novel iteration of it than its Jena incarnations could have foretold. While the foundational insight at the heart of his philosophy remained the same, its embodiment in WL, and indeed the very notion *that* it could be embodied, was evolving. From the beginning, WL was an activity, not a text, an objective and scientific intuition into the structure of thought but also one that is highly personal, coming to life for an individual at a certain moment in time. Every written articulation of the WL – a task that Fichte was always loath to undertake – could only be a sort of exercise book, a series of thought experiments, remarks, and maxims that allow the reader to undertake what is always a unique journey.[2] Just as students must reconstruct their own *Wissenschaftslehren* in hearing or reading Fichte's account, so too does each formal articulation of the WL arrive at its goal from a certain angle. No one version of Fichte's text can be considered definitive, since each approaches the task of WL in a different manner according to different concerns.[3] Fichte saw his role in these expositions not as teacher – still less as master or expert – but as guide, an individual who had himself achieved the insight that he now wished to produce in his listeners and readers but could never construct it in their place.

If facilitating insight was the goal of the presentations of the WL, the obscurity of these – of which Fichte was becoming increasingly aware – was an obstacle. Fichte's philosophy had often been misinterpreted, and its difficulty meant that his words were easily turned against him, as had happened at the end of his tenure in Jena. In Berlin, a more experienced Fichte tried another tactic: approaching the same point repeatedly from different angles. What begin as parallel streams of metaphors are all eventually pulled into the maelstrom of WL; what seems opaque according to one can suddenly become clear according to another.[4] This, too, could be dizzying for students, and expresses a certain frustration on the part of the author-lecturer, who was fighting with language. Words were the inescapable medium through which insight would be produced and the outer form it would take when participants expressed their reconstructions of the system.[5] Yet taken on their own, words were a move away from the insight, a mere mental detritus that hardens into dogmatism and distorts the living philosophy that is WL. In a grand moment of oratory, Fichte would rail against them: "Thus away with all words and signs! Nothing remains except our living thinking and insight, which can't be shown on a blackboard nor be represented in any way but can only be surrendered to nature."[6]

Fichte's solution to this dilemma comes from his own realization, fully articulate by 1804, that the question of how to expose or externalize the WL is in fact the central theoretical question of WL. The nature of language had been buried in the WL all along, but now, aware that discourse was both aporetic and inevitable, the new expression of the WL takes aim at relating discourse itself to the truth established in thought. This would come to be expressed as the split between being and thought central to the theory of truth at the heart of the 1804 text. In concerning itself with the manner in which insight makes itself known in discourse, Fichte is elaborating what Reinhard Lauth has called a *philosophia prima*; following a tradition just as ancient, one could call this presentation of the WL a logic.[7]

While this breakthrough was the product of intense work, it provides no support for the popular myth that has Fichte sequestered in his study, bringing forth an entirely new philosophy amidst the woes of exile.[8]

The nature of such an endeavour – linking from within the confines of discourse the discursive and the immediate – meant that the WL would have to be repeatedly presented and the external formalities of its presentation judged by their effect on the listeners. Berlin was a testing ground for the WL, and both in speech and writing, Fichte multiplied occasions on which it could be given, talked about, or defended. The early Berlin years are, in some ways, the busiest and most public of Fichte's career. He wrote extensively, gave private lessons ("*privatissime*"), and maintained a vast correspondence in which critical transformations in German Idealism would play out. Fichte's lectures, given in his home at Kommandantenstraße 9,[9] include the *Sun-Clear Report* (1801), the WL *New Presentation* (1801–02), and three renditions of the WL in 1804. Concurrently with the third of these, Fichte would lecture on the *Characteristics of the Present Age*.[10]

Of the three versions of the WL given in 1804, the second is universally acknowledged as the clearest. It was Fichte's own suspicion that the first series, thirty lectures that ran from 17 January to 29 March, had been too difficult, that led to the organization of a second series.[11] These consisted of twenty-eight lectures, given from 16 April to 8 June. Fichte lectured in the evenings to a varied public four times a week, with a "conversatorium" (a discussion period) on Sunday afternoons. As many as sixty people could have been in attendance at any given lecture.[12] It would seem that this second series achieved the results for which Fichte had hoped, and if a new, third series was given in the same year, it was simply to accommodate a different audience as Fichte continued to lecture in order to earn a living. Fichte himself seems to have considered the second version the best and most accessible of the three, since during the third series of lectures, he copied out the second in view of publication. Fichte's son Immanuel Hermann accordingly recounts that his father left a manuscript of the 1804/2 lectures ready for publication.[13] It was this manuscript that appeared in volume 10 of the *Sämmtliche Werke* in 1834, under I.H. Fichte's supervision. Historical facts would eventually prove that "supervision" is here a euphemism.

I.H. Fichte was aware that his edition of the 1804 WL suffered from shortcomings, and he apologized for the numerous printing errors it contained in the subsequent volume of *SW*.[14] Decades later, Fritz Medicus corrected these errors in his new edition and was ready to send the manuscript to print when, in 1908, Karl Wendel, a librarian at the university of Halle, wrote Medicus to inform him that he had discovered a hitherto unknown copy of the 1804 WL. Medicus took it to be a listener's copy, a *Protokol*, and used this manuscript, referred to as *Copia*, only parsimoniously in preparing his new edition.[15] Yet a close examination of *Copia* shows that it is no *Nachschrift* or listener's copy but an *Abschrift*, a copy in Fichte's own hand containing information that no listener could have known. Putting *SW* and *Copia* on equal footing allowed for an entirely new edition of 1804/2 to be produced, one that corrects a plethora of hidden mistakes: among other things, *Copia* revealed that I.H. Fichte had surreptitiously provided *SW* with a number of "improvements" that were little more than glosses on the text.[16] The new *Gesammtausgabe* edition of 1804/2, which prints *SW* and *Copia* side by side, offers a much clearer picture of the only rendition of the WL from the period 1800–07 that Fichte had explicitly hoped to see published. For reasons both exegetical and historical, then, the 1804/2 text is the surest foundation for any study of Fichte's middle works.

Regarding the structure of the text itself, the twenty-eight lectures are clearly divided into two sections.[17] The first half (lectures 1–15) are a Theory of Truth [*Wahrheitslehre*] that begin with immediate experience and work up to the absolute, "*esse in mero actu*." Both the starting point and end goal are valences of *Evidenz*, Fichte's term for immediacy. The Theory of Truth occupies itself with the discursive world that lies between these two, elaborating a fivefold transcendental argument structure meant as a corrective to Kant's. Its structure is only clear to the reader once the fifteenth lecture has been completed. It can then be knowingly put to use in the second half (lectures 16–28), alternately called the theory of images [*Bildlehre*], of appearances [*Erscheinungslehre*], or phenomenology [*Phänomenologie*]. Here, Fichte's transcendental argument will seek to identify the truth of appearances, elaborating a logic of discourse that is the basis for all particular sciences.

Beyond this basic division, Fichte is also clear that the whole of the text follows the fivefold transcendental argument. This is itself an expansion of the twofold distinction into truth and appearance. As will be shown later, for Fichte, the basic structure of argumentation is the agreement between what one says and how one says it, between *tun* and *sagen*.[18] This structure plays out in transcendental arguments, which move from immediate experience (*Evidenz*) to mediation in discourse (consciousness) and then back to immediacy (*Evidenz*). That the end-point is logically identical with the starting point means it achieves the same results as *tun-sagen* agreement – indeed, when Fichte is pressed for time, he will simply reduce his argument to an examination of the relationship between content and execution. Yet the fullness of this argument is expressed in five steps wherein *tun* and *sagen* meet through a series of internalizing reversals operated by a mechanism Fichte refers to as the *through* [*durch*]. This can only be explained properly by moving through the WL itself. Essential is that Fichte conceived of the whole of the text as not only using the fivefold deduction or "synthesis" but as being structured by it. Moreover, each of the five moments can also be subjected to five syntheses, thus yielding twenty-five. Fichte only mentions the twenty-five syntheses in passing, and in the last lecture of the 1804/2, where they are spoken of as a *fait accompli*.[19] It would seem that initially, each lecture would have corresponded to a synthesis, following the example set by the 1801–02, which enumerates them explicitly. In the most venerable and most extensive commentary on the 1804/2, Martial Gueroult attempts to identify these syntheses following the pattern of the *"New Presentation of the WL"* (1801–02), for which he also offers an extensive commentary.

Naming the twenty-five syntheses is fraught with difficulties, the first of which is that Fichte's lectures evolve as they progress. For example, Fichte had planned on consecrating the first four lectures to introductory materials[20] and presumably meant to begin the dialectic between realism and idealism (the heart of the theory of truth) at lecture five. The difficulty of lecture four, which contains the theory of truth in brief, meant that lecture five became a review lecture. The three following lectures then expand didactically on what was stated in lecture four. The opposite occurs in the extremely dense lectures that conclude the phenomenology: the twenty-seventh lecture contains two distinct movements, each of which could have been a self-standing lecture.

Yet if Fichte did not outline the twenty-five syntheses explicitly, are we warranted in looking for them? By Fichte's own account, another structure can be seen, one not incompatible with the twenty-five syntheses but which follows broader divisions: the theory of truth is clearly divided into two parts, an introduction and a realism-idealism dialectic.

In lecture twenty-two, Fichte divides the phenomenology into three. Other divisions, based on internal evidence found in the lectures, are possible as well.[21]

Fichte's own lack of concern in naming these is telling. As the analysis herein will demonstrate, the structure of the text, however necessary for understanding the whole, is in Fichte's mind subordinate to the approach one must adopt. Far more important than finding the fivefold synthesis in the structure of the text is to learn how to reason with a fivefold synthesis. In all of its presentations, the WL gives precedence to the dynamic activity of the mind over its static products. Embarking on the journey that is *Wissenschaftslehre* is the essential thing, not presenting some definitive plan after the fact. Any outline of the structure of the WL can only be the personal reconstruction of something alive, more technique than accomplishment.[22]

1

The 1804/2 Wissenschaftslehre Part I: The Theory of Truth

1.1 THE PROLEGOMENA[1]

More initiation than introduction, the first three lectures are meant to cultivate the right disposition in Fichte's listeners. If on the surface, this does not seem to be rigorously philosophical, it is precisely in these generalities that the whole WL is found *in nuce* and from which the rest of the process will be extrapolated. The WL is essentially the science of thought, an orientation in thinking that grounds and situates all derivative ways of thinking particular subject matters. The science into which we are being initiated is a doctrine of right thinking, a work that belongs to the same literary genre as Aristotle's *Categories* but possessing both a subjective dimension and a will to resolve the apparent contradictions that thinking subjects encounter that brings Fichte much further than Aristotle. What Fichte is elaborating, then, is a *logic*. And although this logic is beholden to previous forms of logical reasoning, ranging from Aristotle to Arnauld,[2] its integrative, subjective dimension takes into account the manner in which experience really occurs. It is thus a logic of discourse.[3] More than a simple container of thought, discourse encompasses both its structure and content: for Fichte, to ask what it means to think also means acknowledging that one is already thinking. Thinking is always thinking being – that is, it is experience. Yet the act of thinking cannot be reduced to a simple object of experience. This claim lies at the heart not only of the 1804 WL, where it will come to found all forms of subjective experience, but has been, *mutatis mutandis*, Fichte's argument from the beginning: making the claim again at the beginning of this version of the WL will therefore induce Fichte to articulate, albeit in broad strokes, the moves that have defined the structure of the WL since its inception in 1794: those of positing, disjunction, and reunification.[4]

Thinking is ineluctable, and to present this threefold structure is a way of acknowledging that one must begin one's investigation of what it means to think *in medias res*, from within the dynamism of thought. It is also a declaration of freedom, of willing entry into a system that will come to envelope one entirely; the free starting-point of WL was only ever an affirmation of beginning, the forceful assertion "The I posits itself absolutely" an expression more of depth than breadth. One makes a decision – and a radically free one – to begin examining one's own thoughts. Once within this task, certain incontrovertible facts will present themselves with compelling necessity, and a whole system of thought will, as Fichte says, "construct itself."[5] Fichte's moment of freedom is the decision to begin with philosophy, itself an examination of what one has already been thinking in ordinary experience. It is thus a retrieval of *life*, the dynamic process in which we always already find ourselves, reflectively or not. Going about the business of living always involves following certain bedrock suppositions, axiomatic beliefs that one holds and that form the basis of one's engagement with the experiential world. One simply lives, moving forward according to these axiomatic suppositions, or "maxims." The depth of freedom of the philosopher is found in the ability to probe these maxims while acknowledging their inevitability for human agency. The WL therefore does not seek to abolish these maxims. Its questioning of them is meant rather to demonstrate that these rules for rational behaviour are both the product and manifestation of reason itself: in brief, we are free because we are rational.

The Prolegomena is therefore an initiation into thinking with *maxims*.[6] On the surface, Fichte is presenting the key terms of WL. Yet their meaning will only become clear as one makes use of them. At this point, it is precisely in exploring their status as maxims that one becomes aware of the exercise that lies ahead. By actively introducing his listeners to the act of thinking with a maxim, Fichte is also teaching them how one makes a transcendental argument. Essentially, in experience one encounters certain incontrovertible facts, and one's (maxim-led) engagement with them must be built on the avoidance of performative self-contradiction. To think transcendentally is to perpetually ask oneself, does my *engagement* with experience align with what is *given* in experience? If this line of argument is largely adopted from Kant's critical enterprise, Kant also serves as a foil in the propaedeutic; when judged according to his own transcendental method of argumentation, Kant's affirmations come up short. The critical philosophy contradicts itself and must be re-evaluated in order to sit on the secure foundation of transcendent argument. At stake is nothing other than the freedom and rationality of human existence. If transcendental philosophy cannot yield a coherent logical discourse, the space it leaves open will be inevitably filled by scepticism, which Fichte had always seen – at least since his engagement with Aensidemus-Schulze in 1793 – as the greatest enemy of science.

The first maxims that Fichte presents concern the attitude that one must cultivate when one makes the free decision to examine one's experience in a systematic way. This attitude is characterized at once by intensity of thought (*thinking "energetically"* [*energetsich*]) and by absolute absorption ("*attention*" [*Aufmerksamkeit*]), a passive way of being active that will come to define the new articulation of "intuition" [*Anschauung*] contained in this new version of the WL.

One can reflect on one's existence in an ordinary manner, seeing merely a series of contingent events succeeding each other without looking for any formal connection between them. Yet to not think about the real connection of one's thoughts *in* thought is already a decision – an unwitting form of idealism that ultimately leads to scepticism. Philosophy, says Fichte, is always a matter of *truth*, the unity of a manifold in thought. In thinking, we suppose that truth does exist, that it is always equal to itself and is therefore one. And because this truth is one, it cannot be found merely in the succession of particular experiences but rather "whomever would have it must produce it entirely out of himself."[7] As teacher, Fichte cannot give his students truth. Rather, he can only facilitate the students' awareness of the self-production of truth. Fichte pushes this further, affirming that he, the "I" that is the lecturer, must be erased. The students themselves will have to *perform* this science on their own, not learn it from someone else; they must become Wissenschaftlehrer*s*.

Wissenschaftslehre is a possible system of philosophy, and philosophy's aim is to present the truth. Thus the internal coherence of any proposition is a self-identity. Propositions always imply some content, some object that is *external* to the subject. It is precisely according to this externality that the manifold of experience is encountered. Fichte's technical term for this externality is *facticity* [*Faktizität*]. It refers to the "outer essence of thought,"[8] or knowledge of objects in consciousness; it is what exists externally and is a consequence of something else. For now, the maxims of WL will have to be presented in such a manner. Their initial factical presentation will have to be retroactively shown to be true once they have been posited.

Arriving at the self-identity that is truth from the factical content of the proposition consists in a movement of "*tracing-back*" [*Zurückführung*], Fichte's dynamic expression of the classic problem of the one and the many: "The essence of philosophy would consist in this: *to trace all multiplicity* (which presses itself upon us in the usual view of life) *back to absolute oneness*."[9] The test of any philosophical system is whether it can trace difference back to oneness. To study successive contingency is to do history, not philosophy. The latter requires a principle of unity, "A."

Yet far from seeking some common essence of things, as Fichte's subsequent use of the term "ontological ground" might lead one to believe, he is instead seeking to secure a form of transcendental argumentation, a philosophical proof system that establishes truth in-itself and thwarts the sceptical point of view. The argument that Fichte offers in favour of this oneness as "ontological ground" makes this clear: not only must its content be equal to itself, but the *form* must also be in agreement with the content: *if* experience always makes use of some principle, the principle must articulate content that is consequent with its own rule of application – proposition "p" cannot be denied lest the denier utter a performative contradiction. In the prolegomena, Fichte's example is that of those who claim a philosophical relativism, a kind of scepticism that would make relative historical experience the measure of all things. Essentially, the sceptic makes the assertion: "I claim it is true that there is no truth." It says it will have nothing to do with truth but ultimately posits a truth-statement as maxim for living. Addressing the sceptical claim lies not in arguing with its conclusion of truth as product but rather examining the internal coherence of its propositions. In so doing, it becomes apparent that denying truth as foundational principle for reason is self-contradictory: "I claim that it is true that there is no truth."[10] The premise articulated contradicts the content. Later, Fichte will define this as "a pure absolute contradiction between enactment [*tun*] and saying [*sagen*]."[11] The contemporary name for this style of argument is *retorsion*. A retorsive argument claims that the unity of truth cannot *not* be true. This use of such argumentation makes clear Fichte's commitment to a transcendental philosophy, arguing about possibility-conditions and not causes. The retorsive argument can only have transcendental results, not establishing the existence of this or that but merely the validity of a claim.[12]

Truth, affirms Fichte, cannot *not* be true, whether in its formal self-identity (immediacy) or its expression in discourse. *Tun-sagen* agreement is a means of ensuring this consistency of truth on both levels: this statement that is said to be true, containing heterogeneous elements, must in fact be true in the same way that self-identical truth is true. A proposition "p" must therefore remain equal to itself throughout the process of discursive elaboration. In Fichte's terminology, that which is equal to itself is *absolute*. In any proposition with an internally opposing factor (that is, in which *tun* and *sagen* are not in accord), the absolute, or self-unity, is located outside itself. This manifest contradiction was characteristic of dogmatism. In "all philosophies prior to Kant, the absolute was located in *being*, that is, in the dead thing as thing."[13] Kant taught us that being is inseparable from consciousness-of-being; what *is* is only as thought and one can only think what *is*. Absolute oneness belongs to both the thing and its representation, also the principle of their disjunction. In a Kantian framework, then, truth as absolute is not only unity of thought (representation) and being (object) but can also be broken into these separate, disjunctive terms. Since a proposition is a totality, both unity and its disjunctive terms are posited simultaneously.[14] Representing this in a simple triangular diagram, Fichte claims that "A" (truth in-and-for-itself) splits into B (being) and T (thought). In this diagram, everything, including *A* itself, is only a modification of A. Moreover, all cognition of an object must pass through the B-T separation. All cognizable objects belong to three different domains, which Fichte calls "x,y,z." These constitute a second disjunction of A, simultaneous to that of B and T but necessarily passing through B and T.

With the introduction of the distinction between B-T and x,y,z, Fichte is now in a position to subject Kant's architectonic to his retorsive argument. He asks us to imagine a philosophical system that realizes that the disjunction between B and T is "mere appearance" – that is to say, conceives of true propositions as a reconciliation between subjective and objective poles, between consciousness and existence – but cannot find a way to trace x,y,z back to A. In the final analysis, such a system would not be able to conceive of the unity of object domains as formally unified by A, evading one disjunction in favour of another. This is Kant's system. And while it avoids the errors of dogmatism, it does so merely by postponing rather than resolving the dogmatist error: being and thought resolve into A, but there remains absolute heterogeneity between the object as it is (materially or sensibly) and its perception (or intelligibility). One reaches this conclusion through assessing what Kant had to assume in order to say what he did. When one applies Kant's own transcendental principles to his philosophy, one discovers a fundamental contradiction between its claims and the very enactment of those claims.

Kant rightly conceived of A as the "indivisible union" of B and T. But he did not see it as a purely self-sufficient it-itself, rather merely as the "common basic determination or accident of its three primordial modes, x,y,z … As a result of which for him there are actually three absolutes and the true unitary absolute fades to their common property."[15] Rather than trace the cognition of object-domains back to the common structure of thought, Kant instead erects three external principles for thinking, the three *Critiques*.[16] In other words, rather than posit the absolute of any of the three as the unity of the conditions that gave rise to it, Kant wishes to discover "A" as something external to any of them. Since a ground must ground and not be a consequence, Kant's fundamental claim is reduced to a performative contradiction.

Kant's philosophy therefore makes "three starts": 1) x = sensible experience (the *Critique of Pure Reason*). Here, the intelligible (or supersensible) world seems to totally disappear into a thing-in-itself, a "mere noumenon that has its complete realization in the empirical world."[17] Implied here is the problem of noumenal affection, that of how noumena can affect phenomena. Aware of this problem of heterogeneity, Kant nonetheless does not correct it by securing the foundations of the

Critique of Pure Reason but through a commitment to the independence of morality. The "second start" is therefore 2) z = the moral world (the *Critique of Practical Reason*). Here, "the I comes to light as something in itself through the inherent categorical concept."[18] But this I in itself cannot have the same ultimate foundation as that of the sensible world – it must be a law-giver, not merely a noumenal idea. Hence Kant erects a second absolute, incompatible with the first. Because the "I" is not an empirical object, Kant arrived at a different ground for it. Yet in positing a moral I and its absolute, the law-giver, Kant, also knows that he has not really arrived at the heart of what it means to be an "I" – at the subjectivity that makes human experience what it is. Providing for this means giving an account of the beautiful, the sublime, and the purposive, which are neither cognitions nor moral concepts. What's more, the transcendental unity of apperception (found in the first *Critique*) and the I that is the moral self are so entirely heterogeneous that there is no clear account of how I can at once be a thinking person *and* a moral person without really being two people, the thinker and the moral agent. Therefore, 3) y = the unity of sensible and supersensible (the *Critique of Power of Judgment*). Hence, in the introduction to CPJ (which Fichte calls "the most important part of that book"), Kant declares that "the sensible and supersensible must come together in a common but wholly unknown root, which would be the third absolute."[19] This does not unite the two, instead creating a third absolute because it seeks to find unity in some other thing, i.e., that is *neither* sensible *nor* supersensible but some third thing.[20] If his "common root" were really a root, it would already be present in the two critiques as their ground, not their product. Fichte has forced Kant into a performative contradiction: Kant says "ground" but what ensues is "determination."

The task of the WL, then, will be to act as a corrective to Kant's transcendental argument, seeking the common root of the sensible and intelligible worlds in a single principle *from which both worlds are derived* and not the other way around: "A," says Fichte, divides itself simultaneously into BT and xyz. The insight with which the science of knowing begins (i.e., that disjunctions have their origin in A) is found in both these divisions simultaneously, not just in BT, as it was for Kant. The understanding, moral, and judging selves must be brought together as one self in transcendental unity.

At the outset of this lecture series, the foundation of the WL will therefore be the absolute unity of A, the formal structures of knowing, regardless of its object. Through the successions of different object-domains (and particular objects therein), the knowing self must be equal to itself:

> To begin with, we can demonstrate immediately that knowing can actually appear as something standing on its own. I ask you to look sequentially at your own inner experience: if you remember it accurately, you will find the object and its representation, with all their modifications. But now I ask further: do you not know in all these modifications; and is not your knowing, as knowing, the same self-identical knowing in all variations of the object? As surely as you say, "yes," to this inquiry (which you will certainly do if you have carried out the given task), so surely will knowledge manifest and present itself to you (as = A) whatever the variation of its objects (and hence [38–39] in total abstraction from objectivity); remaining as (= A); and thus as a substantive, as staying the same as itself through all change in its object; and thus as oneness, qualitatively changeless in itself.[21]

The foundational proof that "A" is the common root of all acts of knowing is that regardless of what one knows, one knows that one knows, and this knowing-of-knowing remains the same regardless of the object introduced into consciousness.

This simple realization, which Fichte calls the *insight* [*Einsicht*] into "A," is merely the idea that I know that I know. Knowledge is equal to itself. As I know any particular object, I can be aware of myself as knowing without turning consciousness directly toward the act of knowing. This insight is nothing mystical but a bare logical fact with which we are constantly confronted: for Fichte, the statement "I do not know that I am knowing" amounts to a performative contradiction, retorsion's first victory. Moreover, this has been the unchanging foundation of Fichte's philosophy since the beginning. What Fichte calls insight [*Einsicht, einsehen*] in 1804 is therefore successor to the earlier concept of *intellectual intuition* [*intellektuelle Anschauung*].[22] Insight belongs to a broader metaphor of seeing, undoubtedly the most frequent one in the post-Jena WL, which as a whole signifies intuition. If insight [*wir sehen es ein*] is an intellectual intuition or the knowledge-of-knowledge, it is inseparable from *mere seeing* [*bloß sehen*], which refers to sensible intuition or knowledge of the manifold of experience, knowledge of something in particular.[23]

Knowing-of-knowing, or if one prefers, awareness-of-knowing, "presents itself to you with impressive, absolutely irrefutable *Evidenz*."[24] To say that I know that I know is merely to say something *evident*. *Evidenz* is one of the most important terms of the 1804 WL.[25] It refers to the immediate "thereness" of what exists but also the immediately compelling truth of the insight into the formal unity of knowledge: i.e., "I know that I know" (A = A). That which is evident is immediately credible, and to say otherwise would be to fall into performative contradiction. Fichte is careful to specify that this unity is not T = T, or mere thinking equal to itself, but rather A = A, a formal unity that encompasses both sensibility and intelligibility – WL is not an idealist philosophy.

What, then, is the relationship between knowing and knowing-of-knowing? *Prima facie*, they seem to be as heterogenous as Kant's *x* and *z*, a separation between the object-domains of things and thoughts. Introducing a key aspect of the method that will be pursued throughout these lectures, Fichte claims that this unity of A as knowing and knowing-of-knowing is for now only "an empty seeing"; it has been initially posited factically (externally and hence problematically) and will only be secured as internal unity through the course of the argument. To do so, one of the two, knowing, will have to be "grasped mediately," mediated by knowing-of-knowing. Knowing, in other words, will have to be "inwardly constructed." We cannot seek it externally as a product of knowledge (as Kant did) but rather by means of inquiring into its origins (to which Fichte refers as its "essence"). Hence, if my knowledge *of objects* is mediated knowledge (i.e., in consciousness), I must inquire into how it is mediated by knowledge *tout court*. Hence, to say that we must construct the essence of knowing is actually to say that the essence of knowing must construct itself. This means that the science of knowing (the asking of the question "what is knowing in its qualitative oneness?") and "primordially [*urwesentlichen*] essential knowing" or the identity of knowledge with itself are the same thing.[26] WL is the meta-knowledge of A; it is an inquiry into knowledge-of-knowledge and is substantially A = A. As will later be revealed, the constructive act that is WL and the self-construction that is A are interchangeable. This primordially essential knowing constructs itself and is therefore *genetic*. Yet another key term, *genesis*, is the opposite of facticity. It is the inner essence of thought, the internal possibility-condition of thought; a *genetic deduction* is a tracing back [*Zurückführung*] of all thought to a common root. *Evidenz* (the immediacy of knowing-of-knowing) is therefore purely genetic.

The highest point that facticity can arrive at is "factical *Evidenz*," the mere knowledge *that* there is a link between knowledge-of-knowledge and knowledge of particulars but with nothing to say about *what* it is. For his part, Kant is aware of a "basic law of oneness," but this is not even such a factical *Evidenz*. His highest principle is "y", the external (*post-factum*) synthesis of x and z. As Fichte says, finding the link between a disjunction of two raises a more important question: *how did the one become two?* That is the question that Kant cannot ask. But such a unity must be synthetic *and* analytic – that is, founded in the agreement of *tun* and *sagen*. Because Kant couldn't see this, he couldn't even arrive at the factical *Evidenz* that Fichte is advocating as the yet-unproven mediation of knowledge by knowledge-of-knowledge. The task before us as we move deeper into the WL, then, is a *genetic deduction* of knowing, firmly grounding its relationship with knowing-of-knowing.

1.2 LIGHT AND CONCEPT

In the first three lectures, Fichte developed the concepts of unity, disjunction, and their reunion. This was done primarily through positing the act of thinking as the disjunction of thought and being, of what is and how one conceives of it. There, Fichte suggested that the principle of disjunction of T(hinking) and B(eing), the "A" that we can already presume to be the very act of thinking is also its foundational unity. He also suggested that this absolute unity splits into another division, that of the object-domains of x, y, z. In lectures four to eight, Fichte brings these points together in a reflection on the unity of unity and disjunction, or the conditions of the possibility of thinking A. The fourth lecture contains some of the foundational propositions of the theory of truth, establishing the terms that will be disputed in the realism-idealism conflict and then revisited in lecture fifteen, which makes explicit (and genetic) what was factically posited in lecture four.[27] Fichte was aware of the density of this lecture, and consecrates three subsequent lectures to elucidating it.[28] It is only with the twofold deduction of one of these, the *Urbegriff*, that the prolegomena truly comes to an end.

At the beginning of lecture four, Fichte redraws the diagram by which he depicted A's split into B-T, now incorporating the second split into x,y,z that he had elucidated orally. The new diagram reads thus[29]:

A
B - T • x, y, z

If "A" stands for the absolute (i.e., absolute self-equality), its absolute nature lacks any content – it is not thinking-of-thinking (absolute thinking), or being-of-being (absolute being), but merely the "absolute of absolute," an empty placeholder. Since all absolutes embody immediacy, this empty absolute is *Evidenz* itself (Fichte will relate this valence of the term to the one made explicit earlier, the immediately compelling nature of experience, in a moment).[30] Fichte intends this absolute concept to be successor both to Kant's thing-in-itself[31] and Spinoza's substance.[32] In the WL, these merely factical absolutes will be revisited and integrated into a transcendental system. The space between the dot and the letters that surround it stands for the transition points, or breaks from the absolute-placeholder into particularity. The breaks occur simultaneously and hence are actually one. The first separation downward and left into being and thought is the immediate requirement for cognition, the separation of an object from a subject's perception of it. The further, more determinate separation, downward right into "x, y, z," describes the types of experience that play out in cognition; that is, A, what is immediately self-evident, as mediated by B-T. As we have already seen, these stand for the sensible, the intelligible, and their unity, with reference to Kant's critical project.

The content of the diagram is known from the first three lectures. Left to be elucidated, however, is the role of the point, first as it relates to A, and second (though here only prospectively) as it relates to the exercise in which we are engaged, WL. Fichte begins defining it by saying that WL "stands in the point,"[33] not in A, but then quickly qualifies his statement: it does not belong to either but rather the unity of both. A is an identity outside of itself, an identity with no content yet expressed factically, while the point is mere [*bloße*] genesis, unity without anything to unify. A is the positive and factical expression of what the point says genetically and negatively, through its absence. The point is a mere standpoint, a representation of the attitude of attention, the formal unity of intuition – that is, of thinking and thinking-of-thinking – that the factical A pries apart. The nature of discourse is such that one cannot think one without the other, since what is immediately experienced will always be mediated in thought.[34] The fact that one seeks to *say* something immediate when uttering one or the other leads to a contradiction: "I say that the immediate is mediated" or vice-versa. This contradiction thus constitutes a retorsive argument for the inconceivability of the "real" absolute, that absolute unity for which A is merely placeholder. In brief, the point of the point is to simultaneously factically reconstruct an absolute unity that is immediately and ineffably there, all the while acknowledging that in discursive thought, we have only reconstructed and not fabricated the oneness that is simply there: I *know* that my knowing is the unity of knowing and being, but since I cannot know a unity higher than knowing *within* knowing, I can only reconstruct a factical version.

Awareness of knowledge is intractable but necessary and belongs, with knowledge, to a unity higher than both. To describe this, Fichte introduces one of the chief metaphors of the 1804 WL, light. Light is what provides for the visibility of objects but cannot itself be seen. Like light, awareness-of-knowing is eternally in the background. To be aware of my knowing is to know its bare structure A but not as one knows an object. How, then, can one think light if thought cannot but think it discursively, as if it were an object? This heterogeneity of light and the way consciousness usually thinks is the primary obstacle to arriving at the unity of unity and disjunction.

Fichte resumes this line of argument in four points: 1) We must first conceive of an inconceivable, then negate our conceiving of it – all knowledge is in consciousness, but knowledge of knowledge grounds consciousness. It is in recognizing consciousness's nature that we integrate it into unity. 2) Inconceivability is the negation of the concept, of consciousness itself. Consciousness, which separates, is integrated into pure unity by self-negation. 3) A is *evident*. It only becomes inconceivable when consciousness tries to cognize it *as a thing*. It is the correlate of "pure light." Realizing what pure light is involves letting an object "come to light" and then negating it in order to focus one's attention on the light. But light cannot be cognized. Pure light is "the one focus and the sole principle of both being and concept."[35] Light *shines*, or "expresses itself" [*Auesserung*] in precisely this act of shining. Its activity is the negation of the objects of experience, which are static. The contents of consciousness are therefore mere by-products of the shining of light, a dead precipitate [*todter Absatz*] that light's activity leaves behind.[36] While we are *aware* of an absolute unity that joins the two valences of knowing, light and consciousness, when we try to move back up to the source, particular knowing is cast aside as so many precipitates or useless by-products. The path of reconstruction cannot find its way back to the origins of what was initially constructed; there is apparent incongruity between the two. Here lies the whole difficulty with which the theory of truth (lectures one to fifteen) is confronted. 4) Light is itself inconceivability. It has no qualities.

At the end of this fourfold exposition, we assume that the art of reconstruction is the art of reconciling light and consciousness, the two valences of thinking. Somehow reconciling them *in thought* will be the key to reconciling the incommensurate construction and reconstruction of what is and what appears for us. This reconciliation will not be some object but rather a holding-together of the two, a *grasping* that Fichte calls *Urbegriff*: "In a word, we have to do with constructing and creating the very same primal concepts [*Urbegriffe*] that appear one time as immanent, in the unconditionally evident final being, the I, and appear the other time as *emanent*, in reason, absolute and in itself, which nevertheless is completely objectified.[37]"

The essence of reconstruction is positing something factically in view of making it genetic. And the genetic root of any factical proposition may be itself factical, requiring further inquiry – we have sought a genetic root for the manifold, but only arrived at a higher distinction: light and conscious thought. From here on, Fichte will refer to the latter simply as the concept, shorthand for all thinking that is mediated, i.e., not mere awareness or light. As it stands, then, the division between A (on one side of the point) and B-T; x,y,z (on the other side) has been collapsed into a division between A ("light") and x ("the concept"). Our task is now to unite them in the *Urbegriff.* In general, thinking light and concept is not a matter of thinking sensibility's relationship to the understanding, nor of categories internal to the latter. Fichte, rather, is thinking light, concept, and eventually the *Urbegriff* as categories of reflection – the WL is, after all, a science of thinking, a logic. Fichte has thus consolidated a single concept opposed to light. If in the long term, Fichte has in view a genetic linking of the concept with light (via an *Urbegriff*), some common point will have to be established between these seemingly heterogenous ideas. This will be the work of the *through* [*durch*], the mechanism that will propel Fichte's transcendental argument forward.

The introduction of the *Urbegriff* also reveals something about *Evidenz.* It was implied in the introduction of A as empty placeholder that it was immediate and therefore *evident*. Yet it is not itself "experience," that which is immediately compelling in the world for us. There are, in fact, two valences of *Evidenz.* Within the I of consciousness, objects present themselves with *Evidenz.* So too does knowledge-of-knowledge, awareness of which is represented by light. But to even talk about light is to objectify it, to construct it *as if* it were an object. One is immediately aware of having an experience in the same way that one is aware *that* experience exists at all. It is between these two, in the world of discursive thought, that light shines.

Hence Fichte's retorsive method, the transcendental argument whereby he tests the accord between *tun* and *sagen*, is about maintaining the self-identity of *Evidenz.* A transcendental argument:

1. Accepts that experience is immediately credible (*Evidenz* as immediacy).
2. Asks "why is this experience immediately credible?" discursively elaborating what was there as *Evidenz* in order to understand it in consciousness, and
3. Returns to experience without altering it, now consciously aware of its validity (*Evidenz* as A).

Two static terms, "saying" and "enactment," therefore yield a three-step movement: from experience to *Evidenz* and seamlessly back to experience. It is this third step where Fichte sees the transcendental argument structure of all his predecessors – especially Kant – as having failed. Where he should have returned to experience, Kant instead reifies awareness of the conditions of the possibility of experience, providing a pseudo-ontological ground, the thing-in-itself, rather than a genetic condition internal to the *Evidenz*-cognition relationship.[38]

Fichte will expand this threefold argument into a fivefold one:

> Further, [*Evidenz*] oscillates between these two perspectives: if it is to be really constructed, then it must be constructed in that way. Thus, it must be constructed as oscillating from a to b and again from b to a and as completely creating both; thus as oscillating between the twofold oscillation, which was the first point, and which gives rise to a three or fivefold synthesis.[39]

Fichte's transcendental argument is a fivefold [*fünffach*] one, even if here, at the end of the fourth lecture, the mechanisms according to which it functions remain obscure. Indeed, we are *already* using the fivefold deduction, since the whole WL unfolds according to its movement. Yet in order to describe it properly, one must understand the "twofold oscillation" of *a* and *b*. Initially, it will be put to work in what is to come, the deduction of the *Urbegriff*. For it is precisely in this deduction that its structure will reveal itself.

First, however, a clarification is in order. One can surmise from the tenor of the fifth lecture – one of review and clarification – that the dense fourth lecture was misunderstood, and chief among these misunderstandings was the light metaphor. Just as Fichte's intellectual intuition had been caricatured as an I's creation of its world, so too the knowing-of-knowing of this iteration of the WL seems to have been confused with the consciousness knowing of content. Fichte stresses the nature of this awareness of one's own knowing by evoking attention. Focus is thus shifted from the *performance* of the Jena WL to the cultivation of an attitude. Already in the thought experiment of the Nova Methodo ("Now think yourself thinking the wall …"), the attitude implicitly required is that of *noticing*. One must cultivate an active way of being passive. Now, Fichte is more explicit: his goal in lecturing is neither to teach, nor to effect some change in the listener, but to help create the disposition necessary for insight [*Einsicht*] to arise. This insight will arise on its own. As long as its conditions are laid out, truth will construct itself. Such is the method of WL: given a conditional fact, a series of necessary relationships will appear. Put succinctly, *attention yields insight via reconstruction*.

Making such (largely methodological claims) is grounded in the affirmation of the WL as philosophy of principles. One always philosophizes using a maxim, which is the articulation of a principle, an axiom presupposed in thinking. The WL is a science of principles whose own principles will be genetically deduced.[40] Necessary for its unfolding is a principle (that is, the presumption) of unity and disjunction. Specifically, we assume a connection between light and concept and then attempt a proof. Here, this proof consists in the unity of disjunction itself: the split into B-T; x,y,z happens "in one stroke." There is one separation but two "*fundamenta divisionis*" or modes according to which the division presents itself. These two levels (B-T; x,y,z) are different, but both belong to the realm of consciousness – the division spoken of here is really discursive mediation in thought. If this division is cast as that between light and concept (where light is A and the concept the unity of the two disjunctions), then light shines in the concept, making it intelligible. And where light shines, it is precisely the concept that comes to light. The separation of being and thinking necessarily entails thinking something in particular and vice-versa.

It is precisely this "vice-versa" that lies at the heart of Fichte's argument. Disjunction is itself a unified disjunction, and if one negates its facticity, or external mediate factors, the product is unity. To put it in the form of a retorsive argument, the claim "I say that all discourse is a disjunction" cannot stand. The proposition itself imposes a unity on the very notion of disjunction. Because retorsive arguments provide a transcendental result in the negative, it is therefore the negation of factical disjunction that yields the unity that brings saying and doing in accord. This being certain, we now know that one can arrive at unity from disjunction and disjunction from unity. They are reversible – light posits the concept, and the concept posits light. This reversibility, expressed at the end of lecture four as "oscillation," will come to be called the *through* [*durch*]. Light is always *through* the concept,, and the concept is always *through* light. They are through-one-another [*durcheinander*], and the reversibility (one can start from either L or C) or "throughness" of the propositions (L through C, C through L) will be the backbone of the synthetic deduction. Fichte will now put his deduction (with the *through* as its mechanism) to work in finding a solid genetic link between light and concept, an *Urbegriff*.

In lectures seven and eight, Fichte will offer two arguments for the *Urbegriff*, the first proceeding from the side of the concept and articulating a "proto-idealism," and the second from the side of light, presenting a "proto-realism."[41] The reason for this twofold approach is to have the listener practise the use of the *through* in the context of thinking with a principle. Ultimately, the very *throughness* of the grander argument will come to eclipse the *Urbegriff*, itself only a tentative expression of the genetic link between light and the concept. Thereafter, the *Wissenschaftslehrer* will be confronted with a war of principles, with realism and idealism making conflicting claims about how one must think absolute unity.

Lecture seven argues for the Urbegriff from the side of the concept. Its proto-idealism will mark a major moment in the development of the WL, offering it a methodology that will be operative until the end. Since the separation of light and concept is a disjunction, the starting-point is the nature of such disjunctions. We have already established that they occur according to principles that are also principle of unity, that factical principles are genetically founded in higher ones, and that at the root lies the ineffable principle that is the unity of A and the point. The unity (light) that provides for all disjunction (the concept) cannot be thought from within the confines of the concept. How, then, can we move beyond the bare logical assertion that light is in consciousness as unifying principle and "observe it in its inner form"?[42]

Trying to observe the light leads us to "conceptual *Evidenz*," that is, the realization that I know light is there but that when I try to think it, it disappears. I know that I can think light, but the content of my thoughts about it are not light itself. Such content can only be a representation or image of light.[43] Yet images cannot be dismissed out of hand. An image a proper character, that of being the image of something other than itself – image [*Bild*] is always image-of [*Abgebildet*]. If I am aware of the bare fact of an original light and at the same time perceive an image-of-light in my consciousness, I can infer that light and image-of-light share the same conceptual content. "Should this indeed be the case," writes Fichte, "then an absolute oneness of content is manifest here that remains unaltered as oneness but that splits itself only in the vital fulfillment of thinking into an inessential disjunction, which neither spoils the content in any way nor is grounded in it."[44] Fichte's argument is not that images are always faithful to an original, but rather that in the abstract, the idea of the original and the idea of the image are the same. Fidelity is a matter of degree and depends on content. The identity of light with light's image in consciousness is a formal identity, conceived in us according to the modus operandi of our knowing, the concept.[45] Hence the *Urbegriff* is the unity of light and image-of-light in consciousness *as perceived by consciousness.*

In bringing together light and its image, the product here, the *Urbegriff*, seems to be (at least from the point of view of consciousness) more fundamental than light itself, preceding it. This clarifies the concept-light relationship – we now know that the concept does indeed have its own "primordial" content apart from light: the "image-of" [*Abbild*]. The disjunction is no longer its simple negation but instead conditions its appearance: "Now the same single concept grounds its appearance through its own essential being; therefore, in this concept the image and what it images are posited absolutely, things which are constructed organically only through one another."[46] Image [*Bild*] and what it images [*Abbild*] belong to an organic unity of thought (the concept); in thought, they are constructed through-one-another [*durcheinander*]. The content of consciousness is thus the real light, an "Urlicht", but only inferentially, indirectly, through the *durcheinander.*[47]

While this line of argumentation has its merits and will prove to be essential for the development of the WL, the attentive listener would have noticed that it is only an imperfect application of the *durch*, only a *durcheinander*. A complete throughness would not generate a third thing, an *Urbegriff*, but would itself encompass light and concept and provide a shared genetic root within them – the absolute interpenetrability that the *durch* implies has not been achieved. Here already, we implicitly find all the problems of an argument that proceeds axiomatically from the side of the concept. Fichte will make these clear later (i.e., with the introduction of the category of "idealism"). For now, he will continue to explore the *Urbegriff* by taking another approach, proceeding from the side of light.

Our new starting point is therefore not an *image* of light in consciousness but rather light itself as primordial oneness. If we have already deduced the bare logical unity of the concept and know that this unity is itself light, then we can dispense with any discourse about the image of light. The light is simply there, and we know it to be there. In by-passing discourse about image, this proto-realist deduction immediately arrives at the disjunction at the origin of images and the act of imaging, that of being and thought. This is the real issue that the production of an *Urbegriff* is meant to solve.

Earlier, the consolidation of the concept was achieved through a retorsive argument ("I say that all discourse is disjunctive") as the negation of light. If this is true, then the surest path to light is simply by negating the concept. This will ultimately provide insight into the nature of the B-T split. This realist argument is condensed into one difficult paragraph:

> One term is being, the other – the negated concept – is without doubt subjective thought, or consciousness. Therefore we now have one of the two basic disjunctions, that into B and T (being and thinking), we have grasped this in its oneness, as we should, and as proceeding completely and simply from its oneness, (L = light); and thereby, so that I can add this, too, parenthetically, we would simultaneously have the schema for the negation of the I in the pure light and even have it intuitively. For if, as everyone could easily agree, one posits that the principle of the negated concept is just the I (since I indeed appear as freely constructing and sketching out the concept in response to an invitation), then its destruction in the face of what is valid in itself is simultaneously my destruction in the same moment, since I as its principle no longer exist. My being grasped and torn apart by the [*Evidenz*] which I do not make, but which creates itself, is the phenomenal image of my being negated and extinguished in the pure light.[48]

Here, B is the factical expression of A. T, thought, when taken factically, apart from content, is nothing but the negation of B. But thought, whose principle is the "I" of consciousness, is nothing without content. Deprived of content, the "I" that thinks, or T *tout court*, dissolves into light. This is, once again, a retorsive argument. *The concept cannot be anything other than the negation of L.* Hence, the one disjunction that separates B-T also separates C and L. The lynchpin is the necessary relationship between consciousness and its contents. This is fundamentally the same argument as the proto-idealist deduction but applied in the negative: earlier, it was established that light and its image have the same content: now, when the contents of consciousness are negated, so too is consciousness itself, allowing for the emergence of light. These, then, are expressions of the same use of the *durcheinander* but proceeding from different sides: one from the contents of consciousness to light positively, the other, the same, but in the negative, hence in its positive expression, from light to the contents of consciousness.

In itself, light is perfectly coherent. The appearance of the split into B-T is the product of an insight into something deeper, a dynamic conception of knowing uniting both thinking and thinking-of-thinking in a single act. Absolute unity as absolute act is described by Fichte as *life*. The strength of realism is that it offers – or at least attempts to offer – insight into life. The move to unified life is the negation of insight itself. The factical and the genetic would seem to have the same content, since we are tracing our way back along a path we have always already travelled. But as we posit factically in order to know genetically, we ultimately push the concept – that is, factical knowledge – to its limits. Hence, "the whole of reality as such according to its form is nothing more than the graveyard of the concept, which tries to find itself in the light."[49] In saying this, we have achieved an insight into light as life – it is something that in-itself has no disjunctive terms. We have arrived at "absolute reality" and "appearance" as opposing terms. This announcement is the beginning of both realism and its attendant problems. Reality is not in the concept. Rather, any limits or disjunctions in reality are not real but are found in the concept; the concept can conceive of itself, can grasp itself, and thus is limited. Yet one must ask the proto-realist how one can narrate the inner life of light without involving the necessary mechanics of the concept – from where, then, does the realist speak, if not from the concept?

At this point, such a criticism can only be anticipatory. So far, Fichte has established a twofold deduction of the *Urbegriff* that reveals two ways of philosophizing. Establishing these basic methodologies was necessary to ascertain the possibility of thinking with a principle. Now that a foundation has been laid, the nature of "principled" philosophy can be explored in depth.

1.3 REALISM AND IDEALISM

The *Urbegriff* offered us an insufficient deduction of the genetic unity of L and C. It is only a factical solution. We therefore have only achieved "factical *Evidenz*" or the hollow externality of both light and the concept: "[The concept] lies neither in the light, as what is imaged for the concept, nor in the insight, as the image itself, but rather between these two – we realize that formally in itself this concept is a mere *durcheinander*, without any external consequences[.]"[50] From this point of view, it would seem that the link between ineffable light and the insight into light is the concept, freely posited and not the direct product of light. But the problem is that if consciousness is independent, it annuls light as external. Yet light cannot be the product of the concept.

Resolving this impasse involves examining the foundations of each position: proto-idealism naively took the origins of thought to be found in the mind; proto-realism took it to be found in things themselves. Neither position is entirely false. Both, however, erected a one-sided absolute: for the idealist, the concept, and for the realist, light. Fichte has no intention of refuting these positions but rather to render them genetic and hence collapse them into a single argument. Both proceed according to a principle. What if realism were really the axiomatic principle of idealism and vice versa? Each would therefore contain *mediately* the principle of disjunction found in the other. This would involve correcting our very conception of the *Urbegriff*: until now, it has been "absolutely presupposed" and "according to its external form this is a synthesis post factum."[51] But in its inner essence (absolute unity), it is genetic. In other words, the *Urbegriff* must become genetic.

In seeking this genetic link between the two positions, Fichte announces constant shifts in standpoint that will constitute the idealism-realism conflict, occupying lectures nine to fourteen. If we are to find the principles of idealism and realism in each other, we have no choice but to let the conflict between the two play out, moving through a dialectic of realism, idealism, higher realism, higher idealism, absolute realism, and finally, *Wissenschaftslehre*. This movement will arrive at the genetic link between light and concept, necessary before moving on to the deduction of the manifold of apparent reality, the second part of the WL. What follows will seek to demonstrate that realism and idealism stand neither for schools or individuals but rather for two ways of thinking according to a principle, two "standpoints." The principle of idealism is to always presume that knowledge can only be found in consciousness. Realism's principle is that knowledge is found in the thing and consciousness can be ignored. While Fichte pursues these maxims up to their logical conclusions, these are not the only ways these standpoints can be embodied. Jacobi philosophizes with an idealist principle and Schelling with a realist one, both producing highly original philosophies instructive for the *Wissenschaftslehrer*. Ultimately, however, WL must go beyond these and generate its own principles, becoming "principle-providing" [*principiieren*] for itself.

1.3.1 Realism[52]

The realist position builds on the proto-realist position of lecture eight, from which one can surmise that *if* something appears in consciousness, *then* light must be presumed. The "coming to light" of the contents of consciousness means that light is always immediately present to us: light is *evident*, and only comes into discourse as imaged [*Abgebildet*]. Hence, light is on the one hand immanent life, the absolute unity that subsequently splits into being and thought, and on the other an "objectifying insight."[53] Light is an internality made external by consciousness. Light as life is negated by consciousness when imaged. This proposition is not only reversible (and hence an instance of through-one-another) but its truth lies in its very reversibility – it is only properly understood once the through-one-another has been effected; consciousness does negate light, but when one reverses the structure to see light negating consciousness, it becomes clear that the very split into light and consciousness presupposes the shining of light: "Therefore light's absolute inner life is posited; it exists only in living itself and not otherwise; therefore it can be encountered only immediately in living and nowhere else."[54] This higher vantage point provided by the absolute character of reversibility is the *durch*, the through, at work. Throughout the syntheses of the WL, it will consistently affirm that the initial proposition, in this case "consciousness negates light," only reveals its truth when the terms have been reversed: "light negates consciousness."

Reality, then, does not belong to consciousness and its products but rather to the world of immediate presence – of what stands in the light. Light, life, and reality are all the same – they are the ineffable oneness that negates the concept, the consciousness that we are. This allows us to see into [*wir sehen ein*] the light-concept disjunction. There is no originary split of light and concept but rather a division that is the product of consciousness (the concept) and which from light's point of view does not exist at all: hence, the division of light and concept is itself internal to light, which cannot be taken apart.

Fichte then sets out to find the principle according to which our newly secured realist position thinks. This involves investigating the origins of the original proposition found in consciousness, the negation of light. The absolute split between light and consciousness is derived from the presupposition that absolute unity resides neither in A nor the point but rather in the unity of the two. One then negates all disjunctions to arrive at this unity, thereby abandoning all specificity that either A or the point might possess. Yet this procedure has yielded an absolute that is factical and external. The content may be genetic, but it is formally factical. The locus of the error was its second moment, the negation of all disjunction. Disjunction, too, must somehow be genetically linked to unity, since unity is unity of disjunction. This procedure has let us factically posit something whose content would seem to be true, but we must give up on it at this point, since it does not yield a genetic result. But on what grounds do we claim that all disjunction cannot be negated? Given what has already been established, the question depends on a distinction between inner and outer: light, as immediate, is entirely self-contained; it is inward life. Consciousness of it is merely external. Yet this very externalization is itself internal to light: we see that light, as inward, must have correspondingly "inward" origins. Consequently, the inner/outer distinction is itself merely factical, the product of consciousness. We have, Fichte remarks parenthetically, banished facticity to the side of consciousness.[55] His point is that one cannot draw a line through the fabric of reality, with what *is* (being and light) on the one side and its *representations* (thought and concept) on the other. What is represented in consciousness is what *is*, and this fact is simply evident to us given that we know things in particular. A sceptic who doubts the link between things and their representations in knowing would therefore place herself outside of the very disjunction she seeks to denounce. The sceptic claims, "I think there is no ground for thinking being," a contradiction whose real result is to prove that one is always already thinking being: light is pervasive. The investigation into the realist principle has therefore determined that the concept is disjunction and light the principle of disjunction. Light splits internally into being and thought, an immediacy mediated in the concept. Light is therefore internally diverse and cannot simply be negated as homogenous unity or disjunction.

We have, in fact, already been philosophizing according to this maxim for some time; however, one cannot give an account of these before applying them. The reversal that the *durch* has operated showed us that what we thought was initially a construction is actually a *reconstruction*. Light is not our negation; *we*, as consciousness, are the negation of light, a split internal to the evident shining of light.[56] It requires no deduction because it is not a product of consciousness but rather the negation of a deduction: light simply *is*, and we must simply accept its presence. The whole initial realist position, then, could be summarized as follows: *I initially claim that light divides itself into B and T. But I am just this T that belongs to the division of light.*

1.3.2 Idealism[57]

The realist's initial position of making the light-concept division internal to light does not secure an absolutely genetic relationship. The same facticity initially found between light and concept hasn't been negated but merely foisted onto the concept. The concept's inward essence is a 'through': the imaged light [*Bild*] is through what is imaged [*Abgebildet*] and vice-versa – their content is the same. The true content of the concept, then, is indeed genetic, but its form is factical. "*Bild*" is given, but the "*Abgebildet*" is constructed outside and is therefore factical. The two terms that the through unites require some internal ground that is not merely formal – a genetic grounding of light as content of consciousness. Fichte hypothesizes about how this might come about: "How would it be if the internal life of the absolute light (= o) were its life, and therefore the 'through' was itself first of all deducible from the light[?]"[58] The argument for this would go as follows: If immanent life (light) is to have an outward expression, it must be by means of a through. Such an expression is necessary. Hence the through (of the concept) is the expression of the light's inner life. This granted, it would be the through that divides itself into B and T; it would be the self-mediation of the absolute. The through is the mediated reality of what realism can only express negatively, the absolute. As dynamic mediation, it provides for the different "fundamenta divisionis" of the absolute and hence the manifold of experience as genetic product.

Hence, "the existence of a through presupposes an original life, grounded not in the through, but entirely in itself."[59] But this insight (that the through presupposes life) is itself mediated by a through: life is through the through: to explain the *through* is to employ it. Fichte represents this in the diagram "a – a x b". The first *through*, "a," posits itself in one stroke. The second, the result of insight into the through, mediates it, expanding it into (i) the through and (ii) the through in relation to the life that comes through it. This can be pushed even further back: "a" does not posit "a" and "b" all at once – it does not immediately arrive at the through and the life that is through the through. The relationship is more complex: life is the through's very condition *qua* through – it is what "comes through it," so to speak. Life is the concept of the through, it is the through's intellectual content. The goal of this line of argument is to prove that if it is to be genetic, the concept cannot have an external cause. If the concept belongs to light, light, in turn, must be internal to the concept. There is nothing outside the concept. This is the heart of the idealist retort to realism's initial move, taking apart the immediacy that the realist had forged, wherein the concept was simply shown to be concept of light. The concept, which contains the through, is now a dynamic interiority, itself insight into life: "the absolute concept is the principle of the insight, or intuition, into life in itself, that is to say into life in intuition."[60] To summarize, *if* one thinks, *then* what one thinks *must* be light's dynamism, life. This life does not occur anywhere else other than in thought. If the realist takes *Evidenz* at face value, the idealist wishes to know why it is so compelling.

The idealist refrain is: "reason is the form of outward existence." Life itself is what comes through the through. If existence is rational, it has rational, albeit not directly intelligible, origins. We therefore posit this life-origin from the point of view of existence and then see if, from the opposite direction, the same existence is arrived at. The idealist position is one that moves from *Evidenz* to consciousness and back again by means of the through.

Yet this argument would seem to erect reason, which is not fully genetic, as the absolute. The real absolute principle, life, must be above reason. Reason lives *as* absolute reason. It is not yet life = life but rather life = reason, "mediated by a higher 'through,' so that in this standpoint, it is only derivative."[61] Reason itself presupposes life. Idealism requires that everything be conceived of within the bounds of reason yet does not provide for life's higher truth. This, Fichte says, is "idealism's stubbornness [*Hartnäckigkeit*]."[62] Idealism is stubbornly faithful to its own principle of never leaving consciousness. It is through the rigorous application of this principle that idealism discovers the basic structure of the transcendental method: mediating the immediate (moving from *Evidenz* to consciousness) and then returning to the same experience of immediacy. It taught us that one is through the other and that operating the inversion that is the through is the mechanism of this argument. Yet in its rigour, idealism cannot escape itself: it requires that all philosophy take place in consciousness, yet it cannot find therein the grounds for its own unity. Idealist systems therefore presuppose an external ground, the legitimation of which is elaborated based on this presupposition. The presupposition itself – whether it is Descartes's God, Kant's thing-in-itself, or (to use the example Fichte gives) Reinhold's fact of consciousness – is external and was thus illegitimate in the first place.

In a forcefully poetic paragraph, Fichte asserts that Idealism has essentially destroyed subjective consciousness, which up until now we have merely taken for granted. From the point of view of experience, we cannot rationally access the life that grounds our experience. Our only option is to live it;[63] what reason enjoins us to do is a negation "at the root":

> Let me note in passing that the place for denying ourselves at the root [*Vernichtung unsrer selber in der Wurzel*] is here, i.e., just in the intuition of the absolute, which of course might very well be our root, and which up to now has played that role [*dafür gegolten hat*]. Whoever perishes here [*Wer an dieser Stelle zu Grunde geht*] will not expect any restoration at some relative, finite, and limited place. But we do not achieve this annulment [*Vernichtung*] by an absence of thought and energy, as happens in other cases. Instead, [we do so] through

> the highest thinking, the thought of the absolute immanent life, and through devotion to the maxims of reason, of genesis or of the absolute "through," which denies its applicability here and thus denies [*vernichtet*] itself through itself. Everything has dissolved [*aufgegangen*] into the one = 0.[64]

Here, inner life and outer life are completely separated: "If one wishes to think of them as united, then they are united exactly by this gulf and this contradiction."[65]

1.3.3. Higher Realism[66]

Idealism, then, has ultimately led us to think *realistically*. This reveals realism's maxim: "do not reflect on the factical self-givenness of our thinking and insight, or on how this occurs in mind, rather reckon only the content of this insight as valid."[67] All that is valid about thought is "its inner content." Everything must be negated.

At this point, the merits of both realism and idealism have been clouded by the presuppositions that both espouse. Both philosophize according to an axiomatic principle: idealism posits itself absolutely and lets the consequences of this logically unfold. However, it makes no attempt at exploring its own absolute origins. Realism posits merely "the bare content of thought" but does not think this content – it merely posits it immediately. Neither position offers a full account of itself. The result is an absolute disjunction between inner and outer existence, the reconciliation of which neither system attempts.[68] Since both positions are in the same dilemma – making genetic a factical axiom – we must ask ourselves how to proceed. Fichte chooses realism because it sees the possibility of something outside its principles, which idealism does not. We will have to catch realism in self-contradiction in order to foil its axiom. Here, Fichte is proposing that realism be used as a philosophical foundation that can be corrected by idealism's more rigorous argumentative style. This will allow us to see the disjunction behind realism and make it genetic.

Realism ignores the procedures of the concept and goes directly to the *Ansich* or in-itself, and this is where we must begin. The in-itself is precisely that which is not constructed. As a result, "the in-itself is to be described purely as what negates thinking."[69] This was previously merely factical: realism did not allow for something to exist outside its bounds. Now, realism identifies with its content (the in-itself) as the negation of all thinking. Realism, in other words, has questioned its axiom about only thinking the content immediately and not the method mediated by reason. Reason, as the negation of the in-itself, has been integrated into realism. This position is higher realism. If we stand back for a moment, we realize that we are the beings that have done this negating: "Thus your insight into the negation of thinking in itself presupposes positive thought, and the proposition is as follows: 'In thought, thinking annuls itself in the face of the in-itself.'"[70]

Idealism was grounded in an initial hypothetical statement. *If* one thinks life, *then* life *must* come through thought. It therefore began with our free thinking: we decided to think life. Yet this contingent choice did not take place in a vacuum; idealism has divorced it from the absolutely compelling nature of experience. It takes intuition for granted and does not realize the passive nature of the latter: one cannot decide ahead of time whether one will experience an object or not – one is always already in experience. To ask why it is so does not annul the bare fact of its presence.

Higher realism responds that in intuiting an object, one is aware of one's own thoughts as not being the ground of the object, the absolute. Yet one is also aware that a ground exists, since the object does in fact appear. For idealism, then, appearance is known to have unknown origins. When the idealist analyzes intuition, she seeks an intuition of intuition. Yet such an absolute intuition has no content. To put it otherwise, the idealist position thinks appearance as Spinoza's modes, vindicating Jacobi's complaints about philosophy. Here, freedom is a chimera, experience is illusion, and God the mere dead product of reason:

> [The] negation of thinking over against the in-itself is not thought in free reflection, as the in-itself ought to be thought by us, rather it is immediately evident. This is what we called intuition [*Intuition*], and without doubt, since the absolute in itself is found here, this is the absolute intuition. What the absolute intuition projects would therefore be negation, absolute pure nothing – obviously in opposition to the absolute in itself. And thus idealism, which posits an absolute intuition of life, is

> refuted at its root by a still deeper founding of realism. It may well come up again as an appearance; but, taken as absolute in the way it gave itself out to be before, it is merely illusion. Hence, we do not get past [*es bliebt daher bei*] the previously mentioned fundamental negation of ourselves over against the absolute.[71]

In the above, it is immediately, intuitively evident to us that, from the outset, *our* experience is not the ground of *all* experience, the in-itself – here, thinking's negation is evident. Our thought of this in-itself is precisely its negation. The same thought can be expressed positively: The in-itself's being is negated by particular thoughts. There, consciousness is a product of the in-itself (albeit a by-product), and the constructions of idealism, as merely negative, are actually the self-construction of the in-itself. Higher realism's ultimate position is that the absolute constructs itself, and we belong to this process:

> Thus, the absolute's absolute self-construction and the original light are completely and entirely one and inseparable, and light arises from this self-construction just as this self-construction comes from absolute light. Hence, nothing at all remains here of a pregiven us: and this is the higher realistic perspective.[72]

This self-construction of the in-itself has been seen into, it is intelligible for thought, and so idealism will have a rebuttal. Consciousness does indeed exist; we are aware of it. But it cannot be derived from the in-itself as external to the in-itself.

1.3.4 Higher Idealism[73]

Once again, idealism insists that what realism took to be something in-itself is really something-for-consciousness. If higher realism is indeed "constructed in a clear concept," as it claims to be, it is qualified by our reflection. The highest term, then, would be our reflection. This position is a higher idealism, claiming that it can reflect on the unconditioned in-itself not as something through something else but precisely in-itself. This is idealism's highest point.

A weakness in this position is immediately apparent. Realism thus asks higher idealism: "on what basis do you think the in-itself? How is this even possible?" To this, higher idealism can only answer: "I just do." Realism also had such an insight into the self-construction of the in-itself. This insight (or intuition, here used interchangeably) was taken up into the in-itself as its product, genetically. But now, with higher idealism, a further step is taken: the unification of the inner (in-itself) and outer (my insight). Still, the relationship between my thinking the in-itself and the in-itself remains opaque. What does it mean for me to think the in-itself producing itself? What is produced by the in-itself here, and what did I produce? There is an elusive factical element at work in the higher idealist position that realism has thus far not been able to make genetic. Fichte quickly identifies this elusive element: when the idealist thinks, she is aware that she is thinking – one is aware of one's own thoughts. But idealism is unable to produce a genetic middle term that unifies these two. Higher idealism must always pick one term, either the in-itself or the I think, as factical product of the other. The affirmation *I am aware of myself as thinking when I think the absolutely in-itself*, contains a fluid contradiction: one element must be changed for it to be entirely consistent.

Idealism says that insight into the in-itself just is. One is just aware of one's thinking it. Light is therefore taken for granted – "I simply already find myself in the light, it's just there." If realism sees the light as being derived from the in-itself, for idealism, it must be foundational, since consciousness finds itself always already "en-lightened." In other words, idealism presupposes light and then deduces it from consciousness. This is not the positing and retroactive proving (constructing and reconstructing) that Fichte employs but one that has gone wrong, a vicious circle, wrong because it arrives not at a legitimate transcendental argument but at an external product. Much like Descartes's clear and distinct ideas, here consciousness is made absolute because light initially functions as (external) absolute but only in order to erect consciousness as an absolute from which light would have to be derived.

Whence this external objectification? Idealism has essentially made a mistake regarding the limits of intellectual intuition. An intellectual intuition is not a seeing, or *bloß sehen*; it is an *einsehen*. One cannot see light; one is simply aware of it. Idealism has provided a merely factical seeing, a *faktischer Ansicht*, while the realist seeing into the in-itself's self-construction is a truly genetic one. Fichte then offers a parenthetical "historical commentary," dealing with Reinhold. Fichte interprets Reinhold as being representative of higher idealism's attempt to make the in-itself the absolute – although Reinhold would admit that he has taken this from Bardili.[74] For these two, the thinking of the in-itself of higher idealism is thinking *qua* thinking. Ultimately, Reinhold tries to deduce existence from thought, falling into a Spinozist error. While idealists do indeed employ the foundational moves of transcendental argument structure, they must be reminded that a transcendental argument does not move from essence to existence but from existence to condition back to the same existence from which it began. The idealist loses sight of the agreement between *tun* and *sagen*, where the end goal is merely the enactment of what was initially articulated.

Fichte's historical example is not a mere recrimination of rivals. Its goal is to distinguish his own position – that of WL, to which we are drawing close – from that of higher idealism, with which it is often confused. The higher idealist position "makes immediate consciousness into the absolute," thus establishing an "absolute consciousness,"[75] that is, consciousness of consciousness (the objectification of insight or intellectual intuition). All disjunctions of consciousness would therefore have to be deduced from this self-consciousness. It thinks itself, or thinks the in-itself, which is the same. This absolute consciousness is an absolute I. If this is true, the higher idealist will have to find a disjunctive principle that accounts for both the splitting of the subjective side into multiple perspectives (subjective individuals) *and* the splitting of the objective side into the manifold of experience. The question here is whether idealism's path down is the same as its path up. If not, its absolute remains trapped in itself. We have already answered this question in the negative: idealism makes an illegitimate external objectification of thinking-of-thinking (intellectual intuition), thus transforming consciousness, and subsequently, the absolute itself (absolute I or absolute consciousness) into mere facts of consciousness. Before WL, all philosophical systems began with something factical and posited that thing as the absolute. WL, on the other hand, "lay as its ground … a [*Tathandlung*] which in these lectures I have called … genesis."[76] The WL has never taken the I of which I am aware, the factical I, as a foundational principle. On the contrary, the I of which self-consciousness is aware is only ever a particular I, myself. This

I is produced, while the productive process (*Tathandlung-Genesis*) remains higher.

In spite of its errors, higher idealism provides the WL with a lasting gain; for such an idealism is internally coherent and produces a valid vision of consciousness. Hence, even after going beyond higher idealism, we know that consciousness is self-enclosed and cannot get outside of itself. We now know that the testimony of consciousness cannot be believed and this because its terminus *a quo* and *ad quem* – or what it says and what it does – do not line up.

1.3.5 Absolute Realism; Excursus on Schelling[77]

The final realist corrective to the idealist position therefore accepts that consciousness is internally coherent, but does not have the last word about its own validity. When consciousness thinks, it is indeed aware of itself. But this awareness is internal to its own movement: it is not an external foundation. Consciousness belongs to truth, not the other way around. The ultimate solution, already alluded to earlier, is to posit that "consciousness remains only an outer experience of truth."[78] Consciousness is never the source of truth. The final, absolute realism integrates the idealist position within itself: the self-enclosed consciousness that idealism yields belongs to an overall realist schema: consciousness does not contain or achieve truth, it is not source of its own truth, but rather moves away from it. Structurally (in terms of form), consciousness is the outer appearance of truth.

At the outset of the articulation of absolute realism, we find ourselves before two fully defined conceptual entities. The first is truth (or the absolute, the genesis of light). It is perfect internal coherence and the possibility-condition of all knowing. The second is consciousness, an apparatus that both knows the manifold of experience and is aware of its own knowledge. Neither is the direct product of idealism or realism, but rather, their opposition is the stalemate of the series of correctives that these positions have put forth: realism taught idealism that consciousness is pure externality that does not contain its own truth; idealism taught realism that truth is self-contained and cannot be externalized. We know that in order to arrive at a coherent theory of knowing – a *Wissenschaftslehre* – these will need a common genetic root. Clarifying their relationship and finding this root is absolute realism's task. At the risk of anticipating, we might put the question thus: How does consciousness come to be truth's image? Making what seems to be a long excursus about Schelling, Fichte's initial approach to this question is oblique. The latter is not a caricature of absolute realism any more than Jacobi was of higher idealism. Rather, in much the same way that Jacobi presents a rebuttal to the problems of idealism without ever abandoning its presuppositions, so Schelling's *Identitätsphilosophie* incarnates the typology of realist thinking.[79] Schelling seeks to erect reason as above idealism and realism but on realist principles, only ever anticipating idealism's objections without really integrating its position. He is guilty of realism's outward projection and disregard for consciousness.

Before it was overcome, higher idealism made an absolute I the absolute *tout court*. This was refuted. But in its refutation, realism as we knew it was refuted as well. Realism is no longer an objectivism: its truth has been transformed into an "inner being," not immediately accessible to us. There is no other term with which it can enter into relationship. Now, Schelling had an inkling of this, but produced an *ex post facto* rather genetic synthesis, objectifying the absolute:

> Only one recent philosophical writer (I mean Schelling) has had a suspicion about this truth [i.e., that the absolute is neither subject nor object[80]], with his so-called system of identity; not, certainly, that he had seen into the absolute negation of subject and object, but that with his system he aimed at a synthesis *post factum*; and with this operation he believed he had gone beyond the range of the science of knowing. Here is how things stand about that: he had perceived this synthesizing in the science of knowing, which carried it out, and he believed himself to be something more when he said what it did. This is the first unlucky blow that befell him: saying, which always stems from subjectivity and by its nature presents a dead object, is not more but less excellent than doing, which stands between both in the midpoint of inwardly living being. Moreover, he does not prove this claim, but lets the science of knowing do it for him, which again seems odd: that a system which admittedly contains the grounds for proving our own system's basic principle should be placed below it. Now he

> begins and asserts: reason is the absolute indifference between subject and object. But here must first also be added that it cannot be an absolute point of indifference without also being an absolute point of differentiation. That it is neither one nor the other absolutely but both relatively; and that therefore, however one may begin it, no spark of absoluteness may be brought into this reason. So then he says: reason exists; in this way he externalizes reason from the start and sets himself apart from it; thus one must congratulate him that with his definition he has not hit the right reason. This objectification of reason is completely the wrong path. The business of philosophy is not to talk around reason from the outside, but really and in all seriousness to conduct rational existence.[81]

For Schelling, reason is indifference to subject and object. It does not belong to either but stands above it. Yet Schelling wishes to treat reason as something above and before anything relational, transforming it into an object.[82] Reason has essentially been substantiated into a *being*. What Schelling calls "subject-objectivity," or the self's knowledge of itself, is not grounded in the immediacy of *Evidenz* but in a determinist metaphysical frame. There is no space for a real intellectual intuition in the identity philosophy, since all intuition subreptically becomes object-oriented. As Fichte wrote to Schelling, "one cannot proceed from *being* … but from *seeing*."[83] Fichte and Schelling thus stand before the same problem – that of integrating the isolated spheres of truth and consciousness – but offer radically different solutions; for the latter, indifferent reason, for the former, genetic being.[84]

Leaving Schelling behind, Fichte now moves on with absolute realism. With its arrival, consciousness was rejected "in its intrinsic validity." Yet, we cannot escape it – idealism has taught us that one can't think outside of consciousness. And so when judging, "we must abstract from it." Since "we ourselves occur empirically as consciousness," we are "mediately" entwined in the process.[85] We are ourselves the very appearance of what we are seeking. *We* must genetically deduce our own appearance. In doing this, the maxim we must follow (bequeathed to absolute realism from higher idealism) is: "if never of truth itself, then of this truth's factical appearance."[86] This new maxim is not unconditional, like all previous maxims we have encountered. It exists according to a condition: "*If* truth is to be valid, *then* it *must* ..." This means that it does not affirm the absolute validity of its external product – its validity (or the certainty of its propositions) is internal to its articulation. In this, freedom expresses itself negatively, preventing error rather than establishing truth.

We must abstract from consciousness if we are to find truth. The reason, as we already know, is that consciousness cannot account for itself genetically; it thinks (an outward projection of itself) and is aware of itself as thinking, but whenever it tries to connect these two, it finds itself thinking a third thing, an "absolute I." It moves ever outward. There is therefore a gap between judgment (thinking an object) and intellectual intuition or insight (the awareness of thinking). Ultimately, truth (coincidence of consciousness and consciousness-of-consciousness) is found in existence, where the two factors meet – yet existence is not itself the internal relation of the two – it is "discontinuous" with the process of judgment. Judgments are therefore inexplicably true: I know that my judgments are valid, but on what grounds is this to be explained? As higher idealism claims, we seem to "just know" it. This postulate now returns with a difference. Knowledge is problematically true; there is an inexplicable gap between truth and consciousness. Consciousness constantly tries to transform this empty, barren space into some third thing outside itself; doing so will always result in something merely factical and external. Whatever originates in this gap is merely factical and hence dead:

> This discontinuous projection is evidently the same one that we have previously called, and presently call, the form of outer existence ... For what this means, as a projection, concerning which no further account can be given and which thus is discontinuous, is the same as what we called "death at the root" [*den Tod in der Wurzel*]. The gap, the rupture of intellectual activity [112] in it, is just death's lair [*das Lager des Todes*]. Now we should not admit the validity of this projection, or form of outer existence, although we can never free ourselves from it factically; and we should know that it means nothing; we should know, wherever it arises, that it is indeed only the result and effect of mere consciousness (ignoring that this

> consciousness remains hidden in its roots) and therefore not let ourselves be led astray by it.[87]

The urgency of Fichte's metaphor here – an extended "metaphysical conceit" – is difficult to translate, still more to explain. The objects that one finds in experience are evidently present to us, but this very presence is conditioned by a projection through a space of death, on the other side of which they are only external products of consciousness. To explore this act of projection is to return the object to this place of transformation, the storehouse [*das Lager*] in which their inconceivable transformation from ineluctable to unexplainable occurred. It is here that one finds the invisible root [*Wurzel*] of objective knowledge. The totality of reason's products – including the placeholder "A" – are in this way shown to be a mere precipitate, a *todter Absatz* or residual by-product banished from the self-contained whole that is truth.[88] Consciousness understands what is immediately present by mediating it. Yet its mediated product is no longer the compellingly immediate existence that once stood before it. To switch metaphors, it grasps at rays of light.

Fichte's "metaphysical conceit" reveals absolute realism's position. In declaring consciousness "dead at the root," it has shown that it "proceeds from the in-itself and proposes this as the absolute."[89] This absolute is not constructed by consciousness. It has constructed itself. Yet this is already problematic: The in-itself is defined through the negation of what is opposed to it (consciousness), which means it cannot be absolute oneness. Oneness, the true absolute, would have to unite the in-itself [*Ansich*] (truth) and not-in-itself [*nicht-Ansich*] (consciousness), its two disjunctive terms. Up until now, realism and idealism have each taken for granted that the absolute dwells in one side because neither questions its own maxim; absolute realism's higher maxim allows us to see this most fundamental disjunction of oneness.

And while even now, neither side provides an account of itself, if one assumes oneness to be true based on experience, from there, one can reconstruct what was posited to be a self-construction of oneness. All that remains to investigate is the origin of this disjunction itself. "My experience is immediately true" is, from reason's point of view, an assumption, but one must assume it to be true if one is to get on with both living and thinking. If we do assume it to be true, while at the same time continuing our investigation, we will be able to produce a reconstruction that corresponds to the initial construction of truth, the product of which is before us in *Evidenz*. Awareness of thought provides thought with an immediate certainty. And while thought is not the author of this certainty (as the idealist might think), it finds it immediately compelling and undeniable. Its logical coincidence with thought then provides for the structure of all true propositions; I know that x is true, and I know that in saying it, I am telling the truth. This, in sum, is Fichte's critique of absolute realism. To that effect, he writes:

> How an in-itself and a not-in-itself follow from oneness as simple, pure oneness cannot be explained. Of course, it can be done if the oneness is already assumed to be the oneness of the in-itself and not-in-itself; but then the inconceivability and inexplicability is in this determinateness of oneness, and it itself is only a projection through an irrational gap. This determinateness would have no warrant other than immediate awareness; and actually, if we will think back to how we have arrived at everything so far, it has no other ground. "Think an in-itself" it began, and this thinking, or consciousness was possible. And this possibility has shaped our entire investigation to date; thus we have supported ourselves on consciousness, if not quite on its actuality, then certainly on its possibility, and in this quality we have had it for our principle.[90]

In doing this, we reveal that absolute realism is actually "an idealism." It has fundamentally adopted the methodology of idealism, which moves from intellectual intuition (insight into thinking, awareness) to the ground of thought. Idealism's failed transcendental argument, which arrives at an absolute I, is corrected by realism's affirmation that the in-itself constructs itself. With this, the long investigation into absolute realism comes to a close. This, too, is a merely factical position and on its own premises must be given up. It claimed the in-itself was the absolute and failed to see that the in-itself was merely a disjunctive term, below oneness.

What is left over after absolute realism has been dismissed? "Being," "existence," and "resting" – that is, the terms that composed the now rejected absolute of realism, "being in-itself." While we have negated this as absolute, we also know that since the not-in-itself is mere negation; it shares the content of the in-itself but precisely as negated; I am aware of the true content of my thoughts but also aware of the false form under which they present themselves. We can therefore inquire into the shared essence, or content, of both in-itself and not-in-itself, that is, what *is*. We must, in other words, investigate *Evidenz*.

1.4 THE STANDPOINT OF WISSENSCHAFTSLEHRE[91]

Realism and idealism have exhausted each other. The insight that what is in-itself and what is not-in-itself share the same content, since the latter is merely the negation of the former, has led to the overturning of all idealist and realist maxims. Philosophizing with a maxim (or thinking from principles) has not been abolished; what has changed, rather, is the axiomatic nature of these. The conditional axiom of absolute realism showed us that the validity of experience depends on a self-sustaining truth – we have moved from a merely relational logic, grounded in causes and effects, to a modal one, dealing with necessity and contingency. Here is where the WL, whose position is articulated in this crucial lecture, differentiates itself from all its forebearers. WL will show that it has a contingent rather than necessary beginning, one that validates the free beginnings of philosophy.

Lecture fifteen contains "the basic proposition" (Fichte includes this in its subtitle) and provides an overview both of what has been said, and what will come. It stands between the main parts of the WL, itself the internal relation between truth and appearance (in consciousness): "So then, on a particular occasion I divided the science of knowing into two main parts; one, that it is a doctrine of reason and truth, and second, that it is a doctrine of appearance and illusion, but one that is indeed true and is grounded in truth."[92] The first part of WL, the doctrine of reason and truth, is what the fourteen previous lectures elaborated. We arrived at a point at which the in-itself and not-in-itself were shown to be the disjunction of absolute oneness. Yet these two (being in-itself and not-being-in-itself, ultimately, truth and consciousness) share the same content: being *tout court*. Fichte now asks what this pure being is on its own, and if it can be mentally reconstructed. This "being" at which we have arrived is from itself, in itself, and through itself. It is pure act, "*esse in mero actu*." In this way, being and living are the same thing, the same inwardness. Fichte has just claimed that since thinking is an activity, and awareness of thinking is also activity, their unity lies in pure mental activity that simultaneously performs both. This is life itself. Being is not some dead thing but the very movement of life. This being-life does not exist externally. Rather, everything exists in it. "By its own agency being carries self-enclosed oneness with itself, and its essence consists in this."[93]

Immediate truth is *for us* in mediation, following the structure of discursive propositions. Whenever language tries to speak being, it turns it into a noun. Being can only really be lived yet *is* in speech as "verbal being" [*nur verbales Sein*]. The realm of consciousness is language; it is in language that we project being outward and objectify truth. Language is a nominalization, a living outside of oneself. The whole art of WL is to understand that language is itself the space in which reason comes alive *for us*.[94]

One arrives at reason by "surrendering this substantiality and objectivity." Hence, only being *lives*. Particulars do not. Yet, says Fichte, "we live immediately in the act of living itself, therefore we are the one undivided being itself, in itself, of itself, through itself, which can never go outside itself to duality."[95] In our immediate rapport with the world through knowing – in facing the compellingness of experience – we *are alive*. Put simply, *Evidenz* is. In affirming this, Fichte is also positing two valences of *Evidenz*, First, *being* as immediately alive, within itself; and *we*, as living beings with an immediate rapport to compelling *Evidenz*:

> And surely we know that we are not talking about this we-in-itself, separated by an irrational discontinuity from the other we which ought to be conscious; rather [we are talking] purely about the one we-in-itself, living purely in itself, which we conceive merely through our own energetic negation of the conceiving which obtrudes on us empirically here. – This we, in *immediate* living itself; this *we*, not qualified or characterizable by anything that might occur to someone, but rather characterizable purely by immediately actual life itself.[96]

Earlier, we saw that absolute realism, which claims that absolute oneness must construct itself, must be subjected to the rigours of idealism's method. On its own, idealism came up with a transcendental argument structure that moved from consciousness to condition and yet, instead of returning to consciousness, elaborated an absolute I. Realism insists that idealism remain within the bounds of its own claims. When realism and idealism have exhausted each other, we finally have congruity between a claim of reason and its expression. In the context of lecture fifteen, this is expressed by the two valences of *Evidenz*: between *Evidenz* as immediate being in-itself and *Evidenz* as compelling experience, consciousness is able to know the truth, and say what it knows.

The self-enclosed "*we*" is now all there is. It is even above the very insight into its nature, since this insight is its product. It was only in seeing the common activity of the insight into knowing and the products of knowing that we found the absolute oneness that is activity, *esse in mero actu*. Because we are no longer objectifying being, no longer taking anything that could be a product of anything else as a "factical" absolute, we have proven the maxim articulated in lecture fourteen ("*If* truth is to be valid, *then* it *must* …"). It is true because it is perfectly internally coherent. No consciousness can stand before this *esse in mero actu* as its other and cognize it as object. Objectifying consciousness does exist but not over and against *esse in mero actu*. Rather, consciousness's content "brings only the mere repetition and repeated supposition of one and the same I, or we, which is entirely self-enclosed[.]"[97] The internal structure of consciousness is always the same, providing the same argumentative coherence ("absoluteness") no matter its object. We now have an internally coherent method for evaluating truth within consciousness that itself takes into account the manner in which truth and consciousness relate to one another, without making any appeal to a third thing. Kant's transcendental method has been made fully internally coherent.

Now that we have achieved the standpoint of the WL, having thrown away any factical crutches, Fichte offers a review of the arguments made from lectures nine to fifteen. From where we now stand, the steps already taken – as well as their shortcomings – can be properly reconstructed. First, we "elevated ourselves to a pure through, as the essence of the concept" and saw that a pure *through* "presupposed a self-subsisting being."[98] There proved to be two ways to perform this positing, two paths open to us: an idealism, which starts in consciousness and posits life therein, or a realism, which takes the fact that life ought to exist in itself and goes straight to thinking this in-itself, ignoring consciousness. Each followed a maxim. Idealism's was: "the fact of reflection is to be taken as valid, and nothing else." Realism's was: "the content of the evident proposition is to be taken as valid, and nothing else." Both of these affirmations are mere facts, and so both positions are condemned to facticity. From there, we turned to the in-itself of the realist standpoint. The in-itself was revealed to be the negation of the validity of seeing into what is in-itself. It constructs itself immediately, as *Evidenz.* Insight into it is therefore derived from it: it is evident to us. Then idealism returned: it demanded we *think* the in-itself, which is what we had already been doing – consciousness is inescapable. It said that we are aware of the in-itself's construction, and this is itself its construction. Realism then rebutted: thinking cannot be derived from awareness of thinking; consciousness cannot account for its own truth. This absolute realism faced a new problem: the exclusivity of the spheres of truth and consciousness, through which consciousness, aware of the truth of its judgments, projects its objects inexplicably: a *projectum per hiatum irrationale.* Projection constitutes the maxim of consciousness. It is unavoidable. One overcomes it by dividing the science of knowing in two (knowing and illusion) and integrating illusion into knowing. This highest realism was then judged to be itself the disjunction of what is in-itself with what is not-in-itself. The in-itself turned out to be incomprehensible without the not-in-itself. Truth (in itself) and consciousness (not-in-itself) belong to each other as the totality of knowing, the disjunctive points of something higher. They are *through* one another. Truth and consciousness therefore become the genetic terms of absolute oneness.

The whole realism-idealism dialectic can thus be seen according to the methodology of fivefoldness: realism posits an idealism. Idealism posits a realism. The propositions prove to be reversible. From where we now stand, it is clear that all along, the goal of the *Wahrheitslehre* was to make explicit the form of transcendental argumentation, the fivefold synthesis. We will see it put to work in the next lecture, its structure becoming explicit in its execution.

2

The 1804/2 Wissenschaftslehre Part II: The Theory of Appearances

2.1 THE TRANSCENDENTAL THEORY OF KNOWING: THE "SOLL"

The theory of truth, which found its apogee in lecture fifteen, was an "ascent" [*Aufsteigen*] during which not only all content of consciousness but also the maxims according to which one can philosophize (encompassed by those of realism and idealism) were abandoned in order to reveal the bare, self-reflexive form of transcendental argumentation that is the fivefold synthesis – the move from *Evidenz* as immediately compelling experience to *Evidenz* as immediate being-in-itself and back again. Yet knowledge is not an empty vessel – *if* consciousness arises, *then* it is always consciousness of something. This last phrase is the refrain that will punctuate the rest of the WL, the "descent" [*Absteigen*] that will restore what was willfully abstracted and can now be examined transcendentally. As Fichte is fond of repeating, "we let it all go as just a means of ascent [*Aufsteigen*], until it shows up again on our descent [*Absteigen*]."[1] If the first part showed that "being is entirely a self-enclosed singularity [*Singulum*] of immediately living being that can never get outside itself," now, in the second part, our goal is to "deduce from the first part, as necessary and true appearances, everything which up to now we have let go as merely empirical and not intrinsically valid,"[2] a task that is new to the WL. Subjective knowledge of what is in the world (that is, experience) will be restored according to the rigorous transcendental structures of knowing established in the first part.[3] It is, in other words, an account of how truth manifests itself in consciousness, a "doctrine of appearance and illusion but one that is *indeed true* and is grounded in truth."[4] In this way, Fichte's "doctrine of appearance" [*Erscheinungslehre*] is a theory of truth's images [*Bildlehre*], or alternately, a *Phänomenologie*.[5]

Fichte's phenomenology will consist of three sections and their unity (given its own separate fourth section by way of conclusion): 1) a theory of transcendental knowing, which elaborates a *Soll* (lectures sixteen to nineteen); 2) a theory of ordinary knowing, concerned with the transcendental unity of apperception, a science of mediation that will do for knowing what the first section did for appearance (lectures twenty and twenty-one); 3) a transcendental theory of principles whose goal is to "become what we say, and say what we become" (lectures twenty-two to twenty-five). As WL itself, it unites the previous two. 4: *conclusion*) The unity of all knowing and the WL within the WL itself; the possibility of particular sciences whose structure is derived from that of the WL (lectures twenty-six to twenty-eight).[6]

One of the moves that Fichte made in order to arrive at the standpoint of WL from the idealism-realism conflict was the transition from an *unconditional* (or necessary) maxim, an axiomatic presupposition that was never questioned, to that of a *conditioned* (or contingent) maxim: "*If* truth is to be valid, *then* it *must* ..." This conditioned maxim will now be given a name, the *Soll*, and will prove to be the cornerstone of the theory of appearance. *When* something occurs in experience, *then* certain conditions *must* be present. As Fichte will tell us, this basic logical structure has been operative all along, guiding us through the theory of truth, but is only apparent to us now that the standpoint of WL has been achieved and the fivefold synthesis made transparent. Lectures sixteen to nineteen define the *Soll* and have as conclusion the assertion that being's self-construction is also its externalization; the truth of experience is never disconnected from experience itself. This will establish the possibility-conditions of appearance. *Evidenz*, the immediately compelling nature of experience, will be shown to be both terminus *a quo* and *ad quem* of this transcendental argument, provided for by the internal coherence of the *Soll*. Accounting for this internal coherence is therefore the task of this first part of the theory of appearance.

At the beginning of lecture sixteen,[7] Fichte reminds us of the results of the theory of truth: thought (consciousness) became aware that it shared its content with truth in-itself, and hence an absolute dynamic oneness, *esse in mero actu*, was identified as the absolute. Stated thus, it sounds as if idealism has re-emerged: *I* posit this absolute in consciousness. Any such re-emergence of idealism, however, is accompanied by a realist corrective: if all being is constructed and cannot leave itself, then it constructs itself. In the elaboration of the maxim "*If* being is constructed, *then* it is a self-construction," a realist internalizing movement keeps the idealist methodology within the bounds that idealism itself establishes: it must never leave itself. Of equal importance is that this maxim is equally true when inversed: "Or, as is completely synonymous: We certainly are the agents who carry out this construction, but we do it insofar as we are being itself[.]"[8] This last statement is the genetic version of what idealism (consciousness) had initially posited merely factically. This is achieved by subjecting it to the fivefold synthesis and the method thereof, the *through*. We have now obtained the first explicitly (that is, self-consciously) fivefold deduction, which can be expressed as follows:

a. Insight saw into an absolute.
b. The absolute is the real origin of the insight and not the other way around (*through*).
c. (b)'s conclusion, "insight is the product of the absolute," is also reversible: "we [the insight] are certainly the agents who carry out this construction, but we do it insofar as we are being itself." Hence, an a^2 is affirmed as a proposition internal to the initial a-b relationship.

Expressed according to its bare formal structure, the deduction would therefore look like this:

1. A^1 sees into B^1. This proposition is A^2 (A's conclusion).
2. It turns out that A^2 is true only when reversed: B^1 is the condition of A^1. This proposition is B^2 (B's conclusion).
3. Just as A^1 and B^1 were reversible, so too are A^2 and B^2 (the conclusions of either proposition). This second reversal (or "throughness") is C.

4. C is a higher A^2, the genetic version of the initial factical proposition.
5. C represents two "throughs" $A^1 = B^1 [C^1]$; $A^2 = B^2 [C^2]$. But as pure throughness, $C^1 = C^2$. The logic of inner and outer has been abolished. This last step constitutes *reconstruction*. We trace the same path as what was initially there and which we (ideally) could only presuppose.

This is, as already stated, an ideal construction; for while idealism has been vanquished, consciousness, which follows its maxims, cannot be. Furthermore, the content of this idealistic construction is indeed the real content of the absolute. Yet if this construction constitutes insight into the absolute's self-construction, it merely sees *that* the self-construction takes place. We cannot see into *how* the absolute constructs itself, merely *that* it occurs – there is no insight beyond insight. If the absolute constructs itself and *we* are the agents that carry out this self-construction, then there can be no real disjunction between the absolute (being) and experience. But if such a gap presents itself to us within consciousness, it is because it is an ideal construction of consciousness itself. *We* produce this gap through our act of projection. We will ultimately have to find a genetic *principle* for this gap, since one always thinks following a principle or maxim. In lecture fifteen, it was concluded that the in-itself had an other and so needed a genetic ground above itself and its other. Now, the same thing must be done for the irrational gap: it is an absolute lack of principle, but this lack of what is principled needs a principle. If, in lectures fourteen and fifteen, we moved up from the in-itself (truth) toward *esse in mero actu*, we must now move downwards to the not-in-itself (consciousness).

By definition, to exist on the other side of an irrational gap, simply the product of projection, is to be without principle: there is no principle *in the sphere of existence* that accounts for experience itself. In this sense, its principle is projection itself. Fichte expresses this is a difficult paragraph:

> What could this principle be? The absolute insight, which forces itself on us, that the ideal self-construction must itself be grounded in absolute essence, is conditioned by the presupposition of this ideal self-construction without any ground,

> and thus by this projection we ourselves have made to complete the science of knowing. And so, the principle has been found in what is conditioned by it, and the newer, higher insight that is thereby created can be encompassed in the following sentence: If [*Soll*] the absolute insight is to arise, that, etc., then such an ideal self-construction must be posited entirely factically. The explanation through immediate insight is conditioned by the absolutely factical presupposition of what is to be explained.[9]

Idealism posited an absolute self-construction. Realism rebutted that in order to conform to idealism's own standards (of not leaving itself), it must be internalized, or "grounded in an absolute essence." But higher idealism had made this construction simply by claiming immediate awareness of its own constructive powers. Realism had pointed out that this places consciousness in a state of internal contradiction: it presumed itself in order to posit itself. But what happens if we reverse the question: how does consciousness (idealism) make any true statement at all? Wouldn't it merely presume truth and then always find what it is looking for? Fichte's answers that the fact that consciousness finds its truth internal to its own operations does not mean that it fabricated it. Rather, consciousness has an internal relationship to its conditions, which are simply given.

This is the first articulation of what Fichte will call the *Soll*, for which there will be three deductions in total. It states that *if* [*Soll*] a contingent fact is given, *then* a series of necessary relations *must* ensue.[10] In naming this mechanism the *Soll*, Fichte actually refers to a sentence structure, "*If* [*Soll*] … *then it must* …" the first word of which stands for the whole. The *Soll* is absolutely "hypothetical" or problematic [*problematisch*],[11] not itself a content that must or must not be but a structure within which something else must arise. The *Soll* therefore allows us to think contingency as contingency: should something appear, knowledge will ensue. Should it not, nothing will be known. One might add, "should an object appear, I will know it and be aware of my knowing." The *Soll* articulates, as well, the primacy of activity, of *esse in mero actu*. Without an initial spontaneous act, there is no knowledge. The *Soll* is "absolute construction." It represents consciousness's need to construct itself within itself – even what is received inexplicably from without must be treated by consciousness *as if* it were causally and coherently self-constructed. Since this *Soll* is purely hypothetical, depending on nothing and caused by no other concept, it is absolutely independent "self-making and resting on itself."[12] In other words, what is absolutely constructed, the very possibility of contingency, is itself absolutely independent and necessary. While it initially appears as hypothetical, it is actually something categorical – "the absolute determinateness of essence."[13] Structurally, the *Soll* is essentially another way of expressing *esse in mero actu*. But in our factical reasoning, we have arrived at it as principle. It is the expression of the principle of the gap. And insofar as it is a methodology that seeks always to internalize relations, we have been using it all along.[14]

As implied by the reversibility of the proposition that led us to the *Soll* (*we* see into an absolute that self-constructs; *we* are this absolute), the objective of the *Soll* is to secure the passage from immanent self-construction to external construction. The *Soll*'s principle, its genetic foundation, will therefore also have to simultaneously be the principle of its externalization. *We* are aware of having constructed being in consciousness. Yet, having arrived at the end of the theory of truth, we know that this is projection and that consciousness cannot be taken as unconditionally valid. Our task now is to discover the conditions under which it is valid. The first step in doing this was positing a *Soll*, which initially posits construction as hypothetical (problematic) before extracting some necessity from its structures. The being (the origins) of such a construction should be found in *Evidenz* if it is to be genetic. Hence: if the construction really *is* (the act that is *esse in mero actu*), then it is not based merely in consciousness but being: "if the construction which appears to us is in this sense, then it is not in any way based in the vain 'I' of consciousness that emptily objectifies being; rather it is grounded in being itself. For being is one, and where it is, it is whole; in being qua [*als*] being; therefore entirely and absolutely necessary."[15] In order to save appearances from moving from one merely contingent thing to another, a relation to necessity has to come to light: contingency will have to internalize necessity. The *Soll* is in need of a principle according to which it can always say (discursively) what is compelling about was found in immediacy. What, then, is necessary about the contingent *Soll*?

Thus far, we have established that being is factically (or externally) constructed. Yet this is an internal necessity. Regarding what is external, *we* have freely chosen to undertake this investigation of *external* contingency. Within what is hypothetical therefore arises something necessary: the relation that is the *Soll*. We know that the *Soll* contains something categorical, an internally necessary set of relations, but this internality seems to be foundering: it emerges from something contingent. Its necessity, then, which is in-itself, finds no link to externalization, the not-in-itself or for-another. The *Soll* thus stands at the very juncture of the split into *Ansich* and *Nicht-Ansicht*. And since it holds something in common with both terms and is ultimately projective in its movement, the *Soll* could serve as the middle term between the absolute and the gap. In articulating this, we have not yet arrived at a genetic principle for the *Soll* but have at least more clearly articulated it not just as absolute construction (the form of construction) but also as the principle of appearance. This leads Fichte to undertake a second deduction of the *Soll*, securing its role as principle of appearance:

a. The *Soll* "expresses complete external groundlessness, simple internal self-grounding, and nothing else."
b. To "make it clear from the other side … The absolute assumption is expressed in the [*Soll*], an assumption that is unconditionally allowed to drop, just as it was unconditionally presupposed." Once the *Soll* has been posited, its contingency falls away. In other words: (a) says the *Soll* expresses groundlessness. Absolute groundlessness depends on nothing other than itself (*through*).
c. "The [*Soll*] has been illuminated for us as an absolute that holds and sustains itself out of itself, of itself, and through itself *as such*, on the condition that it exists."[16]

This second deduction makes something clear: the *Soll* bears a resemblance to the absolute – they do not constitute two beings but rather merge. What distinguishes them is that the absolute is *Evidenz* (immediate), while the *Soll* is pure mediation, mediation of mediation. As absolute mediation, the *Soll* mediates the absolute itself (or what is the same, reconstructs it). Whenever something appears, it appears according to a *Soll*, and what appears is the absolute. Projection through a gap is necessary whenever a *Soll* is posited. Yet the projection of the *Soll* is itself necessary for projection to occur. There is a circular relationship between projection and *Soll*. This moves us forward in the search of a genetic principle for the *Soll* and of its externalization: the *Soll*'s factical ground is the act of projection it created. What the *Soll* externalizes is itself in hypothetical-problematic form – it self-externalizes precisely *as Soll*.

Fichte then offers a third version of the deduction of the *Soll*, one that highlights the discovery of the "*Soll als Soll*":

> [We] presuppose a construction of being. On the principle that nothing can be except being, the construction is seen [eingesehen] as arising necessarily from being – of course, with the same certainty it has generally; supposing therefore "If it should be … then ____ must be." But the "should" is something in itself, of itself and from itself as such." This, and in particular the "as" most recently added, is now firmly fixed for you as another new middle point and bearer for the self-producing and self-sustaining "should."[17]

This *Soll as Soll*, or knowing as mediation in, for, and from itself, is caught in a vicious circle. The *Soll* posited projection, but projection presumed the *Soll*. How, then, does one account for appearance when the fact of appearing (projection) presumes its structure (*Soll*) and the structure is necessary to generate the fact (*Soll*)? In this way, the old problem of idealism, which we thought had been laid to rest in lecture thirteen, now re-emerges. Consciousness is looking for the principle according to which being is constructed, but obtaining this principle (for the thing we have already constructed) implies thinking construction according to a universal law. But we have already performed this construction, and so we must already possess this law. We must therefore become aware of what we have always already done, lest we fall back into the attitude of "just doing" that generated higher idealism's problems.

Fichte recasts this question in different terms that better diagnose the problem – that of seeing and its content. I see [*bloß sehen*] but am aware of my seeing – I see into the fact that I see [*Einsehen*]. Yet *Einsehen* and *bloß sehen*, as mechanisms of ideal construction, have a genetic root, formal seeing itself [*formalen Sehens selber*], quite apart from any content. Thinking with idealism, both would therefore be derived from some foundational form of seeing, an *Ur-sehen*. The *Ursehen* is the projective act of seeing but also presumes its own act. As ever, the solution to the error of an *Ursehen* is to bring in a realist corrective, banishing the illegitimate external cause.

Now, back to the *Soll*. In our seeing analogy, *bloß sehen* stood for projection and *einsehen* for the *Soll*. Both occur in a single act and are not the product of some external cause – there is no *Ursehen*, and the *Soll als Soll* is not some higher cause of the *Soll* and projection. The two contain their own principle, which belongs to the single act of projecting. Surreptitiously, idealism has provided the *Soll* with an exemplar, an external thing it copies in producing contingent content – a "*Muster*." This reified archetype is subtly smuggled into the very formulation of the *Soll* itself. The goal of the seeing metaphor was to identify this error: experience has no *prius* that determines its content.[18] When dealing with the *Soll*, we must realize that it does not construct the absolute in projecting it but rather *reconstructs it*. If it "just sees" something, it is because that thing was already given in immediate knowing.

When we arrived at *esse in mero actu*, the true absolute, it was not because realism had constructed it but rather abstracted itself from consciousness. The absolute is the remainder after everything else has been abstracted. Inversely (according to the fivefold deduction), consciousness is the remainder after the absolute has constructed itself. Consequently, the absolute constructs itself, and we are the remainder. To self-posit is to self-construct. Being itself performs the construction. Hence idealism cannot *construct* the absolute – it can only *abstract* from it. The result is idealism's death-knell: "This final illusion is negated here in immediate [*Evidenz*] by means of deep reflection. After abstraction from the highest oneness of understanding, a knowing remains, just because it remains, without any possible assistance from us, pure light or pure reason in itself."[19] The realist corrective to the problem of *Ursehen* is therefore to claim that there is no difference between positing and (self)-constructing.[20] But in the argument we have just made, a perfect equivalency has not been reached. If we start with the absolute, consciousness is a mere remainder and vice-versa. The new problem to be solved is this question of the remainder, whereby the *Soll* renders consciousness into a factical *todter Absatz*.

Fichte then links the foregoing to another protracted case study, Jacobi. For Fichte, Jacobi proceeds from the following principles: 1) "we can only reconstruct what originally exists." On this point, Fichte and Jacobi largely agree, with the former claiming that his WL gives proof of what the latter only took to be a given. 2) "Philosophy should reveal and discover being in itself." Here, too, Fichte concurs. 3) "Therefore, we cannot philosophize, and there can be no philosophy."[21] For Jacobi, since we can only reconstruct and philosophy is aimed at being in itself, it is only in denying philosophy that reason can emerge.

Fichte answers Jacobi:

> We, the we who can only reconstruct, cannot do philosophy: equally there is no philosophy individually and personally; instead philosophy must just be, but this is possible only to the extent that we perish, along with all reconstruction, and pure reason emerges pure and alone; since this latter in its purity is philosophy itself. From the perspective of "we" or "I" there is no philosophy; there is one only [once one has gone] beyond the I.[22]

Jacobi is beholden to idealism's maxim. He misread the earlier WL and didn't realize that there already, one finds no externality in Fichte's "I" and hence no external, heterogenous construction à la Kant.[23] *We* do not do philosophy; rather, *we are* the expression of reason. The move that brought us out of idealism's vicious circle of seeing and which shows that reason is not the product of consciousness but rather the other way around preempts Jacobi's critique. If one leaves consciousness aside for a moment (or regards it merely formally), one sees that reason presents itself as *Evidenz*. Admitting the compelling nature of *Evidenz* (that there is, inexplicably on idealism's grounds, truth in consciousness) turns Jacobi's question upside down: "Therefore, the question about the possibility of philosophy depends on whether the I can perish and reason can come purely to manifestation [*rein zum Vorschein kommen könne*]."[24] Jacobi himself reaches beyond the bounds of consciousness, but without making any kind of genetic deduction, when he claims that we can only reconstruct. Indeed, he contradicts himself: the assertion "we can only reconstruct" is not a reconstruction. Jacobi could only say that this is obvious – in other words, appeal to *Evidenz*. There is no way out for him.

Through this case study, we have identified something necessary in the *Soll*: it always reconstructs and never constructs. Its maxim is *reconstruction*. Its role is to mediate what was immediate, giving voice to what is already there. Yet this does not remove all our difficulties; while there is no more vicious circle between the *Soll* and *projection* that refers us to an external exemplar, the "*Muster*" that is *Ursehen*, its foundation is still not genetic. We still have to deal with the problem of the remainder.

In identifying this illegitimate factical presence, Fichte reminds us of the basic structure of a transcendental argument: "I say: in all derived knowing, or in appearance, a pure absolute contradiction exists between enactment and saying: *propositio facto contraria*."[25] The "*propositio facto contraria*" refers to *declaring* exactly the opposite of what I *am doing*: in essence, a performative contradiction. Mere consciousness contains a permanent contradiction because its truth comes from elsewhere, it always finds itself falling into performative contradiction. Sceptical systems – Jacobi's included – point out this contradiction in consciousness but instead of securing a sound argument, they reject consciousness altogether, performing another version of the same self-contradiction. Realizing the role of performative contradiction in philosophical arguments means that one can refute any philosophical system when one "points out the contradiction between what their principles assert and what they actually do.

The *Soll*'s remainder is the product of just such a contradiction. On the one hand, the *Soll* "presuppose[s] a seeing that is unalterable in its contents" [*tun*]; on the other, it "suppose[s] the insight to be not actual but only possible under a condition yet to be added" [*sagen*].[26] It *says* it is conditioned but *acts* independently. One finds no such contradiction in the absolute: "in the case of absolute reason, what exists, or what it does, is expressly said in it; that it does what is expressed in it in absolute qualitative sameness."[27] Hence this contradiction arises in reconstruction. Fichte offers a fuller account of this contradiction. Now, there is internal consistency in reconstruction – it claims only to *re*-construct what has already been constructed. It knows that its truth is outside of itself and is faithful to its definition. The contradiction lies in the fact that by definition, a reconstruction is superfluous; it follows what has already been constructed and produces nothing new. Yet there is no such superfluous element in the initial construction. Because the construction neither needs nor provides for a reconstruction, the act of reconstructing is *ipso facto* ungenetic.

This contradiction is ultimately the cause of the problem of the remainder. Up to this point, the absolute has been treated as a remainder, when it is in fact the source. It is what remains and persists because of itself, with no external relation. This is itself proof of *re*-construction, since it treats what is purely genetic as the left-over of consciousness. Behind the remainder, one finds a principle: if something is not in-itself, it is *from* another, and if it is not *from* another, it is in-itself. When one thinks (in consciousness) what is in-itself, one is obliged to think using this *from* [*von*], another symbol of the irrational gap. The *from* is a sort of necessary illusion of consciousness, since thought always requires some second term when thinking an object. Thought is always *from* somewhere, even if this somewhere remains obscure. Consciousness always needs a from-another in order to cognize an object; thought is *through* what is *from*-another. Yet the other *from* which this comes is the absolute, the completely in-itself. If we reverse this, we find that the in-itself's self-expression is consciousness, creation through a "from-another." Putting to use what Fichte has taught us, we can explicitly present all the steps of the argument that he has given us by simply applying a *tun-sagen* performative contradiction in a fivefold synthesis[28]:

1. The absolute is what is absolutely left-over after abstraction from the manifold (reconstruction's conclusion).
2. Consciousness always conceives of its products as a *from* (the conclusion of the *from*: itself-from-another, throughness of from-itself and from-another).
3. The absolute's self-expression is an absolute *from*.
4. Consciousness therefore emerges from an absolute *from*.
5. The absolute's self-expression *through* [*durch*] a *from* [*von*] is consciousness.

In sum: If the absolute is *esse in mero actu*, it must act. Its very activity is a self-externalization. Put simply, *light shines*, and is therefore itself an absolute *from*, a *from* through itself. If *we* are the absolute that constructs itself, then this synthesis is the "doing" that corresponds to our saying: *we* are the absolute, and we do what the absolute does: manifest in consciousness. By exploring the principle behind the remainder, Fichte has annulled the contradiction and shown that its expression was the consequence of the old realist-idealist conflict returning. Idealism "just did" something but didn't say it. Realism said it, but gave no grounds for its saying. Each followed a maxim it didn't question.

And so *we are* pure reason. Pure reason is not something external to which we appeal when thinking, it is what we do when we think. Reason and its content have a necessary relationship to one another. This is what the *from* was meant to express: "This oneness permeates the duality in the 'from a–b'; which duality exists only in the absolute 'from' – but not at all outside it in some independence and [in an] independent differentiation of terms – so that [the duality's terms] may be reversed with complete indifference."[29]

What is in-itself and what is for-another are penetrated by light and are completely reversible. They are both *from* one another (there is no in-itself without a for-another and vice versa). Light penetrates this *from*. The relation of the absolute principle to either side is not found as an external third thing but as their internal, genetic link. It comes *through* an *absolute from*. Light, in this regard, is an "inscrutable oneness" that sees both sides with indifference – they are utterly reversible. But if this is how light relates to the *from*, the *from* is itself *from* light – not in a causal way but according to the indifference of its parts: everything 'from' posits light. The possibility-condition of appearance is therefore described in the following way: "there is an absolute, immediate 'from,' which as such must appear in a seeing, itself moreover invisible."[30] We ourselves are the primordial appearance of inaccessible light. Any content, represented by the a-b of in-itself/for-another, is merely structural, the appearance of appearance.

The *from* is the final step in grounding the *Soll*. The *Soll* no longer contains the inner contradiction of seeming to be independent while appealing to what is external. The outward thing to which the *Soll* seemingly appeals is actually internal to it. We have thus accounted for the condition of the possibility of appearance in general.

2.2 THE THEORY OF ORDINARY KNOWING

Lectures sixteen to nineteen established a *Soll* and concluded with the assertion that being's self-construction is also its externalization; the truth of experience is never disconnected from experience. The shared foundation of what *is* and my perception of it is internal to their relation, not a third thing outside them. This shared foundation is a valence of the absolute, "A" as pure activity. This was meant to establish the possibility-condition of appearance, or "transcendental knowing." Now, Fichte will shift his focus toward the possibility of appearances being known, establishing a transcendental unity of apperception, or "actually existent knowing," that secures my representations as really mine. This science of mediation (for consciousness is itself pure mediation) in lectures twenty and twenty-one will do for knowing what sixteen to nineteen did for appearance. The starting point of this will be the *from* as light, the presupposition that accompanies all knowledge.[31]

It is the coincidence of self-creation and externalization, "through" an "absolute from" without remainder, that provides for the two valences of *Evidenz*. Up until now, what the *Soll* takes to be problematic [*Problematisch*] has been merely presupposed. Something posits something else, and the *mechanism* that is the *Soll* is set in motion. But this presupposed thing is not just grist for a series of mechanisms. This absolute presupposition has now revealed itself to be the absolute that externalizes itself in creation, since only the absolute can be absolutely-*from*. Like experience itself, it has proven to be absolutely and incontrovertibly *there*: it is *evident*.

This means that, in addition to what is encountered in experience, there is another valence of *Evidenz*, one we have known about all along and which now has been confirmed according to the syntheses of the WL: the absolute itself is immediately if inchoately present to us, and what's more, it is the same *Evidenz* that we find in experience: because the absolute's externalization (we might say, self-expression) *is* experience; both amount to the same in their immediacy. Knowing is therefore not self-grounding but rather self-producing. And *Evidenz* is the premise from which we explain the structures of knowing, the principle of appearance. *If* the *Soll* expresses the absolute's self-construction, *then* the *Soll* has only ever presupposed exactly what it has posited: the absolute itself. But this does not mean that we have exhausted the WL's phenomenology. Between *Evidenz* as absolute and *Evidenz* as experience lies the world of thought – of mediation. And it is precisely this world of mediation, of knowing, to which we now turn. As one would suspect, this will prove to be an inquiry into *light*.

"The light is an absolute *from*"[32] is the proposition we must now investigate. Light is not itself conceivable, even if it permeates consciousness. It is simply awareness-of-knowing. If one knows, one is simply aware of doing it. This insight (and here we use the term in its narrowest sense, as awareness of one's knowing) is something that one simply does. Its accomplishment is its proof. This itself is the *from*: we simply do it – light simply shines. It is unconditionally presupposed; knowledge of any particular is proof that knowing has occurred. Light enlightens consciousness as "a qualitatively changeless permeation of the *from*."[33] Disjunction is always also through a *from*. More than this, the light is identical with the *from*. Any subsequent *from* is *from* the light. All discursive knowing, which is a series of *froms*, presupposes the *fromness* of light. All this happens in a single stroke through the initial *from* of light. Light *shines*, creating a *from*; acts of cognition are precisely that – activity. But this activity culminates in a separation of knowing and knowing-of-knowing, from which particular propositions can be judged as being true or false. Particular knowing thus presupposes the (inconceivable) separation of knowing and awareness-of-knowing.

To be aware of one's act of knowing (to be aware of the light) is to possess "consciousness of absolute genesis."[34] Our insight, or awareness of knowledge, may seem like a new production, but we are actually simply becoming aware of what we have always done. As pure genesis, pure light appears as producing itself ("from" nowhere, or "from an absolute from") and thus is absolutely *free*: it is beyond the chain of necessity that consciousness requires. But this does not mean that it is something external: it only appears to be so when we stand in the realm of mediation, willfully bracketing out the *Evidenz* that holds what is mediated together.

The validity of our presupposition of light as an absolute *from* can be proven through the coincidence of *tun* and *sagen*: When I know, I am aware that I know without knowing this awareness as object. The locus of this presupposition is the "genetic *we*" that "merges into light." This *we* was the product of the reversal of the absolute's self-production; the statements "the absolute constructs itself immanently" and "we ourselves carry out this construction" are *through* each other. Hence "it has been truly and factically proven that the light can presuppose itself as a 'from,' and that in us it actually does so."[35] It is in consciousness that light shines, where knowing and awareness meet.

Yet a distinction must be made between two acceptions of the *we*[36]: the "*we* that freely posited premises" and "the *we* that merges into light."[37] The first is the empirical *we* of consciousness, whose role is identified with the knowing of objects. The second is the transcendental *we* of awareness-of-knowing, the light in consciousness. The presupposition of the *from* is true in the transcendental *we* of shining light. Yet it is also factically true as an object found by the empirical *we* but as the absence of object rather than object: it is a presupposition. Notice that the empirical *we* always thinks according to the methods of idealism – it wants light to have an external cause that grounds the circular light/fact relationship. From within the world of mediate consciousness, all *we* can do to avoid falling into this error is to concede the hypothetical nature ("problematicity") of the from/light. It therefore becomes knowing's silent companion, presupposed but never known.[38] The light/from as presupposition is therefore the distinguishing ground between "lower, ordinary empirical knowing and higher, scientific, genetic knowing."[39]

This distinction is ultimately one between a transcendental form of subjectivity whose knowledge is a genetic product and an empirical form of subjectivity whose knowledge is factical – that is, of the manifold of experience – and inexplicably *from* elsewhere. The two levels of knowledge here produced, genetic and factical, are the products of two different kinds of *Soll*, one categorical and the other hypothetical-problematic. *We say* that light/*from* is presupposed, but all presuppositions require a problematic *Soll*. That is to say, in the *Soll* as we originally encountered it, a contingent fact was the starting point: *If* x, then there must be … This structure was used in arguing for the *from* as well "if there should be an absolute from, then there must be …" But in the case of the from/light, we have secured a *categorical Soll*, perfectly genetic because its presupposition is identical to its product: here, the *from* is the *Soll*'s presupposition and its content. To be sure, this is only structural, lacking any concrete content: when the *Soll* thinks the *from*, it is categorical – when it turns to anything else, its contents become hypothetical again. The *from* and the *Soll* are therefore both presuppositional – they depend on light coming through an absolute *from* and offer no real account of this. All knowing is therefore hypothetical. What is conditional is the absolute. But this absolute, lying on the other side of a presupposition, finds no place in consciousness itself. It is merely presupposed. It is only when one abstracts from everything that produces consciousness – *from*, *Soll*, we, etc. – that it becomes *evident*.

We therefore have a categorical form of transcendental knowing, but knowing itself, the empirical within consciousness (what is from the *from*) remains problematic. As Fichte puts it: "Our reasoning has proceeded in the hypothetical form of a [*Soll*]; and this to be sure unconditionally as itself knowing, and as primordial knowing, since knowing itself has posited this *from*, then transcended this posited and objectified *from*, which we analyze from below and derive from it.[40]"

As an idealist construct, the *Soll* has a problematic relationship to projection. Should something appear, it presumes the *Soll*'s structure, which is revealed only once something has appeared. The *from*, as we have just learned, only solves this problem structurally – that is, ideally. We now see "a disjunction within the absolute genesis itself, through which it would be *real* and *ideal*."[41] This gap in genesis implies a disjunction between the factical knowing of particulars and the (genetic) awareness of the act of knowing. So far, *transcendental knowing* has been genetically secured, but not *empirical knowing*. In order to root the latter genetically in the former, genesis will have to be applied to itself, eliminating the gap within it.[42] Herein lies Fichte's proof for the unity of subjectivity.

Structurally, the *from* is genesis itself. The transcendental *we* is in fact this *from* immediately. It is the presupposition grounding the light, producing a categorical *Soll* – a being that cannot get outside of itself. In other words, when we turn the *Soll* upon our own transcendental *we*, what emerges is the absolute unity of knowing and knowing-of-knowing, a self-enclosed being that unifies in-itself and for-another. The disjunction into transcendental and empirical *we* is not a disjunction in this one being – not, as realism would have it, in the in-itself. Hence, we have a disjunction into light (awareness-of-knowledge) and consciousness (knowledge). Now, if one of these were able to serve as a provisional absolute, it would certainly be the latter, since within consciousness, awareness-of-knowledge (light) is dependent on a presupposition. Put simply, one can't be aware of knowing if one isn't knowing something. In doing so, we are leaning toward idealism, which seeks the absolute in consciousness – knowing is, after all, the domain of consciousness. On the idealistic account of knowing, consciousness knows, and light simply acts. When I know, I am aware of knowing, and L and C share content (*Bild/Abgebildet*). This means that there is only ever one "I" that knows. There is only one *act* of knowing, and in this act, the subject is unified. All that remains hypothetical now is the impetus of the act of knowing. If the act of knowing is the creation of the I, the coming together of knowing and awareness-of-knowing, its own principle of unity, its genesis, remains a presupposition beyond the bounds of empirical knowing: knowing is "non-self-genesis." Yet knowing is an act that generates an object – it is not mere abstraction but a movement toward existence. We can thus qualify it as *positive-non-self-genesis.* The I is indeed unified in the act of knowing, even if this unity is not found in the object itself. This "positive negation of genesis is an enduring *being.*" We posit a genetic principle within knowing itself – the act that unifies both valences of this *we*. Yet the knowing subject posits a principle outside of itself – the presupposition of absolute act, an external act with an external effect that is thus "non-absolute," or not entirely self-referential. The concrete product of knowing thus results from a negation of absolute act. Knowing's absolute unity, unity of objective knowing and awareness-of-knowing, has a sort of internal non-genetic genesis; its absolute being or the unity of the subject is internal to itself.

In this proof, we see the problem that confronted us in establishing a transcendental theory of knowing – that the absolute and consciousness relate to each other as the other's remainder – has returned. For while it had been removed from transcendental knowing by grounding the *Soll* in its own structures, it was not abolished altogether. It was merely foisted onto genesis itself, and in the theory of ordinary knowing subsists within genesis as the non-genetic remainder when genesis is applied to itself. In the solution just presented, this non-genetic element or gap has not been abolished or thrust onto some other mechanism but rather integrated into the broader genetic structure by means of privileging the *act* of knowing over the static objects of consciousness. What we have really done, says Fichte, is integrate the *projectio per hiatum* into the very mechanism of consciousness. In ordinary knowing, we project through a gap but one that is now *rational* instead of irrational, as it appeared in the theory of truth.

Ultimately, reason's self-construction externalizes itself as an act that annuls itself as absolute. The unity of subjectivity, a sort of lesser genesis, is the *reconstruction* of this non-appearing absolute. This reconstruction is thus the faculty of understanding itself. In other words, the subject is unified in act when it tries to reconstruct the absolute. It performs this reconstruction according to a presupposition that stands in lieu of knowledge of the absolute and thus yields not the absolute itself but the manifold of appearance: "Accordingly, it follows for us that there is no insight into the essence of reason without presupposing understanding as absolute; conversely, [there is] no insight into the essence of understanding except by means of its absolute negation through reason."[43]

This conclusion to the theory of ordinary knowing – Fichte's account of the understanding – is far simpler than its genetic deduction leads the reader to suppose. In sum, Fichte has affirmed that *we* are the *Verstand* that is *Vernunft*'s organ of sight in the world of appearance, not the I of the absolute but rather the eye of absolute seeing. If understanding is a form of mediation, then the theory of ordinary knowing has given us the basic elements of a theory of thinking as discursive act: every expression of thought is founded in presuppositions that must remain presuppositional if the articulation of thought is to be coherent: these are the "silent companions" of what is said, and to attempt to say them would be to invalidate the proposition they mean to ground. The relationship of discourse to *Evidenz* – the very emergence of the world of experience – follows a grammar of which we are now becoming aware. If the first elements were the relationship between what is said and its enactment, at stake in the theory of ordinary knowing was the very emergence of what is enacted as genetic product. This grammar of creation is what will be investigated in the next section, where our task will be to "become what we say."

2.3 THE TRANSCENDENTAL THEORY OF PRINCIPLES

So far in the phenomenology, the appearance of the absolute has been derived from the absolute itself. But there is something still to be discovered in the absolute: its manner of relating to its appearance. We know that "the principle of appearance is a principle of disjunction within the aforementioned undivided oneness and at the same time, obviously, within appearance."[44] This principle is from an absolute *from*. In the last section, we established "absolute self-genesis posited and given a principle, obviously within knowing, which is thus a 'principle-providing' [occurrence]."[45] It is in the act of actually appearing that what appears makes known the principle according to which it appears. But the principle itself was merely the *from*, and we can never bring the *fromness* of appearance to light. The absolute offers no coherent account of its self-mediation. Missing from the phenomenology is an account of the mediation of mediation, or how the mediation that is consciousness emerges *from* the absolute. This account, in lectures twenty-two to twenty-five, is the link between the theory of transcendental knowing found in sixteen to nineteen and the theory of "ordinary" or "actual" knowing in twenty and twenty-one. Fichte calls this link "knowing's being," or the "positive self-negation of genesis," that yields "ordinary, non-transcendental knowing." This section therefore moves beyond particular principles [*Principien*] to explore the very possibility and dynamic structure of "principle-providing" or "principiation" [*principiieren*]. It is in linking these two concepts that the further link between transcendental and ordinary knowing will make itself clear.

In the grand scheme of the WL, we have moved from the immediate experience of *Evidenz* to the mediation of discourse. Now, in accounting for mediation itself, we will be able to link discourse genetically with its objects, returning to experience with a conceptual account of our immediate engagement with it: "Only here will the principle of appearance and disjunction that we seek show itself to us; which then should only be applied to existing (= ordinary) knowing."[46] The completion of the WL is the completion of the transcendental argument. *We ourselves* are this completion, since our act of mediating *Evidenz* is itself WL. *Evidenz* is compelling, immediate presence, and what we say about it (ultimately, what we say about ourselves) must coincide with what it is in the very act of articulating it. We must now become what we say. This coincidence will itself be the manifestation of the "silent companion" that is the *from*-light.[47]

The key concept in the link will be the *we*, the subjectivity that mediates what is evident in discourse. At the end of the theory of ordinary knowing, we were left with an externalization, appearance that would seem to constitute a problematic *Soll* – if some new content occurs, after all, the *Soll* is not entirely self-referential and hence problematic. Yet the two terms involved, the absolute that is given and the appearance that is externalized, were related according to a genetic deduction but precisely as *non-genetic*. If the non-genetic is genetic, we do not have to assume it factically as a presupposition. We can speak of appearance as non-genetically derived from the *Soll als Soll*, categorically.

What, then, does it mean for something to be "problematic," and how is it that the problematic itself has become categorical? "We appear to ourselves … as genetically uniting both terms," that is, the absolute and its appearance. This is core of what it means to be *problematic*. The completion of the WL lies in contending with this inner problematicity. Fichte claims that the problematic became categorical by means of a *through*: we can know that problematicity is an internal necessity of the absolute (and hence categorical) because "we *are* knowing; thus this insight is possible in knowing and is actual in our current knowing."[48] Because consciousness perceives the genesis of genesis as non-genetic, the inexplicability of *Evidenz* is itself genetic. In this sense, the factical *is* genetic. The link is that "we *are* knowing". This lacks a genetic principle however, one that will have to be found later. We therefore have an insight we can hold on to as we move further, seeking the manner in which we are this knowing.

It is the *we* that experiences *Evidenz* and makes it discursive that must come to light. Put plainly, we must realize that *we* are knowing.[49] The proposition is constructed according to a Soll. *If* [*Soll*] we are the being that does the constructing when the absolute constructs itself, *it must be* [*so muss*] that we are knowledge. As with any particular proposition subjected to the *Soll*, this is a problematic (hypothetical) structure that depends on a given – *Soll … so muss*. Yet even the problematic *Soll* contains an internal set of necessary relations. Now that we have established an absolute *from*, *from* which a categorical *Soll* came, we are no longer concerned with the *Soll*'s problematic relationship to projection. Rather, we can watch the *Soll* unfold and pay attention to its inner mechanisms. In this spirit, Fichte asks his listeners what is left when one watches this process but brackets out the hypothetical terms. "Plainly, nothing other than insight's certainty; and because even the insight as such depends on the terms, [it is] nothing more than a purely inner certainty."[50] Cast epistemologically, the necessity buried within the *Soll* is certainty. Within the *Soll*, one finds a *muss*.[51]

Certainty usually depends on some material "whatness" [*Washeit*]. This or that thing *is* what it *is* – it is certainly *that*. But the certainty established in the *Soll* once we have abstracted its terms does not depend on *Washeit*. There is no *Was*. This is a certainty of- and through- itself. When we say that something is certain, i.e., it *is* what it *is*, what is important is not this *what* but rather the identity of the first "it is" with the second "it is." One does not arrive at an "it is" through exhausting its possible "whats" (what a Leibnizian might want to do). "It is" is rather a logical structure, something closed in on itself that is the *support* for any given *what*. As Fichte writes, "being is completely closed into itself, and outwardly, in its properties, is first the condition and support of every 'what.'"[52] Kant knew this but posited the second part merely *factically*, as if the "what" and being-in-itself had no inherent relation to one another. The WL posited the first part of this sentence in the theory of truth and now will prove in the phenomenology that the second part of the sentence has a genetic relationship to the first. This is, in itself, the task of a phenomenology.

Up until now, it has been impossible to say anything concrete about light. We can now say that certainty is a property of light – that is, in a qualified manner light is certainty itself: *light shines*. In its activity it is dynamically identical to itself; its being is its becoming. In this manner, light's presence persists throughout its activity. So with the inner structure of certainty. For something to be certain, it must *persist in* oneness; it is ever equal to itself. And this persisting oneness or unchangeability is the persistence of a quality: "Accordingly, you could not describe pure certainty otherwise than as pure unchangeability; and [you could not describe] unchangeability otherwise than as the persisting oneness of the 'what,' or of quality."[53]

In examining this text, the reader might ask what precisely is in what: is the certain object (that which is) the "what" in an overarching oneness, or is the one unity of being in the certain 'that'? The answer is that both are inseparable. Here, Fichte is collapsing any remnant of an inner/outer distinction between being and appearance, the heart of idealism's tyranny over transcendental philosophy. "Quality is the absolute negation of changeability and multiplicity, purely as such."[54] Certainty is *through* absolute quality. Any particular certain thing (that which is) would therefore be *from* the throughness of certainty and absolute quality. It would carry within it the structure of certainty, always persisting in being what it is. One can therefore repeat the construction of what is certain an infinite number of times and with an infinite number of quantifiable variables and still always arrive at the internal certainty that is from the throughness of certainty and absolute quality. When we construct a "what" (that which is), it will always bear the marks of self-certainty. Lurking behind this affirmation is the old refrain that has come up again and again throughout Fichte's phenomenology: *we* are those who construct being. We view ourselves in the same way we view certainty: light is our very act of construction, bearing all the marks of an internal necessity (certainty). In whatever we construct, we are reproducing the internal consistency that we ourselves carry: "we are what we say, and say what we are"[55] – that is, internally consistent certainty.

Certainty is an in-itself, an immediacy, and so are *we*. Subjectivity subsists in Fichte's system as what is immediately in-itself. Certainty's unchangeability has made us realize that *we* are not really mediated consciousness standing between our experience and the absolute; we are rather *Evidenz* and unravel its immediacy in our acts of thinking. *We are* the absolute origin of the act of thought, the shining of light. The practical result of this is that we are free.

Yet if the *we* is certain, a problem arises: we have just projected outward, as appearance, what is absolutely inner; we are talking about our own immediacy as if it were the product of mediation. Fichte answers that this projection is legitimate, because *we* project ourselves. "Life" (another valence of the absolute or light) is principle in its very immanence. As we saw with the *Soll*, what is problematic must presuppose a principle. What is categorical takes itself as principle. Certainty is therefore its own principle. Structurally, the act of providing a principle *is* the principle of life. Insofar as positing is a projection, a making, "[certainty] is absolute immanent *projection*, and so it is a projection of nothing else than itself, wholly and completely inward as it is."[56] Yet if this content can be self-intuited, it has in some way come outside of itself: the content has been made objective *for itself*. Projection outward *is* the act of self-construction.[57]

The logical framework of certainty is easy enough to comprehend: If I say something certain, what I am saying is in fact certain. The act of saying (*tun*) and the content of what is said (*sagen*) are identical. This itself is a categorical *Soll*: it takes itself for its principle.[58]

Fichte now wishes to make a review of his theory of certainty. This is no mere summary. He proceeds by expounding on three key terms, which he dubs "primary modifications" of "primordial light" [*Haupt-modificationen des Urlichtes*]: certainty (or light); living knowing; and principle-providing [*principiieren*].

Certainty or light. As absolute oneness, it cannot be described, only carried out. "It is always and eternally *immediate* I."[59] But this is a description, putting the statement at odds with itself. This performative self-contradiction will ultimately yield something true. One can secure the coherence of the phrase "light is a living principle" if it is principle-providing [*principiieren*] for itself. This is coherent, containing no contradiction. However, the effect, principle-providing, is projection, a term that is not light itself. Yet it is immanent self-projection (this is what Fichte means when he refers to light as both synthetic and analytic). It projects not through a gap but inward and essentially. Light's activity is projection, and its activity is what it is. This is projection *per transsubstantionem*.[60] The metaphor could not be lost on his audience. In the classic Thomist theory of transubstantiation,[61] God's substance becomes physically present in the world by replacing the substance of bread and wine; these in turn retain their accidents, or outward appearance. Bread and wine thus subsist in the body and blood of Christ just as these carry the substance of God. God never leaves himself but appears under particulars. The relationship of certainty to light is just this relationship of a certain *what* to light: the certain *what* is in the light, and light (absolute certainty) is carried by the certain *what*. This is the insight into "primordially real principle providing" [*ursprüngliche reale Principiieren*] and is a key subject matter for the WL.

Living knowing. We have already said that in providing its own principle, light-certainty projects itself – it relates to itself as the principle that directs its own action. It therefore knows itself, or intuits itself. But intuition is always *from*, and so its self-intuiting is projection through a gap, meaning an externalization. The limits of intuition, which requires a principle, generate an absolute gap. This provides for externalization and the possibility of different "quantities." All things that exist are a "logical" transubstantiation: they contain the inner certainty that is the identity of the absolute, the primordial light. Projection through a gap is therefore "a pure, rational expression of the true relationship of things."[62] This is what it means for the non-genetic to be made genetic: the absolute is both essence and image.

Principiieren. The absolute provides its own principle, intuiting itself "through a gap." This is a consequence of projection, itself a consequence of principle-providing. It is an "absolute immanent providing-itself-with-a-principle [*absolut immanentes principiieren seiner selbst*]."[63]

The next step in our investigation will be to see this *principiieren seiner selbst* as intuition. We must explore the effectuation of this proof, its actual use, and our knowledge of the relation of this structure to the effectuated propositions. Put otherwise, we must "ground the possibility, and justify the truth and validity of the science of knowing's presupposition that living certainty is genuinely principle-providing."[64] But on what basis do we make the assumption that the absolute is "principle providing"? We know that WL = we, and on the same token, light = we. Based on this, an argument can be elaborated. To save time, Fichte does not work out a fivefold deduction but simply articulates it through the accord of *tun* and *sagen*: The I performs itself as immediately self-externalizing act; so does light, etc. The point here is not simply to pass these propositions through the mill that is the transcendental proof structure. Instead, "this mode of proof must fall away and receive its higher premises." And, "when this occurs, the place is revealed where, at the very same time, the I that can act [*könnendes Ich*] and the light that can act fall away, along with all arbitrariness [*Willkür*], the appearance [*Schein*] of which our presupposition certainly still carries."[65] Earlier, we bracketed the problematicity out of which particular judgments arise in order to focus on an inner form that ultimately governs those particularities. We called this certainty, a principle that manifested itself *per transubstantionem* in particular judgments. But the certain *what* put forth by the transcendental we/light was freely posited: more than this, certainty's presence in the contingent *what* is the product of random choice. Our free will is ultimately something factical and arbitrary, mere *Willkür*. We must now focus on the internal activity of the accord between *tun* and *sagen* as a single, self-producing act, such that this *Willkür* falls away.

The self-projection of the absolute must therefore be necessary and immediate, yet *factical*; the absolute self-contained certainty must show itself as necessarily self-externalizing in order to avoid some arbitrary higher principle. On the level of logic, Fichte wishes to secure what was only implied in the key passage on certainty: there, the inner and outer of certainty and whatness was erased; truth appeared *per transsubstantionem*. Now, we hope to prove that this "transubstantiating" is precisely what truth does. Logically, one might say that while a certain proposition requires an internal structure of absolute certainty, such an absolute certainty always also implies a certain "what"; the two valences of "certain proposition," i.e., indubitably true and particular, merge. Predictably, Fichte articulates this in the form of *Soll ... muss*: "Should arbitrariness [*Willkür*] vanish, then an *immediate, factical necessity* of immediate self-production must arise in the *Wissenschaftslehre*."[66]

But can this "arbitrariness" be eliminated, and where did it come from in the first place? Its origins, as one might suspect, were in consciousness. If *I* posits light, then it must pass through an irrational gap: "I cannot predicate anything of the light, unless I just project and objectify [light] as the subject of the predicate." The inverse, of course, is also true: whether I predicate something of light, or light takes something as its own predicate, it is projected through a gap. The culprit, then, is not "I" but predication. To be predicated is to be made into intuition and thus be projected.

We have already said that light projected itself through a gap (it intuited itself) and in this act, immanently provides itself with a principle. Principle-providing is an inner movement that is tied to intuition. But intuition is the product of projection, which is arbitrary. Is principle-providing and the whole movement described up to now merely the product of predication? We know now that a problematic *Soll*, the form of the relation of a predicate to an intuition, contains an internal certainty that ultimately shows itself in certain propositions. We thus know that predication and subsequent intuition do not govern certainty. Rather, we discover them within the mechanisms already established.

In the act of knowing, I am aware of the connection between predication and projection. In thinking, then, I am not only aware of myself as thinking but aware that the process in which I am engaged is discursive. Yet it is not an addition but is merely the elaboration of what was there all along: to claim, "I say what I know, and know what I say" is merely the discursive unfolding of what is simply there, of *Evidenz.* Mediation (and crucially, its relationship to immediacy) is about *situating* objects in discourse. We, as knowers, project and objectify knowing as "a 'oneness through itself,' determined without any possible assistance from some external factor; [a oneness] which I simultaneously permeate and construct in its inner essence and content."[67] The content of the construction of oneness (the self-intuition of light) is arbitrary, product of individual freedom and circumstance. It is simply what is found in experience. Since this content is simply and immediately *evident*, it is unconditionally necessary. I must know *something* in order to know. In brief, projection is the essence of knowing, and there is no projection without predication. Unconditional necessity cannot posit its principle without facticity and vice versa, meaning that predication is the *law* that governs projection.[68]

Consciousness does not escape this law: I know (indeed, I am knowing itself), and therefore, my cognition is subject to law, even if I cannot see this. All projection belongs to this law, and here "formal projection," taken apart from any content, follows an absolute law, or law of lawfulness. Projection always projects according to a law and is *from* absolute law. Absolute law "has real absolute causality on the *inwardness* of the act [of projection]."[69] That projection follows a law *is* projection's act – it is what it does. In its form, projection carries the mark of absolute certainty. Its matter is the unmediated necessary *Evidenz* of experience. To say that projection is law-governed is to assert that both are present at the same time, in a single stroke. Hence, if projection is what it does, "the material expression must simultaneously express the projection's form."[70] The material expression is the *princpiieren*, the providing of a principle. But what sort of principle-providing serves as expression of its own form? It is called *Description* [*beschreiben*], and its introduction signals the collapse of inner/outer that was heralded in the key passage on *Washeit.* It is simply the description of one thing based on the form of another. The principle-providing of projection is immanent to it; what is mediated is always what was immediate. Discourse unpacks *Evidenz.* The content of discourse is *qualitatively* absolutely one but can be infinitely repeated. This is precisely the reconstruction of a pre-construction, or the appearing of life (principle-providing in-itself) as image.[71] Image is mere statement [*nur Aussage*]. Says Fichte, "[description is] the whole simply ideal element, as which we must consider our seeing to be, if we transfer ourselves into the standpoint of reflection, i.e., of 'principle-providing.'"[72] Knowing produces an image, or what is the same, seeing is principle-providing. To see is to see an image and see it precisely *as image.* The thing seen is an object, presented all at once in *Evidenz.* But our knowledge of it has been mediated through discourse and exists for us in a discursive world. To see is always to move from *Evidenz* to discourse and back again but in a single glance. One might put it even more simply, bringing Fichte's argument back to its Kantian foundations: knowing is re-presentational.

But Fichte finds a difficulty in this: *we* were the ones who constructed the insight into absolute law. It is therefore in consciousness. Yet how can consciousness govern or precede an absolute law? In brief, we have encountered absolute law only factically, and "the inference [i.e., of absolute law] itself only *speaks* of a law without being or having one."[73] When we affirm an absolute law in consciousness, the fact of its affirmation contradicts the very definition of absolute law, which should have no antecedents in consciousness. Were this in fact the case, construction would itself be mere reconstruction, and the truth in discourse would be nothing but a simulacrum. Lurking behind this problem is a deeper disjunction, which contains the key to its resolution, that of "the inner living difference" between subject and object as two forms of life. This is ultimately the sceptical problem that stems from the idealist position come back to haunt us once more. It asks, if everything is reconstruction, how can our representations correspond to anything at all? There would be no real world but rather only two reconstructions: a secondary one that faithfully reconstructs the first and then a more primordial one *that lies.* The sceptic therefore argues that the absolute law is itself the product of *Willkür*, something merely arbitrarily posited. The culprit, again, is *Willkür*. If one could just prove that the primordial reconstruction were *necessary*, then it would cease to be *re*construction and, as original inner expression of the law, would become the law: it would cease to be the external application of the law, and become the very activity of the law itself. Merely in stating this, we already have the beginning of an answer: in its inner conformity, law is identical to itself: no matter how often one reproduces content, the original remains untouched. Even the sceptic cannot doubt this identity.

This, the reader will recognize, is the *Bild/Abgebildet* argument structure first found in lecture seven and which became the hallmark of idealistic argumentation. If we are to legitimize absolute law, the sceptical problem will have to be banished for good, and to do this, we must return to the very argument structures of idealism that the WL has made its own. This, then, is Fichte's ultimate "refutation of idealism," his version of the Kantian proof. As far back as the proto-idealist argument for the *Urbegriff*, idealism's argument style is characterized by a distinction in the nature of what images are. We can now revisit that distinction with greater depth: An image is always an image *of* something, a reconstruction. A reconstruction constructs what is already given. Intuition, the construction of image, always follows a rule: reproduce the content *as image*. This presupposition of a law of imaging is precisely what makes reconstruction (image-making) reconstruction. When reason points to an image and declares it to be an image, it has arrived at something certain. This is an "ideal positing": we presume it as we do it. Yet it is simply another name for discourse, for the mediating of what was already present immediately. As ever, idealism's vicious circle has been corrected through realism and internalization: in its own movement, it finds the source of what it produces. "So, what we have undertook to prove yesterday is completely proven, 'The law itself posits itself in ourselves.' Image as image is the *nervus probandi*."[74] What answer does this give to the sceptical objection that idealism raised? The sceptic cannot doubt *that* he is speaking, otherwise his own sceptical claim would amount to nothing.

What earlier was called *Aussagen* is now recast as image. We can therefore subject knowing to the same argument as image: knowing is neither an image nor an original but is internal to the relation of the two. In order to recognize what is immediately present, *we* must reconstruct it *as* image: we do not create the image from an original but rather reconstruct what is given. Experience itself, as given, is already an appearing but an immediate appearing that is reconstructed (imaged, made mediate) by consciousness. It is the consistency of the act of construction between these that constitutes the law of projection, of knowing itself. This act is itself immediately present to us, another valence of the same evident-quality. The very structure of knowing, then, is image, but image of image, an image whose projection allows for repetition. Knowing must be identical to itself before it can know anything else. The law of the identity of knowing as it pertains to the possibility of knowing anything else is a law of image. Ultimately, to say that thought is always discursive is to posit it not as some heterogeneous, mystical thing-in-itself unavailable to conceptual thought but as a primordial image, a play of light. Put simply, in knowing, predication is always presumed.

This positing of primordial knowing as image qua image is "the total removal of the material,"[75] the extraction of the last factical element in Fichte's argument for the coherency of the WL. We have now become what we say and say what we are: in the act of knowing, there is no difference between form and content, and the transcendental argument meant to reconcile discourse and *Evidenz* is complete: the solution is a theory of knowing as absolute image. We can no longer say that the absolute necessarily externalizes itself; rather, its structures have been redefined such that internal/external is no longer a useful way of describing it, either logically (according to being) or epistemologically (according to knowing). This is the true meaning of "we are what we say, and say what we are"; subject and predicate, *we* and our object, consciousness and *Evidenz*, now all have an internal relation, not as original and copy but as absolute image and image.

We have now arrived at the highest point of WL, the integration of the phenomenal world into the absolute:

> Here we are immediately absolute knowing. This is an "image-making process" [*ein Bilden*] positing itself as an image, and positing a law of the image-making process as an explanation of the image. With this everything has been unfolded, and is completely explained and comprehensible in itself. The terms come together to form [*bilden*] a synthetic cycle, into which nothing else can enter.[76]

We have done this through negating *qualitative oneness.* We allowed for multiplicity by negating the conceptual oneness to which we have been beholden all along. The last step was the internalization of the absolute law *from* and *through* which predication comes. A different kind of oneness, oneness of image, allows for both quantity and quality, unity and multiplicity, to coexist in a single structure.

Consequently, WL itself has lost all particularity. It has now reached a point where its constructs constitute a science of thought *a se*, a *logic* in the way that the stoics – or for that matter, Hegel – used the term. It is a science of discourse, a discourse on the nature of discourse itself. Yet more than this, it is a living science, one manifested in the world of humans. *We are* the WL. Our philosophy is not a dead letter, a mere conclusion at the end of syllogism, but a reasoning and philosophizing that is precisely what it means to be a rational being.[77]

2.4 THE UNITY OF THE *WISSENSCHAFTSLEHRE* AND THE POSSIBILITY OF PARTICULAR SCIENCES

The last three lectures (twenty-six to twenty-eight) are a disquisition on the WL itself, partly a review and summary but also an exploration of the link between WL as logic and the transition to the particular sciences that are derived from it, much as image is derived from image as image. While one could call it Fichte's speculative Sunday, he means it to be the foundation for the move toward concrete disciplines of knowing; there is no sabbath for *Wissenschaftslehrers* – or rather, the sabbath is what structures their activity as they go about their work each day. In the end, these lectures seek to portray the WL as *life*, the very activity that founds experience and manifests itself in it.

At the beginning of lecture twenty-six, Fichte offers a program for what remains. He now wishes to investigate the question of how *we* have become WL and to investigate the two "further conditions" of this becoming, the one transcendental, the other ordinary. Just as transcendental and ordinary knowing were united in the phenomenology (in its theory of principles), so too must the WL and particular sciences be united in the WL itself. This link, something of a meta-WL, itself genetic, belongs to the internal movement that is life. Hence, we must now prove that life is inseparable from WL. Fichte also announces that this will "raise entirely new topics."[78] Implied is that particular sciences will emerge from a common source, internal to the WL: our very awareness of ourselves as WL.

In order to be absolute knowing, we must be certain of it: not only must we be aware of ourselves as knowing that we know, we must know *that we are* this knowing in the act of knowing, that we are WL. We already know that knowing carries with it the marker of certainty – that certainty appears within a certain *what* and necessarily so. What does it mean to take this whole process and, as we are now doing, insert it into a problematic *Soll* (if we are certainty, then we must be just this certainty)? This is, as Fichte says, an expression of inward certainty, and no matter where we begin – with "I am certain" or "this is certain" – we arrive at the same. And in both cases, we "presuppose the nature of certainty." If we see both statements as being through one another, we "presuppose that the essence of knowing is known."[79]

In the exploration of certainty in the theory of principles, it embodied a "oneness of qualities". The key to the argument there was claiming that certainty is pure unchangeability and unchangeability was "the persisting oneness of the 'what' or of quality."[80] But now, such a qualitative oneness has been abolished in favor of absolute image. Our characterization of certainty must therefore be adjusted to this new regime. Certainty is therefore "essential, immanent self-enclosure (as absolute being was previously seen to be)."[81] In doing this, we are offering a *description* of certainty. Description, as we saw, was principle-providing [*principiieren*] that serves as expression of its own form. Description is therefore an "originary concept" [*ursprünglicher Begriff*]. But how can one *describe* certainty? Normally, the laws of discourse require a "certain what" to appear in order for the whole movement that is WL to be accomplished.

In order to see how this is possible, we must re-examine the origins of description. In the last section, we saw that it emerged out of the concept of law. Law is "a principle that, in order to provide a principle factically, presupposes yet another absolutely self-producing principle."[82] In other words, something functions according to a law when it presupposes the principle of *something else* in order to be posited. The mutual relation of the two principles (of the thing posited on the one hand and of the thing presupposed on the other) is description. WL itself functions according to absolute law – it is always *from* a law. Judgments integrate two terms, their being posited and their presuppositions, in discourse. Hence "description is an inward immanent projection of the described."[83] Earlier, in lecture twenty-three, this projection – that is, discourse – went from being a problematic internal projection through a gap, or superfluous words that fill up a conceptual oversight, to a necessary part of the absolute's internal movement. Description does not exist in a gap, but rather saturates the interiority of the absolute. It is "just pure ideal *seeing*, or *intuition*." Such a seeing is a "projection that recognizes itself as projection … immediately, in itself and negates itself as such." By this, Fichte means, "'Seeing X' means not regarding the seeing as X, thus negating it. In this negation, seeing becomes a seeing, and something seen arises simply if it abstracts from X." In the act of seeing, one sees what is seen and negates seeing as object. Description of certainty is a *pure seeing*, the purely formal description "of an enclosure within itself."[84] Yet this description has a negative moment, the negation of pure seeing when something is seen. As we established with the *from*, there can be no remainder in the WL – the *todter Absatz* of consciousness was itself incorporated into the absolute as being from a *from*. This same movement can now take place on a higher level: "*Being* is what [certainty] intuitively projects in this negation of itself in which it still is. Because it projects this within, and by means of, its own ineradicable essence, this essence is an *expression*, an intrinsically self-expressive being."[85]

The astute reader might accuse Fichte of being redundant. This, is, essentially, the whole argument of the phenomenology expressed according to the paradigm of seeing. It was announced in lecture sixteen in different terms, those of insight into the absolute. There, Fichte arranged it in a fivefold synthesis, the clearest expression of it up to that point. Here, once again, was that synthesis:

a. Insight saw into an absolute.
b. The absolute is the real origin of the insight and not the other way around (*through*).
c. (b)'s conclusion, "insight is the product of the absolute" is also reversible: "we [the insight] are certainly the agents who carry out this construction, but we do it insofar as we are being itself." Hence an a^2 is affirmed as a proposition internal to the initial a-b relationship.

Now, having achieved WL, Fichte repeats this synthesis more explicitly. Liberated from facticity, he can express it using a "purely formal description." It is not the synthesis applied to anything in particular, but rather the fivefold synthesis applied to itself. Since *image* and *seeing* are the idioms according to which this has been achieved, this is what the formal description of the fivefold deduction uses:

a. Seeing sees into another, life.
b. But in so doing, it negates itself. Life is in fact the ground of seeing (reversal).
c. Seeing is part of life, life's own inwardness (life through seeing, seeing through life).
d. The terms therefore constitute a single movement, an externalization generated by the throughness of both terms (genetic version of seeing into life).
e. The genetic seeing into life is itself reversible; this externalization is internal to life; facticity belongs to genesis (reconstruction).[86]

Key here is that factical appearance remains at the end of the deduction. This is precisely what the transcendental theory of principles achieved. The factical has not been made into something identical with the genetic. Rather, it has been integrated into the genetic deduction as a necessary non-genetic element. Writes Fichte: "The drive for coming out of oneself always emerges in appearance and is struck down; undoubtedly, it can form [*bilden*] the appearance of freedom and genesis themselves, but it does not enter into truth."[87] The drive to externalize that is internal to truth is what grounds quantities. Unifying quantity with the principle of quality (oneness) will provide for ordinary knowing's primordial appearance.

At issue here is the constitution of a "qualitative oneness of being" out of the absolute image, in which all differentiation is abolished. In the act of externalization, then, the absolute image is construed as qualitative oneness. It would seem, then, that qualitative oneness and externalization are the reciprocal moments that proceed from absolute image. Certainty is to be found in the movement of externalization, between the certain thing and certainty in-itself. From this emerges a foundational claim: discourse is always discourse about something, or as

Fichte says, "objectivity and genesis are entirely one."[88] Transcendental knowing presupposes ordinary knowing. Fichte expounds on this using the metaphor of sight that has become integral to the phenomenology's presentation: "seeing permeating itself as *seeing* necessarily surrenders itself as something *independent* and posits an absolute *being*. The latter enters into a further synthesis, which yields a description of certainty as an enclosure into itself."[89] In the act of seeing, the capacity to see ceases to be about itself. It is about the visible world. This circumscribed – though not finite in the mathematical sense – world of seeing is what we might call seeing's *intentionality*, the "aboutness of seeing." Since seeing is given over to this world in its act of seeing, this act is the positing of an "absolute being" an objective outer world that is not seeing's construction but reconstruction. This intentionality of seeing requires a differentiation between "seeing" and "seeing permeating itself as seeing," that is, between sight and seeing. Fichte now clarifies that if one admits sight, then seeing necessarily ensues: "if *seeing* is *posited as seeing*, then it follows that seeing actually takes place; or, seeing *necessarily* sees." There is no substantive sight without the act of seeing. Fichte likens this to the classic ontological argument, whereby one proves the existence of a thing merely by means of the thought of it. Fichte does not mean to revive this old argument, which according to his own transcendental method would necessarily fall prey to idealism's vicious circle. The point, rather, is to prove at a merely formal level what we have been doing all along: that to posit something is to reconstruct what it has already made itself out to be. The act of seeing brings sight into existence and as *reconstruction,* such that "sight" is the inner essence, or the thought of seeing. In seeing, I know there is seeing of seeing. If thinking seeing (one could also say "thinking intentional thought") yields its inner essence, mere sight, this thinking of seeing, is inseparable from the act of seeing something in particular.

Fichte thus clarifies his position on intuition: there is no intellectual intuition without sensible intuition and no sensible intuition without intellectual intuition.[90] This ultimately means that arguing for the bare existence of something is not meaningful, since it is not discourse *about* anything at all. The true inner essence of existence [*Existenz*] is *Daseyn*, the determinate being-there of something seen precisely *as something in particular.*[91]

Following Fichte's "actual" (as opposed to ontological) argument, it would seem that seeing is living. Seeing may well be an absolute negation of its independence (an affirmation of its intentionality), but this intentionality, or relating, is the totality of what seeing does. Herein lies the subject-object relationship – in active living, which is seeing. This is the "absolute insight of reason" or "absolute reason itself."[92] The act of seeing is coextensive with life itself. Reason of reason, the normativity of reason, is the act of thinking. And the act of thinking is always thinking *about something.* And we are this absolute reason, since we think. Reason's norms are internal to its own act of thinking. Reason provides its own normativity. It is therefore intrinsically genetic. Put simply, the act of reasoning always carries with it its norms of action, otherwise it would not be reason. Reason *exists* in acts of reason.

A question now arises, one that has been lurking for a long time and only ever obliquely addressed: if reason subsists within life, how do we account for the fact that *we* posited the insight into reason *freely?* The question is made more complicated by the fact that *we are reason.* To say "I posit," "we posit," and "reason posits" are all synonymous. We are reason insofar as we carry out the acts of thinking, and we do so freely. *We* decided to embark on the journey that is WL, and while contingent decisions might be structured according to a problematic *Soll*, these, like the problematic *Soll*, are *from* a categorical *Soll* – they belong to the structures of rational thought. Writes Fichte, "We appear to ourselves as yielding ourselves to the original law of reason by a free act, and now, gripped by it, as made into [*Evidenz*] = certainty. This surrender and this [*Evidenz*] appear to us as able to be repeated indefinitely."[93]

We freely posited absolute reason because we are rational, and we were all along. We are free because we are rational. This is a not a subjugation of human freedom and moral agency to an absolute reason, a spinozist God. Rather, it is a radical affirmation of human freedom. Freedom is a constitutive part of reason.[94] Reason always manifests itself in the discursive sphere of human action. Reason, in this sense, is itself *free*, all the while presenting itself with all the markers of normativity that we can discursively mediate whenever experience presents itself as *Evidenz.* To act freely is to act rationally, in spite of the facticity of particular choices.[95]

Hence, ordinary knowing, that of our everyday actions and judgments, is precisely the crucible wherein transcendental reason is brought to bear. "Our life, or the life of reason, does not escape from its own self-objectification."[96] The factical world and the rational world are the same: the factical belongs to the genetic, the certain thing to certainty, the free to the rational. The presupposition we began with – that transcendental knowing presupposes ordinary knowing – has now been tested and validated. And just as facticity is the place in which genesis is found (ordinary knowing the locus of transcendental knowing), so too are specific domains of knowing the place in which WL will manifest itself. No matter what one chooses to reason about, one will find oneself employing the transcendental laws of thought discovered in WL. Reason has but one life, even if it factically appears in innumerable ways. And because this choice of subject matter is free, the condition of the possibility of the appearance of absolute reason is freedom – even if freedom is ultimately a product of rationality. Freedom and reason comprise a single movement, which like intuition is at once inward and outward (intellectual and sensible), a drive that is beyond the spatial logic of externalization. It is here that one finds the force and originality of Fichte's theory of appearance – not a mere *Scheinslehre*, or theory of the image as copy of original, but of manifestation or *revelation*: something that reveals its truth in its appearing.

We have now arrived at "the border of a *philosophia prima*."[97] What does Fichte mean by this expression? In the foregoing, a first basic distinction of appearance was identified – its very appearance as such. A further distinction into types of appearing would constitute just such a first philosophy. At the beginning of the last lecture of the WL, Fichte states that instead of offering a detailed account of these further determinations, he will seek to give one concluding lecture on WL itself. WL is a *principiieren* and not itself a series of principles or even the appearance of principles.[98]

In what remains, Fichte will thus offer a rapid account of how one moves from WL to thinking according to particular principles.[99] The goal here is to find a way of establishing consciousness's progression within the WL, moving through various levels of self- and object-awareness as it learns to think. The exercise that is WL consists in holding both together in one's awareness, or as Fichte says, standing in a middle point and ignoring one's own objectification of that point. Therefore, the absolutely original disjunction of reason is tripartite: *being and making; making of being;* and *making of making.* These are the three steps whose shared genetic source will allow them to be unfolded in a fivefold synthesis.

True oneness is absolute image. Its first disjunction is into the possibilities of imaging: image and object (thinking and being), thinking of being, and thinking of thinking. This introduction of quality, of qualitative oneness, allows for the existence of quantity – of a manifold of images (which *we* are as conscious subjects). This is also the first and broadest problematic *Soll* that can be applied to WL itself: if WL is to arise, then a consciousness in which it can arise must be posited. Knowing always comprises an outer unity of the object (immediacy) and inner multiplicity of the subject (mediation in thought). This, of course, follows the form of the *Soll*: the categorical *Soll* is self-grounding, positing the problematic *Soll*. The categorical *Soll* thinks itself as principle, and other principles are *from* it: it is principle-providing. The problematic *Soll* finds some contingent principle. Hence the movement from absolute image down to qualitative oneness – that is, pure imaging as union of thinking and being to image-of-something, of multiplicity – is the movement from principle-providing to principles.

Here, Fichte is not seeking to recapitulate the phenomenology but rather to highlight that for consciousness, disjunction is fourfold: from absolute qualitative oneness necessarily arises subject and object as opaque, or only relating externally to one another [*stehendes Subjekt/Objekt*], each being itself a mere factical externality for the other. With the introduction of quality and quantity arises the possibility of change, or the persistence of subjects and objects in successive mental states: I am always aware of myself *as* thinking, and of my object *as* being thought [*stehen im absoluten realen Bilden des Subjekts/Objekts*]. These four standpoints are contained within the movement of the WL:

1. Thinking the factical object. One takes nature as principle of thought. This yields *materialism* (realism).
2. Thinking the factical subject. One takes personality as principle of thought. This yields *legality* (idealism).
3. When the subject begins to conceive of itself as a product of oneness, from which both subject and object are

derived, its principle of thought becomes one of action and not stasis. If one takes the activity of personality as principle of thought, it yields *morality* (higher realism).
4. If the same is done to the object (as necessary correlate to the subject) and one takes *dynamic* nature as principle of thought, one arrives at an "inwardly living God" rather than (only) externally manifested life: this is *religion* (higher idealism).

These are standpoints rather than object-domains: one can think nature from the point of view of religion and vice-versa, but thought will always be coloured by the standpoint one has adopted. These standpoints are therefore ways of thinking in general according to a specific principle, similar to idealism and realism. The difference, of course, is that the *Wissenschaftslehrer realizes* that a particular standpoint works according to a principle: she adopts the standpoint as hers, knowing full well that it is the product of a *principiieren*.

This means that each standpoint contains the other standpoints (and itself, its narrowest acception) within itself. Each also contains the unifying principle of the four, which is WL. This constitutes twenty-five standpoints (e.g., 1.1. Sensible sensibility, 1.2. Sensible legality, … 1.5. Sensible unity; 2.1. Legal sensibility, … 5.5. Unity of unity). Moreover, the range of possibilities of knowing itself is fivefold and functions according to the fivefold synthesis. The last category of each standpoint, the unity of that standpoint, therefore also represents a moment in the overarching fivefold progression of WL. Each of these uniting moments represents the completion of a synthesis, the overcoming of a point-of-view by a particular transcendental argument, thus moving up to a higher point of view.

These twenty-five standpoints, then, are the whole of WL. WL has proven itself to be a science of science, both a rule for thinking and the source of the division of knowledge into particular disciplines. Yet the work done in this last lecture, the move from principle-providing to principles, can still be expanded. Moreover, one wonders how Fichte would go about elaborating these particular sciences. "Perhaps," he says in closing, "there will be time and opportunity this coming winter for applying these principles to particular standpoints, for example religion, which should always remain the highest."[100] Both religion, the highest standpoint, and the question of principles itself, will be explored in subsequent works.

PART TWO
The Berlin Lectures to 1806

PREFATORY REMARKS: PHENOMENOLOGY AND FEELING

The 1804/2 lectures end with a declaration on the fivefold nature of all science. WL is science-of-science, and from it stem four particular sciences, interpreted as moments or standpoints of knowing. Science therefore has a static, objective moment (nature), a static subjective moment (right [*Rechtslehre*]), a dynamic objective moment (ethics [*Sittenlehre*]), a dynamic subjective moment (religion [*Religionslehre*]), and a synthetic moment, the WL. Fichte's promise to lecture on religion, the highest of the standpoints, the following winter, therefore gives the impression of announcing both a program and a system; philosophical inquiry would seem to be exhausted by the five standpoints, and Fichte consequently will treat each of them in turn, descending from the *philosophia prima* down to a philosophy of nature.

Such a program, however, was never carried out. After completing 1804/2, Fichte began a third set of lectures on the WL, and concurrently, a set of popular lectures ostensibly on the philosophy of history, the *Characteristics of the Present Age* (1804–05). Once the third series on the WL had been complete, Fichte offered a new set of "scientific" lectures, concurrent with the ongoing "popular" lectures that are the *Characteristics*. The title of these, *Principles of the Doctrines of God, Morals, and Right* (1805), is telling: these are not lectures on the standpoints of religion, ethics, and right, but rather on the manner in which the WL provides these with principles, allowing for their appearance in a world of subjective freedom precisely as being derived from or "principiated" by the WL. After these lectures, Fichte would leave for Erlangen, where a different audience, different concerns, and above all, a different articulation of WL would lead to a different approach. Upon returning to Berlin, he gave lectures on religion, *The Way Towards the Blessed Life* (1806), which were popular rather than scientific in nature. War and exile would then bring this phase of Fichte's career to a close.

The first Berlin period therefore cannot be seen as a systematic exposition of Fichte's philosophical system, despite the strength of its exposition of the WL. The *Blessed Life* is a series of popular lectures. Scientific expositions of ethics and right were accomplished in the Jena period, with the *Foundation of Natural Right* (1796–97) and the *System of Ethics* (1798), and would be revisited during the last period of Fichte's career, in 1811–12. These provide the model for the manner in which the particular sciences can be rigorously presented but are disconnected from the 1804/2 WL. Finally, the philosophy of nature is altogether absent from Fichte's philosophical output.[1]

This is further complicated by a difference in literary genre: of the three works that follow the 1804/2 WL, two, the *Characteristics* and the *Blessed Life*, are popular lecture series. The idea of a distinction between the "scientific" or "philosophical" and the "popular" is not new for Fichte. From the beginning of his professorship at Jena, Fichte's main "scientific" work consists of the WL and the formal expositions of the four sciences derived from WL, science-of-science. Still other scientific works are meant to mediate between the WL and its four scientific derivatives. Such works include the *Principles*, as well the several iterations of the lectures called *Tatsachen des Bewußtseins*, given between 1810 and 1814. These all have to do with the transcendental application of WL – which has no content of its own – to the world of particulars. In addition to this serious academic work, Fichte produced two types of "popular" works (mostly series of lectures) aimed at a broader audience. The first category consists of those works meant to make the WL more easily intelligible. Among these are *Concerning the Concept of the Wissenschaftslehre* [Über den Begriff der Wissenschaftslehre] (1794), *An Attempt at a New Presentation of the Wissenschaftslehre* [*Versuch einer neuen Darstellung der Wissenschaftslehre* (1797), the two introductions to the WL (1797–98), and the *Sun-Clear Statement*

[*Sonnenklarer Bericht*] (1801). The second category consists of works aimed at the spiritual, intellectual, and personal edification of the audience. Even in the Jena period, these lectures were often given in Fichte's home on Sunday afternoons. Their scheduling, tone, and subject matter give them the flavour of a sort of philosophical church service. These works include the three series of lectures on the vocation of the scholar that began his three professorships in Jena (1794), Erlangen (1805), and Berlin (1811); the *Vocation of Humankind* (1800); the *Characteristics* and the *Blessed Life*; and the *Speeches to the German Nation* (1808).

This kind of popular work, meant to be "uplifting" or edifying discourses (to borrow a phrase from Kierkegaard), follows a distinct methodology, which Fichte makes explicit in the second lecture of the *Blessed Life*.[2] A scientific lecture confronts errors in thought and by means of their systematic refutation lets truth arise on its own; it uses, in other words, the transcendental argument structure elaborated in the WL, applying it in a manner exemplified by the protracted realism and idealism debate we have just seen. To put this in the language of 1804/2, the philosopher seeks to uncover the maxims according to which others think and tests their internal coherence. This is an application of the philosopher's skill that would be impossible if she were not already in possession of the truth. A popular lecture dispenses with transcendental argumentation and depends on this natural sense of truth. If the sense of truth can subsequently be cultivated into philosophical method, so too can it merely be confronted with what is true and understand it. In the language of the WL, one can grasp what is true as *Evidenz* without subjecting it to transcendental arguments. The person capable of doing so has the right disposition, but this disposition or attitude – ultimately that of attention [*Aufmerksamkeit*] – has not been formally educated and built up into philosophical dexterity. The non-philosopher who approaches truth with an open mind is not already entangled in the outgrowth of an erroneous philosophical maxim from which she would have to be freed before truth could manifest itself. Indeed, it is in this spirit that in 1797–98 Fichte wrote two introductions to the WL: one for the student who already has a system and one who is, so to speak, philosophically open to the appearance of truth. It is the latter group who stand to gain the most from the popular works. Fichte's task as popular lecturer, then, is to cultivate the right disposition in his listeners, enjoining them to *pay attention* so that they might become aware, on the level of feeling, of their immediate rapport with truth.

Even accounting for literary genre, the gap between what Fichte had announced in 1804 and what he subsequently produced cannot be entirely explained. Historical circumstances no doubt played a role: the need to earn a living through private lectures, the disappointments of the Erlangen experience, the desire to found a university in Berlin, intellectual rivalries, and the outbreak of a war that would redraw the borders of Europe and redefine German identity all influenced Fichte's work. What is certain, however, is that the three series of lectures given during the first Berlin period that are *not* renditions of the WL are all indebted to its conceptual framework: the *Characteristics* and the *Blessed Life* both make explicit use of the fivefold synthesis to structure their main arguments, and the *Principles* is a deeper treatment of the notion of principle-providing found in 1804/2.

Taken together, these texts represent not an expansion but rather an *application* of the WL to particular subjective experience in this world. The 1804/2's expression of subjectivity, the *we*, is an empty placeholder with a strict scientific function: the transcendental foundation of the possibility of subjective experience as appearance of the absolute. Now, this structure must be confronted with the real world – the thought and felt experience of particular individuals must be able to subsist within it. Such an application of WL is aimed at reconciling two aspects of human experience: human action is at once always goal-driven and determined, seeking to achieve defined ends according to established and reliable sets of means, but it is also free and intersubjective – not only is one free to engage with the world in a self-consciousness way or not, one also cannot predict the actions of others. In sum, experience is intelligible because of a bare logical structure, and the WL's theory of truth reveals its mechanisms, but human experience is not exhausted by determinist mechanisms because the locus of experience is the world of contingent facts. The WL's second part, the phenomenology, sought to reconcile these two aspects, the necessary and the contingent, on the level of a logic of experience. Their practical reconciliation, applied to real-world events in time, will require metahistorical a priori principles and thereafter a scientific investigation of these principles as united to the possibility of *a posteriori* content. This is achieved in the philosophy of history found in the *Characteristics*.

Building on this, the *Principles* will theorize the concepts required for subjective experience explored by a philosophy of history. In sum, it will claim that knowing has an encapsulating logical structure that is always present in free subjective activity and that works within the framework of the human spatio-temporal realm, the world. This claim can be eloquently summed up using the language of 1804/2: in order to act as a free subject in the world, one must be able to stand *in the light*. One does this with immediate conviction – the unspoken logical foundations of human action cannot be deduced before one engages in activity in the world; indeed, one is always already an agent in the world, and as the 1804/2 has taught us, unspoken foundations must remain in the shadows if discourse is to make sense. This immediate self-positing in the light is referred to as a *Selbstgefühl*, a "feeling of the self." With the *Principles*, then, feeling emerges as a central concept in the first Berlin period. Ultimately, feeling consists in adopting the attitude that is appropriate for the experience at hand. This makes explicit what was only gleaned from 1804/2 with great difficulty: experience is always accompanied by its own set of norms, and if these can be discursively elaborated *ex post facto*, one has from the start an immediate, intuitive rapport with them in *Evidenz*.

This feeling-driven phenomenology reaches its summit in the *Blessed Life*. As a popular work, its goal is ultimately to teach its audience how one lives with the knowledge that one is the image of an ineffable God. The answer, of course, is dependent on the WL's phenomenology (more aptly in this context called by its other name, *Bildlehre*) but becomes genuinely subjective through feeling, described in this text using the language of standpoint. A standpoint is perhaps broader than a feeling, but the two are intimately related, and each standpoint from which one can consider one's existence, as described in the *Blessed Life*, has an identifiable feeling associated with it. Religion is the highest particular science, and its object is therefore the same as the WL but cast in the subjective language of feeling – the scientific terms "absolute" and "truth" are transformed according to feeling into "God" and "love." Where WL is a science of discourse, religion is a science of the subjective, felt dimension of discourse, the rapport that one has, according to feeling, with the truth-content of any kind of discourse. The bare logical structure of the 1804/2 WL's phenomenology shows how discourse relates to its truth. Religion shows how any truth can be spoken with real personal conviction.[3] Finally, the WL is a philosophy of life. Said with the conviction of a free human subject, it is a *Blessed Life*.

3

The Characteristics of the Present Age 1804–05

3.1 FICHTE'S PHILOSOPHY OF HISTORY

History had been a concern of Fichte's from the beginning of his career. Already in the early sketch *Chance Thoughts on a Sleepless Night* (24 July 1788),[1] he began to thematize history in terms of the corruption of humanity and its vocation. A few years later, Fichte had conceived of (but never wrote) a second part to his *Contribution to the Correction of the Public's Judgment on the French Revolution* (1793)[2] that would have examined its historical conditions.[3] From the beginning, Fichte was convinced that history has a *telos* and that a priori principles guide its progression. But unlike Rousseau and Kant, who both saw nature as the measure of this progression,[4] Fichte accords this status to religion, which as highest standpoint and popular presentation of the WL's theoretical philosophy will provide history with a self-contained transcendental ground. However, Fichte would not seriously engage with these themes until the turn of the century, beginning with the *Vocation of Humankind* (1800) and the *Letters to Constant* (1801).[5] The delay occurred because the foundational tasks of establishing a moral and ethical philosophy, embodied by the questions of natural right and a system of ethics culminating in a theory of intersubjectivity, had to be in place before addressing the question of history, meaning that Fichte could not possibly have done so before 1799.[6]

It is only in 1804–05 that Fichte produced a text that directly confronts questions related to the philosophy of history, in a lecture series called *The Characteristics of the Present Age*. While this text cannot be called Fichte's philosophy of history (a treatise he never wrote and the reconstruction of which would have to draw on numerous texts that span his entire career), it is a direct engagement with the question of the individual's place in history. At least superficially, this is the most unlikely moment for Fichte to have done this. The 1804/2 WL as *philosophia prima* makes a programmatic announcement about the sciences that are to be derived from it and exhaust the standpoints of human knowing. Indeed, in 1804, the validity of a *philosophia prima* depends on its ability to provide principles for these derivative sciences.[7] The philosophy of history, however, is not one of them. Moreover, Fichte expressed a certain contempt for the study of history itself. He once opined to Friedrich Schlegel that he would rather "count peas" than study history.[8] Known for his ill humour, Fichte may have simply been polemically reiterating a foundational point: philosophy is not concerned with mere empirical facts but with the foundations of free human interaction. As Fichte saw it, the march of history was akin to physics: both were empirical sciences that described necessary relations in the factical realm.[9] Why, then, write a work that is ostensibly a philosophy of history in 1804–05?

The motivation for writing the *Characteristics* is largely dependent on the circumstances in which Fichte found himself. The Napoleonic wars were at their apogee (the battle of Austerlitz would take place one month after Fichte completed the lectures on the *Characteristics*), and the Holy Roman Empire was falling apart. Fichte's Berlin audience may have had the impression that their individual lives were being swallowed up by world-historical forces. As preoccupied as ever with the question of human freedom, Fichte most likely felt compelled to find a way of negotiating the relationship between *my* history as free individual, coloured by intersubjective interaction with others who also have a history, and "world history," the seemingly inexorable rise and fall of empires.[10] Fichte seeks to address the free subject's feeling of helplessness in a series of popular lectures; these were literally a form of "uplifting" discourse meant to help the audience members become aware of their free rationality and lift themselves above the feeling of chaos that world history may have created. This goal is sometimes obscured by Fichte's vituperative rhetoric: ours is decidedly the most decadent period of history.[11]

While remaining "popular" in genre, the *Characteristics* advances its arguments using philosophical means. Fichte seeks to reconcile the free individual's history with world history using the structures he established in 1804/2. The vehicle of this reconciliation is a *Weltplan*, or plan of world history. The history of the world unfolds a priori and teleologically, directed toward an end. This single movement can be described according to the fivefoldness of the WL: time unfolds according to a transcendental foundation that presents itself in five successive moments or "ages." History has an a priori component, the *Weltplan*, and an *a posteriori* one, the contingent events that populate it, the products of free human action. The *Weltplan* is regulative and does not predict the course of history. Moreover, because rational action always takes place in the realm of the contingent, particular individuals at certain times and in certain places serve to advance the *Weltplan*; certain peoples or even individuals can be ahead of their time, others behind. Regression is also possible.

Fichte's core argument is that *we* belong to some standpoint that governs our intersubjective relations, and a shared standpoint can be characteristic of a particular period in time. Because of this, the *Characteristics* must investigate some period in particular: hence its consideration of the "present age." There are no a-historical perspectives any more than there are a-subjective perspectives. This is consistent with Fichte's overarching project regarding the reconciliation of individual freedom and the broader structures of necessity in which those individuals live. It is the interplay of necessity and freedom, the categorical and the problematic, that provides for both subjective activity and its entry into history. If this is described abstractly in 1804/2 according to the different valences of a *Soll* (the problematic *Soll* comes *through* the *from* that is the categorical *Soll*), at the end of the Jena period, in the *Nova Methodo* WL, it is described as intersubjective interaction. Others are not a limit imposed on my own subjectivity; rather they issue a summons [*Aufforderung*] to interaction. It is the other's free actions that condition my own actions as free. Writes Fichte, "the subject has freely chosen; it has absolutely given to itself the nearest determination of its own activity; and the ground of this latter determination of the subject's efficacy lies entirely within the subject alone."[12] The causality that governs my actions is both within me and outside of me, in others.

I am incited to act because another acted freely, a gesture I receive as an invitation to act freely within the confines of a response. For Fichte, free activity is always a determinate activity.[13] Freedom and necessity in history work according to the same structure: one always finds oneself in a historical context, surrounded by groups of people with shared presuppositions. These were elaborated through the free interaction of individuals (they are problematic *Solls* that came *through* the categorical *Soll*). I then relate this entire structure to individual action of my own. These condition, but do not fully determine, my actions. As a historical agent, my encounter with others gives me a framework and a goal, but never compromises my agency as a human subject. The unique contribution of the 1804/2 to this structure is the consciousness integration of *my own awareness* of the structure into the structure itself. The fivefold deduction is completed through my own awareness of belonging to it and being integrated into it; in Fichte's words, insight is the product of the absolute, and *we* ourselves *are* this insight.[14] That I am aware of my own status as a free historical agent, elaborated by and elaborating the context for free action, means that I am able to reach a meta-historical standpoint – that is, knowledge of the a priori factors that govern historical progression.

This introduces a necessary moral dimension into history. Not only do I act freely as a historical agent, but my ability to think the a priori foundations of a historical progression lets me morally evaluate historical events. The point of history, then, is not to merely recount the contingent facts that make up the past but to be able to make ethical decisions that prevent catastrophes rather than merely reckoning with them. While his friend Schiller had declared that the world's history is the world's judgment, "*Die Weltgeschichte ist das Weltgericht*,"[15] Fichte instead seeks metahistorical criteria in order to evaluate the ethics of historical action. Such (a priori) meta-historicity is the *sine qua non* of free action in history. Schiller's poetic aphorism is, to Fichte's mind, a justification of external force, a victor's account of history.[16] In this perspective, history is only secondarily about the past: it is meant to allow for free action in the present in view of results that will impact the future.[17]

The contribution of the *Characteristics of the Present Age* to the phenomenological progression in the 1804/2 period lies in negotiating the relation between the *a priori* and *a posteriori* elements of subjective experience in time, a fundamental aspect of the absolute's appearance. In this way, history is a transcendental condition for consciousness. It belongs to the condition of the possibility of the application of WL to real-world experience and is not itself a philosophical standpoint. Religion, ethics, and law all happen *in* history, not adjacent to it.[18]

To its credit, the *Characteristics* is a highly readable text. The lectures were well-prepared and were published as pronounced in 1806.[19] Fichte had intimated in the fifth lecture that, in order to combat false reports of the contents of his lectures, he was reading from a manuscript that would subsequently go to press unaltered.[20] The lectures themselves were delivered on Sundays at midday, beginning on 4 November 1804 and ending on 17 March 1805, running concurrently with the third presentation of the 1804 WL (1804/3) and then with the *Principles of the Doctrines of God, Morals, and Right*, both of which were held during the week. The popular lectures that were the *Characteristics* had been conceived for a broader audience. Fichte had advertised them as such and rented a lecture hall at the Academy of Sciences to accommodate a large number of people. His gambit succeeded: 138 people subscribed to the lectures, including much of Berlin's high society: a Prussian prince, ambassadors, military officers, pastors, philosophers, ladies of the nobility, and bourgeois professionals all attended. A member of the Berlin Academy complained, "Our Academy finds itself in a precarious situation. It has been besieged by the *Wissenschaftslehre*."[21] Fichte had conquered Berlin's elite set, accomplishing an extraordinary rehabilitation that few would have thought possible when he left Jena in 1799. The ruling political class – some of whom were loyal students of Fichte – were intent on ensuring that he stayed in Berlin. At the time, the city had no university, and so it was arranged that Fichte would teach in Erlangen during the summer and then continue to give popular lectures in the Prussian capital in the spring and winter.[22] Despite complications in Erlangen, when the University of Berlin was founded in 1810, Fichte would be named first rector. Fichte's second ascent to prominence – steadier and more successful than the first – begins with the *Characteristics*.

The text itself is composed of seventeen lectures. Each lecture contains a unifying theme, clearly identified by Fichte himself in a summary that accompanies the published version.[23] While Fichte does not group the lectures thematically, many are continuations of what was exposed the previous week, allowing certain lines of continuity to be seen. The first lecture explores the idea of a *Weltplan* and outlines the five ages that belong to it; lectures two to eight offer a diagnostic of the present age, situating Fichte's present within the *Weltplan*; lectures nine to fourteen examine the progression of history in its political expression, seeing the development of the state as analogous to that of history itself; finally, lectures fifteen to seventeen begin to explore the *a priori* principles of subjective action in history, a task that the *Principles* will take up more rigorously once the lectures on the *Characteristics* have drawn to a close.

3.2 THE WELTPLAN

Fichte announces in the first lecture that he is not providing his listeners with a systematic philosophy of history but a series of lectures offering a philosophical portrait of the present age.[24] If elements of a philosophy of history are to be found here, it is via the philosophical analysis of the concept of an "age." A philosophical approach is one that traces all multiplicity back to absolute unity and conversely deduces all multiplicity as stemming from this unity. The first part of this formula refers to the tracing-back [*Zurürckführung*] of the 1804/2 WL,[25] the second, to the protracted phenomenology begun as a theory of appearance in the second half of 1804/2 and further developed in subsequent lectures, including these. In affirming this, Fichte is announcing one of the key aspects of the *Characteristics* – a philosophy of history must proceed a priori, following a transcendental structure.[26] The empiricist can observe the world and list events that unfold in time, but without an a priori ground from which history can be evaluated, these are merely a collection of occurrences, with no means of delimiting the boundaries between this age and another. The philosopher, however, enquires into the very concept of age or era: from the a priori concept the various modes of historical appearing are derived. Fichte therefore founds his theory on the fact that historical events are a form of appearance, and as appearance, they can be traced back to a source and grouped into exhaustive categories – all of this, of course, strictly a priori. This will involve an a priori description of all of time [*die gesammte Zeit*] and the ages into which it is divided.

In establishing an a priori concept of "ages" and then of this age in particular, Fichte does not exclude the empirical but rather assigns it an extra-philosophical task. Because knowledge of the age to which one belongs is dependent on observation of events, one cannot reflect on history without admitting empirical fact. Yet there is a difference between holding empirical fact up to its transcendental ground on the one hand and letting the empirical itself adjudicate history on the other. Examination of the empirical content of history is therefore the frontier at which philosophy stops and history proper begins.[27]

History, therefore, has a single foundation, an a priori concept: time. Like any practical concept, time develops according to action, being subsequently divided into several, successive concepts. These concepts are the "ages," the concepts from which the essential characteristics of a certain moment in history are derived. The progression of ages according to time is called the *Weltplan*, and it is teological in nature: the history of life in space and time is moving toward a definite goal, that of the free exercise of reason.[28] Deducing the fives ages from time therefore involves conceiving of the necessary steps toward this goal. The first and broadest distinction that can be made is between life and freedom. Freedom is the first determination or quality of human life. But freedom is an activity that belongs to human life: it is possible for humans to act in a way that isn't free. It follows that at one point, humans did not direct free action toward reason; the moment then arose when they did. *Time,* as it were, has now emerged from its foundations: there is a period *before* freedom and one that proceeds from its introduction. This does not mean that there was a time before rational behaviour. Indeed, where there is life, it is governed by rational norms: reason is the fundamental law of all human life. In this first segment of history, reason is at work not as free activity but as natural force. People behave rationally but not self-reflectively – that is, instinctually. Once freedom is introduced, individuals recognize the principles that govern their action. This is not a determinist knowledge of the outcomes of action but simply the awareness of free action. This means that there is an intermediary term between reason as instinct and free reason, a middle segment of time: consciousness of freedom.[29] But before consciousness of freedom can be fully achieved, reason must be progressively liberated from instinctual rationality. The middle term is therefore further divided: in a society where reason manifests itself as instinct, the weak rule over the strong in an arbitrary manner. When a distinction was first made between rational and arbitrary laws, some individuals would have become aware of their own drive toward free self-determination. This drive toward self-determination requires conscious, systematized use in order to achieve its goal – a science of action is therefore required. This science consists in consciously managing all human interaction according to the norms of reason. It is only exhausted when humanity has conformed to the original image [*Urbild*] of reason.[30] This end, of course, plays a regulative role; it is only in some eschatological scenario, in some collective afterlife, that this complete conformity might be achieved. Fichte's intention here is to establish history's end, its teleology, which is not itself internal to history: the space of historical action is where freedom is continually directed toward reason.[31] This movement is carried out by a series of mediations that first make humanity aware of its capacity for free rationality, and then internalizes it. The movement ultimately yields five ages or moments of history:

1. The age of the unconditional domination of reason by instinct; or the age of innocence (immediate rational instinct).
2. The age of domination by external authority; or the age of the emergence of sin (mediated rational instinct).
3. The age of liberation from external authority, giving rise to unregulated (purely negative) freedom; or the age of the completion of sin (indifference).
4. The age of the realization of freedom's orientation toward truth; or the age of the emergence of justification (mediated free reason).
5. The age of the practice of the art of reason; or the age of completed justification and sanctification (immediate free reason).

These five ages do not correspond to specific dates in human history. Nor are they linear and successive periods. Fichte uses the word *Stand* to describe them. They therefore ought to be understood as the spatio-temporal incarnation of the *Standpunkte* found in the last lecture of the 1804/2 WL, the appearance of shared worldviews. Their description as "ages" is part of Fichte's program of providing a complete, transcendental account of appearance, a phenomenology. Such an account can only be completed if it takes into account all the modalities of intersubjective interaction of standpoints: that is, how individuals agree and disagree on the ends of action across space and time.[32] Moreover, Fichte announces that the completion of the cycle of ages would be nothing other than a return to its origins. Just as WL involves construction and reconstruction, a movement from *Evidenz* back to itself mediated by consciousness, the history of intersubjective encounter is a movement from right relation back to itself via conflict, with subjectivity gaining awareness of the rational norms that govern those relations along the way.

3.3 OURS IS THE THIRD AGE

Fichte conjectures that we live in the third age and will develop this thought in lectures two to eight. The first two ages, those of immediate and then mediated rational instinct, can be conceived together as one long period during which reason is blindly dominated by instinct. Conversely, the last two, those of mediate and then immediate free rationality, are marked by the informed or clairvoyant use of reason. The present age brings together the heterogeneous principles of the two divisions of ages: blindness and clairvoyance, constraint and freedom, mediacy and immediacy. It is, both in the technical language of philosophy and the language of the everyday, the age of indifference.

Fichte will justify this claim not only with empirical observation but also by asserting that a deductive path, starting from the notional definition of each age, helps situate the present in the *Weltplan*. If the first and last ages are regulatory, then the space of historical action belongs to the second, third, and fourth ages. Given their natures as standpoints, these three must coexist throughout history. If Fichte is thinking about the a priori foundations of history, his age must lend itself to this kind of reflection. The second age does not provide this, since it is only with its consummation that one becomes aware that one is a free historical agent. On the other hand, the fourth age consists in an achieved recognition; it is suitable for this kind of reflection but less so than the third age. If the key to history is meta-history, then the third is the space where the becoming of free action is discursively worked out. Having been freed from external constraint, the historical subject considers its own position before others in time. It is here that freedom does the work that allows for its self-possession, the place where reflexivity will arrive at self-reflexivity through awareness.[33] Whatever else might be said about the third age, it must be remembered that it is a necessary moment in freedom's rational self-possession and indeed, is itself a description of this transformation.

The third age is constituted by the progressive liberation, individual by individual, from blind authority. The instrument of this liberation is the concept, that is, discursive understanding. As specific instances of external authority are brought to light and explicitly thought out, individuals are able to realize that to reason is to be free. Seen from within, the maxim of this age is "to admit as certain only that which has been clearly understood."[34] This is also the maxim of the fourth age. They differ only in application. The third is unaware of its own free rationality and uses concepts as if they were ready-made, engaging in a naïve idealism: the concept is the measure of being.[35] The fourth age, however, that of the scientific employment of reason, does not elevate the concept above being, nor the opposite, but rather seeks to apply concepts to being as present in experience. The third age is the age of idealism, where the limits of the concept determine a priori what is conceivable and what is not; the fourth age brings this same maxim a realist corrective, using the concept to discursively reconstruct what is found in experience. The third age, in other words, does not seek to offer a genetic account of its own rational activity – moreover, it does not see the need to do so. This is the reason for its qualification as the age of empty freedom: the fulfilment of its maxim is found in that which is inconceivable, beyond the concept's reach.[36]

The third age's idealism emerges from the rational instinct of the first two ages. This instinct governs collectively, its goal being life, the survival of humanity. Life as immediate totality has been replaced by an individually possessed concept. The result is an individualism that mistakes its own rational faculties for that of reason itself.[37] This individualism is the primary fault of the age. It consists firstly in an epistemological error, considering that subjects are the authors, *ex nihilo*, of their own thoughts. As Fichte demonstrated in the WL, cognition is a complex process of spontaneously elaborating in discourse what one finds in experience, a necessary ingredient of which is the awareness-of-thought that one cannot simply fabricate. As Fichte reiterates here, the subject of thought is not an absolute subject but always a determinate one. Taking this false epistemology as a starting-point and erecting the individual, the "I," as the goal of life, the third age reduces life to mere self-preservation, constituting not only an epistemological error but a moral fault. If only that of which I can conceive exists, then my own existence enjoys a privileged status.[38] As in the WL, idealism leads to a form of scepticism, one with the practical repercussion of self-centeredness in the interpersonal realm.

Another consequence of this idealist individualism is empiricism. Since the instinct for survival and self-preservation that the individualist elevates above all other forms of moral activity belongs, in humans, to the species rather than the individual (survival is the product of rational reflection on one's needs and environment), it seeks the means for self-advancement in experience in the empirical realm.[39] The problem is not that these individuals turn to experience in order to know (it could not be otherwise) but rather that they deny the possibility of anything objective and a priori that governs their knowledge of the empirical world. As in the WL, when the idealist is asked how she came to know reality, she answers, "I just do it."[40] The grounds for knowledge remain inchoate. On the level of experience, one simply takes things to be true because one has perceived them.

Against the individualism of the third age, Fichte declares that the proper exercise of rationality is directed toward the good of the whole. The greatest virtue of the rational being, writes Fichte, is to forget oneself, the greatest vice, to think only of oneself.[41] In this affirmation, Fichte's WL, ethics, and religious thought converge in a single imperative. We have seen how the WL, the theoretical foundation of Fichte's philosophy, traces the manifold back to the one, seeking the genetic root of consciousness. While the WL was able to move on, in its second part, to the reconciliation of subjectivity and appearance in a transcendental phenomenology, it remains abstract: strictly speaking, the WL has no content. The interactions between subjects is governed by the logical foundation that is WL, but the appraisal of their actions belongs to a moral-ethical philosophy. The derivation of a *Sittenlehre*, an ethics, from the WL was one of the chief tasks of the Jena period and culminated in the theory of the "summons" [*Aufforderung*] of the WL *Nova Methodo*. There, Fichte concludes that a constitutive part of individual freedom is a summons to limit this freedom in recognition of that of another.[42] Recognition and self-limitation are the foundation of Fichte's theory of subjectivity. Feeling, the bridge between a purely conceptual check [*Anstoß*] and the richer, more subjective *Aufforderung*, will also return in the Berlin period, receiving extensive treatment, as we shall see, in the *Principles of the Doctrines of God, Morals and Right*. Moreover, Fichte will bring this theory of subjectivity a step further in the Berlin period: as the biblical allusion of "losing oneself" suggests, Fichte's phenomenology of subjectivity will move into the domain of religion. There, in the *Way Towards the Blessed Life*, the subject that is summoned to limit itself achieves true interiority, transforming a feeling of summons to limit one's freedom into a calling to lose one's own life in order to gain life itself. This general calling of humanity is linked to another more determinate vocation, that of the scholar's life. Fichte's priority whenever taking up a university chair was to give lectures on the vocation of the scholar. The *Characteristics* intimates the same structure: one forgets oneself in view of serving the whole, the life of humanity itself. Since the life of humanity is expressed in ideas, to forget oneself in service to the life of the human race as a whole is synonymous with living one's own life in service to ideas.[43]

The work of putting oneself at the service of humanity lies in striving to image reason through one's own free activity. In its activity, the individual achieves an absolute identity that is the external image of reason's own activity: a life lived in conformity with reason loves itself. Pride, then, is not only a moral and religious fault but an intellectual shortcoming: while the true scholar seeks to understand what is found in experience through the knowing application of a priori principles, the dishonest scholar seeks to bring the world into conformity with his own principles of self-preservation, all the while appealing to experience and common sense as the arbiters of truth. These philosophers – the *Aufklärer* or "enlighteners" whom Fichte mockingly calls *Ausklärer*, "obscurers"[44] – are the product of idealism unchecked and unrecognized, their inability to conjugate experience and the foundations of knowledge resulting in philosophies of idle chatter.[45] Ultimately, the *Aufklärung* does not constitute a step forward but rather a historical regression, since it fails to acknowledge that the free exercise of reason is norm-governed. Just as humanity was emancipated from the tyranny of nature, of wild chaos before the advent of civilization, by recognizing reason's norms, so too is it freed from external authority. To ignore the normative character of reason is to be thrown back into a state of bondage.

Moral and Intellectual progress through the *Weltplan* are intimately linked. Fichte now introduces a third factor, religion. If theoretical and practical reason have been able to discursively speak of progress by relating contingent facts to a priori norms, the same progress can be immediately experienced through religious feeling. Christianity in particular provides Fichte with a means of speaking about progress in an immediate and felt way. The Christian conception of time is a linear one directed toward absolute truth, the fulfilment of revelation, and the return of humanity to God. It is this fundamental orientation toward truth that makes Christianity a vehicle of progress. However, the movement forward must itself be accomplished by individuals who break through from one age to another. While one might think that they would do so by some act of self-valorizing heroism, they do it, paradoxically, by self-sacrifice, preferring the progress of humanity to their personal satisfaction. This paradox is not immediately apparent to individuals who think according to the precepts of their age. The genius of Christianity is to convey this through religious feeling, by means of the Christ figure. It is necessary, writes Fichte, for a forebearer to show us the path of self-sacrifice. Such is the action of an individual who is already fully realized, one who inhabits the highest standpoint, adjudicating history from the point of view of WL. This Christ sacrifices himself completely, giving humanity an example to follow. The real miracle of Christianity, Fichte stresses, is that the Christ shows others that he is *not* in order that life as a whole might *be*.[46]

Similarly, the idea through which humanity itself is known is given a religious sense. This idea is an autonomous thought, carrying life within it, animating matter. The members of the audience familiar with the WL would recognize here a realist corrective to the third age's idealism, culminating in the ineffable absolute. It is this absolute that provides for particulars via a problematic *Soll* and not the other way around. Using the same language as the 1804/2 WL, Fichte calls the idea the root of life, as opposed to the "death at the root" that the presumed autonomy of particulars represents.[47] What is alive lives because of life itself. Fichte finds a religious expression for this philosophical affirmation in the Gospel of John: "It is not the flesh that lives, but the Spirit."[48] This is the "immediate proof" of one of the foundational propositions of the WL. The goal of a popular philosophy is not only to bring it to consciousness but to enjoin one's listeners to embody it in daily life and activity. Individuals should strive for life in the idea, or "life in the Spirit," the religious standpoint from which one sees the ultimate reality, the self-same idea that is the absolute, life, or God. This, says Fichte, is beatitude. Only its first step, that of self-renunciation, is painful. Once one consents to begin this journey, the rest of the work is an evident path to beatitude and hence no work at all. As with the WL, the system constructs itself, and one need only consent to begin. Crucial to Fichte's phenomenology is that these experiences take place in time. The teleological development of the idea in time is itself history, the trajectory of the activity of human intersubjective action as it moves toward truth; that the one absolute gives rise to particulars is the expression of time, the linearity of the subjective that can be intellectually and mediately grasped by philosophy (that is, WL) and immediately grasped in a religious eschatology.

Understanding the religious sensibilities of the third age are therefore key to understanding its fundamental character. Assessing the age's relationship to Christianity leads Fichte to make an important distinction. There are, he writes, two forms of Christianity: Johannine, based on the Gospel of John, and Pauline, based on the writings of Paul. John's God is the true God, truth itself, the truth-life that Fichte sees as the dynamic absolute of the WL.[49] The Johannine Jesus presents in a popular, accessible manner by means of an "inner proof" what the *Wisseschaftslehrer* arrives at through the proper use of reason. Because Johannine religion is based on eternal truth, it is as old as the world and is not subject to evolution. John is not interested in anchoring Jesus in the world of first-century Palestine, nor in providing him with a genealogy; John's unique goal is to present Jesus as the image of the living God. Paul, and the other Evangelists who follow him, harbour different concerns, obscuring the essence of Christianity with mere *a posteriori* facts. Fichte sees Paul as presenting a merely historical, contingent religion grounded in empirical events. In contrasting these two figures, Fichte is arguing that the content of history is culture, culture's broadest expression is religion, and if religion has no a priori foundation, there is no means of differentiating between progression and regression, worship and idolatry, right and wrong action.

The privileging of a "Pauline" *a posteriori* salvation history has had, according to Fichte, a broad and negative impact on the development of culture. It elevates discursive reasoning – the concept – above truth itself, unknowingly placing *a posteriori* conclusions (one might say "non-genetic" conclusions) above the one truth. This deformation of reason is the beginning of the end of Christianity, the first moment along the path of intellectual decadence typified by the third age. If Catholicism, with its emphasis on external authority, is the religion of the second age, the Protestant Reform is the great religious event of the third age. And if Fichte agrees that the Reform was a religious emancipation allowing individuals to cultivate true interiority, its emphasis on the Bible as text, ignoring the oral tradition from which it came, led to the proliferation of religious writing. As it is practised in the third age, Protestantism is a religion of the letter [*Buchstabe*], its real source of revelation the printing press. As representatives of *a posteriori* "Pauline" religion, both Catholicism and Protestantism have failed. In religious terms, overcoming the third age implies a reform far more radical than Luther's, one that moves toward a "Johannine" religion based on the absolute truth of inner experience. In this respect, Fichte's proposed form of Christianity is ahead of its time, declaring that the historical Jesus is of little importance; it is Jesus the Eternal Word, the *Logos*, that is essential for Christianity.[50] It is at once prophetic and ancient: true Christians need no covenant, no messiah, no forgiveness: they need only realize what has always been true – that they live and exist in God.

What would Johannine Christianity look like if put into practice? Fichte's central prediction is that it would ultimately lead to a reconciliation of philosophy and religion, scientific and popular expressions of knowledge, and at its broadest level, of thought and feeling. The gap would be bridged between scholars and laymen. Both groups would arrive at the same immutable truth, the latter intuitively and immediately, via an authentic interior life, and the former through intellectual inquiry grounded in immutable, dynamic, absolute truth. Moreover, philosophers [*Wissenschaftsler*] would be able to convey their scientific findings in popular lectures, communicating in an immediately comprehensible way the absolute truth that was attained discursively. The preacher and the philosopher would only be separated by differences of idiom. More important, both would come to conceive of all forms of knowledge as derived from one absolute truth, all determinate standpoints the derivatives of a science of science. The thinker of the fourth age, then, the Johannine philosopher, is a *Wissenschaftslehrer* – not in the sense that the reconciliations just named would turn all thinkers into disciples of Fichte. Rather, the Johannine religion that is Fichte's ideal would transform our collective relationship to knowledge: the goal of scientific exposition would not be to communicate a series of facts but rather to assist people in reconstructing some truth for themselves.

3.4 THE STATE AS LOCUS OF HISTORY

So far, Fichte's critique of the third age has dealt mostly with its intellectual life, which elevates the concept above being. In order to move beyond critique and establish a positive theory of intersubjectivity in time, another, more inherently relational approach is required. Fichte achieves this through an investigation of the state (in lectures nine to fourteen). The political situation of the age is the key to understanding the interactions between individuals and, more than any other aspect of human life, is historically conditioned. It is here, then, in examining the history of the state that leads up to the third age, that Fichte comes closest to elaborating a philosophy of history, seeking to describe the a priori concepts that allow the state to move from one age to another. The deduction of the fives ages is repeated here, but this time concretely, with attention to the necessary subjective element that the historical progression contains.

Fichte begins his remarks with a "metaphysical proposition": what really exists, exists necessarily and necessarily as it is.[51] That which is true, the conjunction of being and knowing, can neither come into existence nor be modified. That which is true and exists independently is what we commonly call God. The existence of God is knowing itself. The world exists as knowledge. It is mediately (through knowledge) what knowledge is in-itself: God's existence. As existence, externalization, and image of God, knowledge exists as self-consciousness, the spontaneous power of the subjective intellect. The starting point of the intellect's path to internal clarity is always an act of particular knowing – knowledge of an object. An object is determined and could be otherwise, meaning that the intellect is constantly determining an object *as* something particular. The object, when equal to itself, is eternally so – from here come the laws of physics and the philosophy of nature. When confronted with the spontaneity of the unified subjective intellect, the object is seen as belonging to a linear series, which is time. Empirical science applied to a totality of objects in their temporal progression is history. In the examination of history, philosophy reaches its lower limit; it consists in the evolution of factical objects, of the indeterminable transformation of what is contingent. If history could be genetically determined, it would be necessary, and hence atemporal. History is therefore the factical repetition of certain necessary forms but whose future content always remains hidden in the shadows of facticity: a priori progression does not mean necessary content.

Hence, the philosopher must presuppose some indeterminable factical content from which one can move up toward philosophy and philosophy of history; the historian presumes the conditions of contingent facts in order to provide an *a posteriori* account of temporal, factical succession. Fichte now wishes to provide, from a philosophical perspective, an account of the conditions of contingent facts. The existence of self-consciousness means that knowing splits [*spalten*] into individual self-conscious knowers. That knowledge is therefore discursive and interpersonal, but also mutually intelligible and communicable, implies the use of language.[52]

Reason always manifests itself in the discursive world of human action, that is, by means of individuals interacting with each other through language. And while this manifestation follows norms, it is fundamentally free: it is humanity's determination and vocation [*Bestimmung*] to show itself to be the free manifestation of reason. Yet humanity's limited exercise of freedom must have its genetic root in some greater freedom – particular free acts, in other words, must be traced back to a source. On this basis, Fichte concludes that at some point in its history, humanity must have been perfectly rational. This state of perfect rationality is not the achievement of humanity's finality, which is *becoming-rational* by means of freedom. This *Ur-rationalität* would have been without effort or freedom. The ideal people, the "*Normalvolk*" who possessed this pure rationality show that insofar as humans live in community, their actions are always governed by the norms of reason. The vocation of humanity is to become aware of this rationality and to freely accept it. The *Normalvolk* had no history, since they were not conscious of contingency, and did not behave freely and reflectively; they merely did what was obvious. It was the introduction of counterfactuals – of the idea that one could live and behave otherwise – that would have provoked the realization that necessity is always enacted factically: there is no rational activity without a contingent realm of facts. Thus begins self-awareness, and free rationality along with it.[53] This transition is prehistoric, and any details on the original cultivation of collective self-awareness through awareness of facticity would be more mythological than historical; yet the simple fact that a transition occurred from assumed rationality to conscious rationality can be posited a priori. Within this a priori development of reason, it is only once facts achieve real importance and are seen as transition points that they are recorded as history.

The time of innocence represented by the *Normalvolk* is the political component of the first age. Human interaction is perfectly rational, and so relations of authority do not take on the juridical aspect they acquire with the advent of history; here, authority is not an external constraint but something that is immediately compelling. When freedom first emerges from the realization of contingency, so too does the state as we know it, a body that imposes external authority on individuals. While the state is inevitably an institution of constraint, it is a rational organization and is host to the free actions of individuals. In order to highlight the state's role as container, Fiche introduces, in addition to the non-state of the *Normalvolk*, the heuristic concept of an "absolute state," a fifth age in which individuals place all of their power in service to the life of the human race, sacrificing their own inner life in view of the external realization of the idea of humanity in the state.[54] The individuality of every member of the species is negated in favour of the whole; conceptually, no higher individual good is possible, and so individuals exist in mutual submission to one another.

The absolute state represents an unattainable perfection and is as apolitical as the world of the *Normalvolk*. In reality, constraints are imposed on individuals unequally. In the most primitive form of the state, where freedom is only nascent, this inequality is total, with a few members exploiting all others for personal means. It is also possible that mutual submission be accomplished only negatively, by means of laws that prevent personal interests from interfering in the accomplishment of ends. It is not that such a state is without law; rather, these laws are not established according to their content but only their form, in favour of oppressive rulers. In a second period, the state's laws are more considered: a collective cooperation is ensured by force of law. A third period sees the laws imbued with real positive freedom: following the law becomes a matter of personal ethical drive and not merely a protection from others. In terms of the *Weltplan*, one could see the following correspondence:

1. First age: *Normalvolk*, no state.
2. Second age: total inequality, empty legalism.
3. Third age: imperfect mutual submission: negative freedom.
4. Fourth age: perfect mutual submission: positive freedom.
5. Fifth age: eschatological ideal, consummation of the absolute state.[55]

In sum: absolute freedom culminates in complete mutual submission; government and freedom are reconciled on the political level just as freedom and necessity are on the epistemological level. The finality of the state is therefore no different from that of the species: that all interaction be governed by the laws of reason.

In examining this development, a pivotal intervening factor must be taken into consideration: the advent of Christianity. For Fichte, church and state will follow a parallel development according to the same a priori principles. Factically, Christianity does indeed emerge in history at a particular time and later comes to define whole ages. Yet Christianity's truth, which exists *a priori*, does not originate in time. Moreover, its manifestation occurs in three moments that roughly correspond to the second, third, and fourth ages. But like history itself, its consummation is not in time: as long as there is a state, there is a church. Before and after, in the first and fifth ages, there is no need for either. Both church and state develop externally in time but only as images of absolute truth, to which they correspond in greater or lesser degree. While the political and religious organization of a society have the same ultimate goal – the realization of reason in freedom – religion will provide this with a subjective, interior dimension; in this regard, it is the state's role to put in place those structures that allow for the realization of humanity's vocation, a religious question that is accomplished interiorly, through the agency of individuals.[56]

3.5 IN SEARCH OF HISTORY'S PHILOSOPHICAL PRINCIPLES

Drawing on this religious question, Fichte then articulates history's philosophical principles in lectures fifteen to seventeen. It is from the principles established by religion that the moral behaviours [*Sitten*] of an age are derived. Morals are themselves a series of principles dependent on the higher, generative ones given by religion. Morals are the principles in use that govern the intersubjective interactions of individuals and, having become second nature, do not come to immediate consciousness in being employed. Principles are that which guide action without themselves being manifested in action. Morality [*Sitten*] provides principles of inner determination – of the meditated actions of individuals – while, once removed from morality (and even further from religion), right provides principles of outer determination – of human interaction as it appears objectively and externally.[57] All three sets of principles have a shared finality (the free use of reason), and cooperate with each other in achieving this task: moral and legal structures allow for the personal realization of interiority, while religion helps inform the legal establishment of equality among members of humanity.

Fichte insists that among sets of principles, religion has pride of place. As principle-provider for more restrained principles, it consists in the discursive attempt at expressing that which is complete and self-contained.[58] To understand its relationship to bare conceptual principle-providing [*principiieren*] is to become aware of consciousness without transforming it into an object. It expresses in popular language the coincidence, in action, of knowledge and awareness of knowledge. The religious behaviour of a society therefore represents its level of awareness of the integrity of its own activity. In truth, *tun* and *sagen*, saying and doing, coincide. To place oneself in truth is to speak from it knowingly. Fundamental to religion is therefore the practice of attention, an active way of being passive that allows one to realize that being constructs itself, and we are the ones who carry out this construction.[59] It is in attention, then, that the cultivation of interiority consists. Fichte consequently denounces all forms of religious practice that consist in mere externals, whether the civic worship of the churches, the romantics' cult of feeling (which ultimately degenerates into the religion of the second age, Catholicism), or the empty morality of Kant's categorical imperative.[60] In brief, for the person who inhabits the religious standpoint, freedom is the end and principle of all action; the external and internal constraints of law and morality, respectively, give way to a normativity of freedom.[61] The authentically religious person, writes Fichte, possesses eternal life immediately and totally and sees this state as going beyond the individual, being omnipresent. To attain the religious standpoint is to live a blessed life.[62]

Fichte's search for principles in this context is therefore a continuation of the phenomenology begun in the WL. If the WL articulates the passage from principle-providing [*principiieren*] to principles themselves, it leaves inchoate the relationship between philosophy as meta-principle, as the science of principles, and religion, which is both highest particular principle and expansive, popular expression of philosophy's scientific conclusions; it also does not provide for the relationship between this highest principle and lower, more restrained ones. Now, at the end of the *Characteristics*, it becomes clear that the field that allows for the discursive consideration of these different standpoints is history. Particular sciences have an irreducible factical element (in the case of the WL, this element is the possibility of problematicity, the very concept of contingency itself). Facticity occurs in succession, hence in time, and both the concept of time itself and the juxtaposition of factical objects in it must be governed by a priori principles. Just as intersubjectivity requires both an a priori account of subjectivity itself and an accompanying account of the free agency that explains its drive toward ends, so too do events require an a priori account of their teleological progression.

Religion, as highest standpoint, is therefore the point of view from which history must be adjudicated. The reason is that religion's content is truth, which is self-contained and immutable. It consists in recognizing in all life a necessary development of the one life, that of God (in religious language) or the absolute (that of the WL).[63] This recognition is in no way derived from empirical facts. Nor can it consist in contemplative flights, which would be empty superstition. Rather, it always has a necessary factical element, concomitant with which one becomes aware of its ultimate unity. This one life, moreover, is not the product of blind necessity, nor did it simply arise out of nothing. If it is truth, it is equal to itself, and its appearance in the factical world must be teleologically oriented back to itself; in brief, the conjunction of being and knowing in the absolute is not only life, it is *blessed*, its factical progression oriented toward returning to the truth from which it originated.

4

The Principles of the Doctrines of God, Morals, and Right 1805

4.1 DETERMINACY AND VOCATION: FICHTE'S SEARCH FOR PRINCIPLES

Early in the fall of 1804, Fichte placed an announcement in the *Jenaische Allgemeine Literaturzeitung* advertising three series of lectures for the coming winter: one on the *Wissenschaftslehre*; a second on the "foundational principles of the doctrines [*Lehre*] of God, inner right and outer right (habitually called those of natural theology, morality, and right)"; and a third series of popular lectures offering a portrait of the "characteristics of the age."[1] The first and the third of these, the WL 1804/3 and the *Characteristics of the Present Age*, would begin on 4 and 5 November, respectively. While the lectures on WL came to an end on New Year's Eve, 1804, the *Characteristics* continued until 17 March 1805. The second group of lectures announced by Fichte, given the title of *Principles of the Doctrines of God, Morals and Right* [*Principien der Gottes- Sitten- und Rechtslehre*], went from 6 February to 30 March 1805. It had most likely been Fichte's intention from the start to offer two series of lectures throughout the winter, one scientific and the other popular. While the second category ran for the whole season, the first was divided in lectures on the WL and the *Principles*. This would have been necessitated by a practical aspect: the seventeen lectures on the *Characteristics* were only given on Sundays; the other, more technical lectures were given during the week, proceeding at a more rapid pace. Moreover, the reformulation of the WL had been Fichte's constant preoccupation since arriving in Berlin, and both in presenting it for a third time and linking it to the principles of particular sciences, he would have been able to elaborate much extemporaneously. If we accept the hypothesis that Fichte was copying out 1804/2 in view of publication at this time as well, one could easily imagine him seeking to correct the misunderstandings that may have occurred as he gave the earlier set of lectures.

Both the 1804/3 WL and the *Principles* are driven by Fichte's concern to make clear something that he had taken for granted in 1804/2: that the WL was both synthetic and analytic and that this be understood in a single insight, one that could accompany and structure any kind of discursive thought. Fichte had supposed that through his correction of Kant's critical project, his readers would come to see the synthetic-analytic nature of WL as a matter of course.[2] He had presumed too much, both in thinking that his listeners – who were not academic philosophers – had a grasp of Kant's philosophy and that they had understood it as Fichte had. The 1804/3 WL therefore eschewed the gradual, synthetic process of the two earlier presentations and gives equal weight to analysis. Concretely, this means that Fichte thought his audience had become dependent on his explanations and had to be propelled up to the highest insight as quickly as possible, "utterly independent from all discursivity [*Ausdrücke*]."[3] One presumes Fichte felt that 1804/2's complex philosophy of discourse had been misunderstood, with listeners possibly taking the phenomenology and its theory of images to be a sort of emanationist theory. Fichte corrects this by placing more emphasis on genesis: "knowledge is genetic not in its *own* emergence, which proceeds outward from 'A,' but in its emergence *within* [A]."[4] This approach proved to be unsuccessful; without the pedagogy that had made 1804/2 accessible, questions abounded, and Fichte multiplied the number of *conversatorium* or conversation periods in order to accommodate them. His notes, apparently written and rewritten as the series progressed, remain fragmentary and difficult.[5] Fichte himself would eventually realize that this new approach was untenable.[6] The lecturer's mounting frustration was surely one of the causes of the bitterness found in both series of lectures from the autumn of 1804. As one of Fichte's listeners, the prominent philologist Georg Ludwig Spalding,[7] wrote to Schleiermacher on 24 November 1804, "When popular, nasty. When not nasty, incomprehensible."[8]

Indeed, when Fichte was not railing against Schelling in the 1804/3 WL,[9] he was decrying a corrupt and decadent present age.

Still, the work accomplished in the fall of 1804 has its worth, and its preoccupations would come to inform the *Principles* that Fichte would begin in 1805. One sees in the 1804/3 WL a phenomenological preoccupation with time – a topic that does not intervene in 1804/2 – that serves as a compliment to the *Characteristics*' preoccupation with history. The *Principles* will ground the idea of history in the concepts of time and drive. In so doing, it will also correct the teleology found in the *Characteristics*, largely inherited from the *Vocation of Humankind* and the *Letters to Constant*. Humanity's destination or calling to arrive at the fifth age takes on, in the *Characteristics*, an open-ended conception of the future that might easily fall prey to a romantic enchantment with possibilities. The *Principles* postulates the full cooperation of *a priori* and *a posteriori* elements through action in time; its conception of the future, grounded in the word *Bestimmung*, therefore plays on both valences of the German word: at once "calling," or vocation, and "determination." We cannot determine the future, but it is certain that future agency is something determinate; as was learned in lecture twenty-three of the 1804/2, to be autonomous is to be determinate. In essence, a phenomenology can only occur in conjunction with spatio-temporality, in the limited totality called the world. It is this concept of a world and its relationship to the absolute that is the main preoccupation of the *Principles*.

The main point of these lectures is summarized in the foundational synthesis [*Grundsynthesis*] of lectures nineteen and twenty. Knowing has an absolute structure (the absolute or "God") embodied by spontaneous intellectual activity (morals [*Sitten*] in the broad sense of concrete activity) in the spatio-temporal realm ("right"). This material is largely elaborated out of lectures twenty-two to twenty-five of the 1804/2 WL. However, it wishes to go even further in giving Fichte's phenomenology a properly subjective dimension. Hence, the conceptual language still present in 1804/2 is replaced by more properly subjective language (e.g., feeling, clarifying, finding, etc.) mostly retrieved from the Jena period. The central problem of this text is that of reflection, as manifested by a tension between the concepts of immanence and projection. This rearticulates the problem found at the end of lecture thirteen of the 1804/2 WL, the last step before arriving at WL itself. There, we found ourselves confronted with two enclosed spheres, those of truth and consciousness. They were reconciled in WL itself, the synthesis of in-itself and for-another. In the *Principles*, these will have to be reconciled in the phenomenological realm of subjective, lived experience, generating spatio-temporality from within the spatio-temporal itself: experience in the world is the product of a genetic deduction *in time*.

Reading and interpreting the *Principles* is a difficult task. Fichte intended his notes to be merely an aid to his oral presentation, and they contain numerous abbreviations, sentence fragments, and obscurities. This is exacerbated by the constant shifts in vocabulary and imagery found in the text – luckily, many of these are simply reiterations of the basic duality of the *Principles*, immanence and projection. Still, even the most astute reader is often required to reconstruct rather than interpret. Complaining of its fragmentary state and convinced that it did not contribute substantially to his father's opus, Immanuel Hermann Fichte refused to include it in SW, his critical edition of his father's work.[10] The *Principles* would first be published by Reinhard Lauth in 1986 and subsequently included in GA in 1989.[11] Contrary to I.H. Fichte, Lauth considers the handwritten manuscript, found in the Fichte-Nachlass of the Deutsche Staatsbibliothek, to be "in a perfectly legible state." [12]

The MS consists of twenty-three lectures in which no absolute division can be made. Nonetheless, the text can be divided based on the structure of its arguments into prolegomena (the first lecture) and four major sections.[13] The first section (lectures two to seven) establishes the paradox of the absolute's activity as an immanent projection. The paradox is encompassed by a twofold movement called reflection, in which the absolute moves away from itself in its spontaneity and back to itself in determinate knowing. The unity of these two moments is established by freedom, and the conclusion is that if there is a world, it is for free consciousness. The second section (lectures eight to thirteen) aims at making genetic what was only factically posited in the first section. The world that is for consciousness is known in experience, not only by means of reflection but through *feeling*. Feeling makes genetic the externality of the world and incorporates itself into reflection's movement as a *Selbstgefühl*, a subjective self-positing in light. Knowing always implies this standing-in-light of the I, even if it cannot be objectively deduced. If knowing arises, then a non-objectified I must be presupposed, meaning that knowing always involves more than what it makes explicit. The third section (lectures fourteen to seventeen) establishes that the free individual is the product of the absolute's act of generating facticity. The absolute thus expresses itself by means of free individual consciousness, as I. Since particular actions take place according to succession, the I's performance of the absolute's self-construction takes place in time. The I as moral agent in time is itself the standpoint of the absolute. That the I carries out contingent choice in the world according to time and does so following the laws of necessity established by the absolute (the *Soll*) yields a moral imperative. This "free imperative" is the I's *Bestimmung*, evoking both meanings of the word: at once call and determination, the union of inner and outer in activity. The fourth and final section (lectures eighteen to twenty-three) reconciles necessity and contingency without leaving the contingent realm of discourse by thinking modally, allowing us to conceive of the absolute as necessary, free, and manifesting in time. This manifestation in the temporal realm implies the absolute's manifestation as a multiplicity of I – of its manifestation as *we*, the free appearance of reason in the world.

If the WL is discourse about discourse, or a treatise on the conditions of discursive knowing, the *Principles* seeks to establish the possibility of the three types of discourse. The first two sections establish first factically, then genetically, the possibility of a subjective presence *in* consciousness that cannot be an object *for* consciousness. This entails the possibility of discourse about God, in particular, the presence of God in the world. The third section argues that action is always a free particularization of necessary structures. In particular action, necessity as compellingness or obligation occurs simultaneously with belief in the efficacy of one's free actions. This signals the possibility of moral discourse, both in the way a subject can situate itself before the moral law and how the latter can be articulated. The fourth section shifts from the free moral action of a subject to the necessary multiplication of subjectivity in time. When agency moves from *mine* to *ours*, it loses the content of its interiority (the inner life of others is not the ground of my action), and what remains are the external norms of our interaction. These norms are those of *right*, a discourse about how subjects live together in the world.

4.2 THE PROLEGOMENA

Fichte wastes no time in setting forth the goal of this series of lectures. He declares in the first lecture that he intends to articulate the principles of the doctrines of God, morality, and right, deducing all other characteristics from their essential being. The methodology to be employed is neither completely analytic nor synthetic but "purely deductive,"[14] presupposing nothing. And because nothing has been presupposed, the initial definitions of the doctrines that will be offered are only tentative. As with the WL, facts will be initially posited and proved later, once they have been put to use.

The first of the three doctrines is that of God. Here, the word God signifies what it always has in "true Christianity" and for all those who, according to Fichte, have clearly thought the concept before – the absolute, *ens a se* and *per se*, which carries within it what is and lives.[15] "God" here implies a personification, evoking an issue that was central to the WL: an absolute principle available to us in discourse cannot be a true absolute, since it would not be entirely genetic. Yet one in fact does speak about the absolute, and it appears in discourse as the reified ground of discourse itself, as "A." Now, the same problem is evoked, using the more subjective language of *God*: The central problem of God is that of the externalization of what exists *a se*.[16] It would seem that God moves out of himself as cause [*Ursache*] of the world; this world outside of God nonetheless finds its truth entirely in God and must somehow be identified with him. As with the WL, Fichte's listeners will be forced to think the solution to this paradox for themselves, moving beyond mere factical (and presumably historical) opinion [*Meinung*] and consider the question philosophically.

The second doctrine is morality [*Sitten*]. In an aside in the *Characteristics*, Fichte examined whether or not this term is useful.[17] Now, he claims that it can be preserved insofar as it is used philosophically. On its own, *Sitten* can refer simply to an empirical concept of custom [*empirische Begriff der Sitte*]. But here, this idea must be elevated to a philosophical a priori; instead of simply considering it a science of action whose a priori premises or maxims rest inchoate, a real ethics [*Sittenlehre*] involves articulating the connection between the principle of moral action (the maxim according to which one acts) and those actions themselves. Articulating this link involves eliminating the arbitrary element found in everyday human behaviour (called *Willkür* in the WL) in order to clearly see the consistent externalization of a principle.[18]

The final doctrine is right.[19] In both common parlance and scholarship, right and morals are often confused. For Fichte, they are to be distinguished, with morality having as object free action and right having as object a stable and firm state. Right lies in the stable relationship of rational individuals among themselves; that is, it articulates static norms. Philosophy of right, says Fichte, is not a moral philosophy but a philosophy of nature. This is because nature and right are respectively the objective and subjective poles of thinking factically, or statically. When right, as subjective factical thinking, comes to conceive of itself as the genetic product of oneness, its principle becomes one of action and not static being, leading to moral philosophy.[20]

In defining the subject matters of these lectures, Fichte has gone from highest to lowest, starting with the absolute conceived as God and the world's relation to it (religion – subjective dynamic thinking), then moving to the relationship between interpersonal action and its principles (morality – objective, dynamic thinking), and then the stable relations between rational individuals (right – subjective, factical thinking).[21]

The task before us is to establish principles that link these object-domains with their governing concepts – in other words, to find the principle of application or realization of each of these domains. In doing this, our guiding principle must be the WL, unity of all unity and disjunction and therefore the principle of the separation [*Spaltung*] of the object-domains. We have found them historically, meaning we need not deduce or justify their factical existence. But since they exist precisely as intellectual disciplines, they have been genetically linked to WL itself and thought according to this science of thinking. The search for principles is therefore an application [*Anwendung*] of WL.

Taken on its own, the WL is "the *Daseyn* of the absolute," its existence in the world.[22] Factically, the immediate application of this in language is *God*. That is to say, thinking factically, and merely accepting what is acted upon in the everyday world without reflecting on its principles, Fichte's contemporaries would have unreflectively called the being-there of the absolute "God." This factical necessity of language, imposing normative expressions for this or that group at a given time, means that even beginning to think the application of WL leads us to be entangled [*verwickelt*] in the question of God "against our will."[23] If God's *Daseyn* is the expression, in language, of the absolute's *Daseyn*, then the other two concepts, morality and right, are derived from this: they are also linguistic expressions but ones that belong to the WL; their appearance is linked to a willful abstraction of the insight into absolute *Daseyn*. The emergence of particular domains of knowledge as self-standing therefore arises because knowledge has not been traced back to its source.[24] In religion [*Religiosität*] (the everyday expression of what is scientifically the doctrine of God), morality and right disappear, enfolded into this broader standpoint. Crucial to this discourse is the fact that each particular discipline of knowledge constitutes standpoints that relate to each other as concentric circles: because religion shares the same object as WL, it contains all other standpoints.[25]

In what follows, Fichte will not offer a comprehensive exposition of religion, morality, or right, but rather their principles. In establishing these principles, he will arrive not at complete doctrines, but rather standpoints.

4.3 IMMANENCE AND PROJECTION AS THE ABSOLUTE'S EXISTENTIAL ACT

The goal of this first section (lectures two to seven) is to establish the state of affairs within which a "doctrine of principles" [*Principienlehre*] operates, factically positing the elements of an argument that will be made genetic later on. The central claim involved is simply that the absolute appears. It has a *Daseyn* or presence in the world. From this foundational claim arises the disjunction that will remain with us for the rest of our investigation, and the solution to which will be the consummation of this text. If the absolute appears, then it is at once immanent, or self-contained, and projecting, moving outside of itself to establish something concrete that is not the absolute. The reconciliation of immanence and projection is therefore the central problem of the *Principles*. The initial problem of this section is that of "immanent projection": knowledge is the external existence of the absolute (God), but this absolute is a self-enclosed totality that can never leave itself. The movement of immanent projection will initially seem to reify intellectual intuition, privileging sensible intuition. The counterargument, which turns sensible intuition into the product of intellectual intuition, amounts to the same: elevating either side above the other leads to a category error, confusing knowing with awareness-of-knowing and illicitly giving the latter some concrete, external content. The solution will be to emphasize *Daseyn*'s dynamic nature; it is the absolute's existential act, and within this activity, that is, in the moment of knowing, both valences of intuition are identical.

This is achieved through repeating these same arguments but in broader terms,[26] using the more sophisticated tropes of image and light rather than those of immanence and projection. Through these, it will become clear that the contradiction between projection and immanence cannot be treated as external, as happening between the absolute and external consciousness. Rather, it is entirely contained within the absolute. Immanent projection is both outward movement and return to the source, constituting a single act called reflection that is internal to the absolute. The problem of *Daseyn*'s appearance is therefore enveloped by that of reflection's inner mechanisms; there, the same solution to the same problem will have to play out on a broader level. Within reflection, these terms will then be reconciled as necessarily externalizing on account of freedom. Freedom, as intellectual spontaneity, is the principle of the reconciliation of immanence and projection and is ultimately that which accounts for the absolute's externalization as *Daseyn*. The first section concludes with using this to draw a conclusion about about the God-world relationship: freedom is a constitutive part of the world: the world is for free consciousness.

Fichte begins this section by offering a review of the intellectual foundations required to think a doctrine of principles, that is, the WL. While most of Fiche's listeners would have been present for at least one rendition of the 1804 WL, some were not. Fichte reassures the newcomers by saying that there are many avenues into the WL; here, he chooses to employ the concept of *intellectual intuition* [*intellektuelle Intuition*] as entryway.[27] If in the 1804 WL, the absolute was presented as *esse in mero actu*, with thought being the element that had to be integrated into an existential framework, here, the absolute is described as knowledge – or more appropriately, the absolute act of knowing. The *esse in mero actu* of the *Principles* is a *noesis noeseos*, "thought thinking itself," a change in vocabulary that will continue in the Erlangen WL of 1805.[28]

Knowledge is the external existence of the absolute. This external existence is not a remainder or merely contingent determination. Rather, "existence is the inner enclosure that in externalizing itself encompasses and delimits itself once more – and this act of external self-encompassing does not reside in simple immanent, inner *Daseyn*."[29] While knowledge can be described in a self-contained fashion, as absolute knowledge, this absolute knowledge is *from* the absolute, to use the language of the 1804/2 WL.[30] It structurally contains the absolute in its activity, thereby giving presence to the absolute when acting. Knowledge is the absolute as externalized presence-of (what Fichte calls *Daseyn*, "being-there"). Knowledge as *Daseyn* is the absolute "*aufgefaßt*," a bivalent term that refers to both understanding and externalization. This "making present" of the absolute externalizes it through some activity and also gives it content, the necessary correlate to particular activity, which is always *about* something, whether sensible or intelligible. All of this applies to self-contained absolute knowledge, alternately called knowing-of-knowing, insight, or intellectual intuition. One can further conclude that to be aware of one's thoughts is to exist *as* thinking: we see into [*Einsehen*] the fact that knowing and *Daseyn* are immediately the same thing [*unmittelbar dasselbe*]. *Daseyn* is not an external image of knowing; any such image could only be a particular determination [*besondere Bestimmung*]. Knowledge implies *Daseyn* and vice-versa. Knowledge is the absolute's *Daseyn*.

Hence, in external existence, in image, one always finds the absolute (structurally) as well as absolute knowing (as intellectual intuition, or awareness of knowledge). In order for particular acts of knowledge to take place, there must be a passage from the absolute to absolute knowledge as *Daseyn*.[31] This seemingly impossible passage from an absolute that is completely immanent to an activity that projects it outward is the central question we must address, that of accounting for the absolute's relationship to knowledge; it is the hiatus between God (absolute) and world (knowing). We know that *if* knowledge is, *then* the absolute *must* be present, for knowledge is the absolute's own externality. In itself, this assertation only establishes the bare externality of knowledge, the existence of a world whose content is yet to be determined. Yet the fact that something appears *in* the world is precisely what constitutes its nature as world, as the enclosed realm of contingency and particularity.

Daseyn is always immanence *and* projection, both immediate identity with the absolute and a mediated expression of content:

> Out of the *Daseyn* of the absolute comes the internally autonomous *Daseyn* of this *Daseyn* – the first goes with the second and they are inseparable – knowledge. Knowledge of knowledge = *consciousness*: no knowledge without consciousness and vice-versa. Both *Daseyn* of the absolute; the first unmediated, the other mediated.[32]

Daseyn, then, functions according to the same pattern as intuition: in the latter, intellectual and sensible, knowing and awareness-of-knowing, always accompany each other; in the same way, *Daseyn* is always accompanied by a *Daseyn* of *Daseyn*, a pure externalization of world-possibility. Just as I am aware of thinking when I think something in particular, so too am I aware of my actions taking place in the world, in an enclosed totality, when I act.

Yet how can a self-enclosed totality such as the world be the externalization of another self-enclosed entity, the purely immanent absolute? *Daseyn* of *Daseyn* is the pure possibility of externality, the projection of the absolute. The absolute is pure act. The projecting movement is ultimately from absolute as immanence to absolute as projected, manifest in the act of projecting. There is one absolute, but it can be considered either from the side of projecting or projected. Since the absolute is always equal to itself and never leaves itself, its projecting is immanent to itself. Fichte will qualify this paradoxical statement later. For now, he presents it factically as a maxim: the absolute's activity is immanent projection. This can also be expressed by saying that "[The absolute] externalizes itself as *external* ([the external] precisely of the absolute). It therefore describes itself and constructs itself again in its *inner activity* as such, as absolute."[33] The absolute externalizes itself – this is what the absolute does. It then reconstructs itself within itself precisely *as itself*: the externalizing absolute. In this statement, the absolute presents itself according to three valences of *Daseyn*: as constructing (*Daseyn*-of-*Daseyn*), as constructed (existing *Daseyn*), and their unity, *Daseyn* itself. To this "threefold I" [*dreifaches Ich*][34] one must add (though not externally but as genetic root) the absolute itself. This fourfold relationship constitutes the absolute's *Daseyn*, with all four being posited simultaneously in an act of immanent projection. In this simultaneous fourfold positing resides the internal, original disjunction [*Urdisjunktion*] that accounts for appearance. This fourfold distinction therefore contains the whole problem of externalization.[35]

This synthesis of *Daseyn* and the absolute also describes the conceptual relationship of the three particular sciences (religion, morality, right) to the WL, according to a fivefold synthesis. The difficulty of its expression is due to the exclusion of the evident starting point, nature; indeed, Fichte has reworked the deduction to make it coherent in the absence of this "natural" starting point in order for his lectures to remain consistent. Despite its absence, the structure of the deduction is clear:

1. *Daseyn* has insight [sees into] the absolute (it knows *that* it is *Daseyn*: *Daseyn*-of-*Daseyn*).
2. The absolute is the real origin of insight: it externalizes itself as *Daseyn* (*through*).
3. *Daseyn* is an internal movement of the absolute that never leaves itself (immanent projection).
4. *Daseyn*'s insight into the absolute (the intellectual intuition that yields *Daseyn*-of-*Daseyn*) and the absolute's self-externalization are *one* movement (complete *throughness*, or reversibility, of the terms).
5. Externalization is internal to *Daseyn*; *Daseyn* is the internal, genetic reconstruction of the absolute.[36]

If knowledge is an externalization and *Daseyn* (external existence in general) can be presupposed, then a *Daseyn*-of-*Daseyn* is necessary. Knowledge belongs to consciousness, and consciousness is always aware of its own act. In the same way that one cannot posit thought without awareness of it, so too is *Daseyn* always accompanied by *Daseyn*-of-*Daseyn*: the pair positing/posited are inseparable. We saw this because we were able to elevate ourselves to the insight into the self-reflexive nature of *Daseyn* through a free act of thought: we are consciousness itself and are aware of our thoughts. Intellectual intuition, then, structures not only *Daseyn* but the possibility of our discovery of it: were we not consciousness, we would not have had insight into the absolute's *Daseyn*.

Fichte now examines the nature of the proof of this deduction. Knowledge belongs to the immanent absolute, immediately present to itself and able to be other than itself. Yet what is known belongs to consciousness, the discursive realm that is projected, "out there." We therefore find ourselves before a contradiction between the absolute's self-identity and its self-positing: if the absolute is immediately present and consciousness is discursive, how can consciousness relate to the absolute? How, in other words, can *Daseyn* and *Daseyn*-of-*Daseyn* coexist? Ultimately, this problem depends on a category error, confusing awareness-of-knowing (intellectual intuition) with knowing of particulars (sensible intuition): to say that all knowledge is absolute knowing itself does not imply that the absolute knows itself as unique object: rather, it is itself the very activity of all knowing. Consciousness, then, would be the product of a higher, self-constituting consciousness (awareness of knowledge, or intellectual intuition).[37] Yet this would seem to secure the absolute's externalizing in knowledge at the expense of self-enclosure, of the absolute's immediate, ineffable truth. This is the opposite of the initial contradiction: if before, intellectual intuition was taken up into sensible intuition, now, sensible intuition is seen as the product of intellectual intuition. We banished contingency from one domain only to find it in another. The solution will not be to eliminate it but rather accept it and provide it with a foundation.

Neither sensible nor intellectual intuition should be privileged over the other; they are identical in the unified act of knowing. This pure act is the absolute, and its *Daseyn* is therefore *existential act* [*Existential Akt*]. Particular, more definite *Daseyn* – individual being and knowing – belongs to this pure, living act. To say that it is living is to affirm that it is dynamic, genetic, and self-enclosed. The absolute is totally self-enclosed as *act*: its own activity is never beyond its identity, since it is what it does. Knowing belongs to the pure act of the absolute. In activity, we find the unity of knowing and its awareness, the unity of sensible and intellectual intuition. The solution to the earlier contradiction – which always seemed to privilege either knowing or awareness-of-knowing – is to establish their identity in the unified act of knowing. Such an act is always particular and always spontaneous. In brief, the existential act is where the absolute, as pure act and unified intuition, appears and is always the free act of an individual. The free individual act is, in Fichte's terms, a "ray of light" [*Lichtstral*], a spark of pure activity in the moment of coincidence of knowing and knowing-of-knowing. The knowing subject is therefore duplicitous [*Duplicität*]: partly factical, appearing in the world, yet, in its judgments, animated by light. What is manifest in the existential act is light; light, even if intangible, is the "immediate *Daseyn*" or animating force of the existential act. We can know this by means of intellectual intuition: when knowing takes place, light must shine: the absolute must manifest itself.

Yet the fundamental problem faced by immanence and projection, that of the external relationship between projecting and projected, remains. We have arrived at a single act that encompasses both of these, but what is projected, consciousness, is still *outside* the absolute. There is still a fundamental tension between immanence and projection. This will lead to the repetition, on a higher level, of the arguments already made but now using the more sophisticated tropes of image and light rather than those of immanence and projection. This switch in vocabulary inaugurates two series [*Reihe*] of terms: light-projection-activity on the one hand, and image-immanence-resting on the other. Through these, it will become clear that the contradiction between projection and immanence cannot be treated as external, as happening between the absolute and external consciousness; instead, they are entirely contained by the absolute. Immanent projection is both outward movement and return, constituting a single act called reflection, internal to the absolute. The problem of *Daseyn*'s appearance is therefore enveloped by that of reflection's inner mechanisms; there, the same solution to the same problem will have to play out on a broader level. The question at hand is how the absolute can seemingly leave its own immanent core by means of its own activity without really leaving itself. On the one hand, the absolute is intransigently immanent. On the other, its activity is light, creative and without borders, responsible for particular acts of knowing. Linking immanence and projection involves seeing into light as light, as activity. In inquiring about the nature of the absolute's activity, we must therefore ask, how does light appear? And how does it *enlighten Daseyn*?

Fichte's investigation begins with the series light-act-projection and moves toward its opposite, image and immanence. This first series is grounded in the existential act. As activity rather than stable category, the existential act is the absolute's own power, its acting-out [*Aussen*Akt].

Its structure coincides with its activity. This, says Fichte, is the definition of an image, a delimited totality that is immanent and autonomous, and that depicts something other than itself: "Thus externality and activity immediately permeate each other [in the existential act], and are simply one. Externality, however, is *image.* The existential act is therefore image in an absolutely substantial way; it is image, wholly and inalterably, and nothing more."[38] The existential act is an activity, more precisely, the activity of imaging. What it images is the absolute. That the original thing it depicts – the absolute – is not itself knowable does not detract from its image character; one need not see the original in order to know *that* an image has the character of an image. One is aware that it is simply *image-of*, that it has been constructed *as* image. In addition to my awareness of the image *as* image when beholding it, there exists a second order awareness internal to image, providing for its intelligibility. The composition of every image contains elements that are not immediately visible and cannot be separate from the whole.[39] The subject's confrontation with an image therefore involves two levels of meta-cognition, of awareness-of: in a restrained sense, being aware that the image is internally coherent and in a broad sense, knowing that it is the image of something – whether or not there is a known original. Any such original cannot be a blueprint but a pure act of imaging [*Abbilden*]. Put otherwise, a purely imaginative scene, such as the product of an artist's fancy, is, as image, still image-of. If I am aware that something is an image, I am aware of it being the product of some activity but also as depicting some activity: in the image, *Daseyn*, *Daseyn*-of-*Daseyn*, sensible intuition, and intellectual intuition all converge, the two former categories being its objective poles and the latter its subjective poles. In the image, form, content, and execution occur simultaneously and interactively. For this reason, the absolute can only appear *as* image.

As a delimited product, an image is an externalization. If the existential act is an image, we can rightfully say that *Daseyn* is at once internal to it while being necessarily externalized and objectified. Yet Fichte does not conceive of the concept of image as a static product – it is not merely another term for the manifold of experience. The image was meant to be a genetic solution to the factical problem of conceiving of intellectual intuition as a mere factical seeing of objects. It must be dynamic. The image, therefore, is not a concretion of light or the abrupt end of light as it reaches an opaque surface: it is rather the reflection of light, its doubling over onto itself, dynamically, as it effects a return movement. Image *as image* (i.e., the existential act) is reflection, and its factical existence as something visible is the product of its genetic existence as reflection. The reflection of light is the inner law that guides the existential act.[40] Reflection is the law of existential act. A law is a guiding principle whose application presupposes another principle.[41] The principle that reflection presumes is: light can never leave itself. Hence the emergence of an image is the product of light "turning back" upon itself [*zurückgebogen*].[42] In reflection, light's interior *is* its exterior; in this way, its self-representation and self-intuition coincide. If law-giving shows that positing is always accompanied by predication, awareness-of-knowledge is always predicated of knowledge and vice-versa. Where images are manifest, the shining of light is presupposed. Here, neither intellectual nor sensible intuition has been given a dominant position, but each has been predicated of the other in the single movement that is the turning-back of light upon itself. The answer to the question, how does light appear in *Daseyn*? is therefore: as reflection.

Reflection seems to have solved the problem of the externalization of the absolute. But upon closer examination, it has in fact generated a new contradiction: it takes knowledge to be the external product of the absolute. Knowledge externalizes as existential act, or image. This movement is called reflection. But if reflection is a self-intuition of the absolute as existential act and this existential act is God's (the absolute's) *Daseyn*, then reflection never left its ground. Yet there is indeed a world outside of God, concrete products of reflection that are not the absolute. The question, then, is how this world came from God without leaving God.[43] Put otherwise: if reflection constitutes its own essence by turning back on itself [*zurückgebogen*], then it is a self-intuiting. The question, then, is whether the constitution of image, the product of reflection, is not an illegitimate use of inner (or intellectual) intuition, confusing a mere awareness of intellectual activity with the creation or imaging of something. In the language of God and world, the question is whether the world can simply be seen as some by-production (a precipitation) of God as he leaves and returns to himself. This contradiction, then, is a higher form of the contradiction found earlier in immanent projection, and reflection has thus far pre-emptively solved it in favour of immanence, just as was done earlier.

Fichte will solve this question by placing the absolute and reflection in a proposition that, despite being posited contingently, contains within itself a necessary relationship. The first step is to reorient the question. If the existential act is the external form of the absolute, then it is a determination that is also an essential element of the absolute. How, then, can a determination [*Bestimmung*] be essential? The existential act's relationship to the absolute can be considered according to three terms. "A" stands for the absolute as immanent, "B" for the absolute as projective, and "C" for the existential act, consequence of immanent projection.[44] "C" exists as duplicity, projected by and immanent to the absolute. The projection of immediacy is knowledge-of-knowledge as determination. It is pure unity of knowledge and its self-awareness, apart from content: the absolute's own self-reflection is its content. But this is precisely what consciousness is: the unity of knowledge of content and awareness of one's own knowledge. "C" is therefore consciousness. But must this determination of A/B exist externally? Not necessarily. Yet "C" is indeed the factical product of A/B, meaning it is a contingent expression of the internally necessary structure of the absolute in its two valences, immanent and projecting.

It is now clear that, without naming it, Fichte is making an argument according to the *Soll*, which would have been familiar to his listeners. The argument essentially claims that *if* [*Soll*] the absolute externalizes itself, *then* it *must* externalize itself as reflection. This reflection, in turn, must be contingent but bear all the markers of the absolute, meaning it is particular consciousness. The hypothetical *Soll* that yields consciousness is here *from* the categorical *Soll* that expresses the absolute's self-relation.[45] Consciousness, as a self-enclosed sphere, is *through* the *from* that is the categorical *Soll*.[46] This posits a hiatus or gap between the absolute and consciousness, but, as we learned from the 1804/2 WL, one can project *rationally* through a gap. Such is the case once it has been established that the absolute's content is its very action, its dynamic principle. Once this becomes the case, the particular *Bestimmungen* or determinations of the absolute become accidental, the bearers of a consistently self-same act.[47] This, proposes Fichte, is the very nature of autonomy: the contingent individual bears within it a constant necessary structure;[48]

the introduction of particular content is the free introduction of a contingent element that does not modify the necessity of the structure, even if the fact *that* there is content is one of its essential elements. The necessarily factical is the bearer of freedom; it is the "I" of consciousness. Its external existence contains an element of contingency, but its inner life, its intellectual structures, are necessary. Freedom, therefore, exists in a restrained sense, conditionally and not in itself, but *should* light appear, *then* freedom will belong to it.[49] Absolutely inner freedom must exist externally, as "I," in the realm of particular action. Only rational beings are free, and they are free because they are rational. The solution to reflection's contradiction is therefore the same as that of projection but repeats the solution on a higher level: the free individual is no longer merely a spark of consciousness, a ray of light, but itself a necessary product of light's reflective movement.[50]

If the existential act must externalize itself as it is internally, it must appear as something contingent. In this world, it is thus interiorly contingent and dependent on the absolute. There is a hiatus between the contingent essence of the existential act and the necessary self-referential essence of the absolute. Insight was able to negate this hiatus by rendering rational the absolute's projection. This secures the content of the existential act. Yet the same must now be done for the form. The immanence and projection of the absolute, "A/B" must be reconciled with "C." In the end, a contingent particular will have to set in motion the act of reflection and contain all its necessary mechanisms. The solution will be to establish freedom, in the form of intellectual spontaneity, as the principle of reconciliation of immanence and projection. The form of the existential act is freedom – or more precisely, freedom as intellectual spontaneity.[51] This spontaneity must occur in consciousness, hence in a particular act of knowing, of which the subject is aware. Spontaneity, then, externalizes.

To say that spontaneity externalizes means it is both substantial light *and* freedom. This will lead Fichte to make a distinction: earlier, he spoke of the existential act (the consequence of projection) as "C," the product of A/B (the absolute as immanent and projecting). C proved to be a modification of light, the ray of light that provides for intelligibility – the ability to refer all content found in a problematic *Soll* to the categorical *Soll*. Materially, this moment is free because of the necessary contingency of a problematic *Soll*. But formally, the freedom or spontaneity of this same act is to be distinguished from it. This second, spontaneous movement is "D." This distinction makes clearer the "turning-back-on-itself" [*zurückgegoben*]: both C and D constitute a single outward movement of externalization, but D is the more properly outward moment, the shining of light, while C constitutes the return, the cognizing of what is intelligible. C-D is a single outward movement folded over into itself. It thus repeats externally the movement of A-B. Indeed, if the absolute is pure activity and manifests itself in the existential act, then (at least from the point of view of consciousness as embodied by C-D) C-D are the "higher members" [*höhere Glieder*] that come to envelope A-B, including freedom as a real fact in what was initially only a movement of projection and immanence.

Fichte concludes that if the spontaneity of knowing, the free element of light's activity, is necessary to its inner constitution, then there is an affinity between intellectual intuition and freedom. To be aware of my knowing is a doubling-over, part of the "turning back on itself," since it refers what exists to the discursive mechanisms of understanding. If I do this, Fichte posits, repeating the foundational claim of WL, then I am aware of having done it. But if the initial outward movement was spontaneous (free), then I am aware of it having been spontaneous. The awareness of my knowing is also the awareness of my freedom.[52] In other words, consciousness is always self-consciousness, and self-consciousness is *ipso facto* free. It is in consciousness that freedom and necessity are reconciled, the former being the first accident [*erste accidens*] of the latter.

However, elevating C-D above A-B and making consciousness the locus of freedom has a consequence: while materially, it seems to dissolve the hiatus, formally, it creates a new one: consciousness, as unique locus of the reconciliation of freedom and necessity, seems to be autonomous. This autonomy of consciousness unwittingly posits a necessity whose origins are outside itself, making it a form of idealism. Fichte solves this problem through performing a reversal (or, in the language of 1804, a "through") by means of insight: C-D cannot be superior to A-B, since the C-D movement is internal to A. "C" belongs to A, and we, consciousness, are A's spontaneity. The proof is that in knowing, consciousness is aware of itself as not being the origin of knowledge. *That* there is another order of knowledge at all (awareness of knowledge) gives rise to the insight that we know only *as* externalization, as consciousness. The "external" idealist presupposition is thus internalized, since the necessity at the origin of consciousness's inner structure actually belongs to the absolute as immanent, from which consciousness arises. The return movement that is C is therefore not a ferrying of mental content back to the absolute but a reflective process whereby the structures of consciousness are shown to be that of the absolute – the return movement is to spontaneity what intellectual is to sensible intuition. Every act of knowing is the product of a hypothetical *Soll* that is *from* the categorical *Soll.*[53] In this way, knowing as externalization of the absolute is the expression of the absolute's truth. Truth is always in the act of knowing – or, quite simply, truth appears. A final consequence of the broad movement whereby C-D are integrated into A-B is that the "I" cannot be viewed as absolute, as it briefly appeared to us during the ascendancy of C-D. This is a consequence of the reversal operated: consciousness is the absolute's appearance, its existential act, and not the other way around.

The fact that the existential act *is* constitutes it as image – not as a particular image but a primordial one, the very becoming of a conscious "I." More than image, it is imag*ing*, *bilden* as verb rather than noun; it is a self-enclosed totality free to image or not image. By now it should be clear that in the duality God-world (another way of expressing the absolute-existential act duality), "world" is in fact the "I" of consciousness, the former being merely a static expression of what the latter represents dynamically and genetically. This does not mean that experience – the world "out there" – is generated by an "I," but rather that if "world" describes an intelligible totality, then it only *is* insofar as it is *for* consciousness.[54]

The "I" is the imaging of the existential act. Far from being some absolute creator, the "I" is only the image of the existence of the absolute. It has *insight* into its own truth – it knows *that* it is from the absolute – but cannot directly cognize itself as a true, free being. Indeed, as was said before, the "I" of consciousness can only yield the negation [*Vernichtung*] of the absolute. The result of this hearkens back to a key element of the 1804 WL: "Consciousness has been rejected in its intrinsic validity, despite the fact that we have admitted that we cannot escape it."[55] Now, in the *Principles,* Fichte puts it thus: "I = world. Negation of the I = God within us."[56]

Ultimately, the truth of the conscious I belongs to the absolute, expressed as image. The coincidence of truth and freedom is found in the absolute. The absolute does not act freely; rather, it is, as act, freedom itself. Freedom is not an "existence" but is the determination [*Bestimmung*] internal to the existence of substantial light, that which *enlightens* or animates consciousness as it knows. The particular existence of this freedom is *within* its externalization. The act of the absolute, freedom itself, is therefore the stable core of the conscious I, a power [*Vermögen*] that it possesses. In other words, what animates consciousness is the en-folded (or "turned over onto itself") light within it. In each free individual, there is a play of light, a possible activity that is the product of the absolute. Ultimately, light itself, the activity of the absolute, is the foundation of all particular acts of the I. The factical world and all its discrete particulars have their origin in the shining of light.

With this, the first part of the *Principles* draws to a close. We have arrived at substantial light itself and seen in its very appearing "another appearing" – the conscious I and its attendant field of experience, the world. Moreover, we have elevated ourselves to the point of their disjunction in facticity and unity in *freedom*. Freedom is what mediates immanence and projection, the free shining of light itself that we called earlier "immanent projection." What remains to be discovered is the genetic root internal to the absolute/consciousness (God/world) dyad. If, as it stands, we understand that facticity is simply *from* absolute genesis (the shining of Light), we have accepted this *fromness* as being simply there, as itself a factical object of reflection. What is missing is precisely what a doctrine of principles ought to add to a *philosophia prima*: consistent rules for the application of maxims according to genetic principles.[57]

4.4 THE GENETIC DEDUCTION OF THE ABSOLUTE'S EXISTENTIAL ACT

In the first section (lectures two to seven) immanence and projection were reconciled through the concept of freedom, the free shining of light. While this conclusion is indeed the product of deductive reason and argumentation, it is only factical. Following the methodology established in 1804/2, what was initially posited will now have to be retroactively proven: we must demonstrate that our reconstruction of a state of affairs in thought corresponds to the absolute's initial construction – as the necessary genetic product of the absolute itself (in lectures eight to thirteen). There is, in other words, a contradiction between *tun* and *sagen* at work. In its manner of functioning, this contradiction is similar to that of higher idealism. When asked on what basis it thinks the in-itself, higher idealism replied that it "just does."[58] Yet this saying could not be enacted on its own grounds but rather on those of its opposite, realism. When we ask it the question, "how do you know what you think you know?" a contradiction appears.[59] The same has now occurred with the existential act: consciousness *says*: "I have the power to bring the manifold of appearance to light." But on what basis does it make this claim? Unless it can offer some proof for its claim, consciousness would be positing its own power [*Vermögen*] as a third external term[60] and thereby contradicting itself – it would have claimed reconciliation while further fracturing reality.[61]

For Fichte, this contradiction lies in an illegitimate presumption. In the factical externalization of freedom, we became aware of our knowing, but we have presupposed *that* we know this before anything in particular was known. We established an en-folding of light before anything in particular came to light. This contradiction was first found at the beginning of the last section, where awareness-of-knowing was privileged over knowing of particulars and was therefore transformed into a sort of Ur-knowing from which knowledge of the manifold arises.[62] Here, it occurs in more determinate fashion, specific to the question of externalization. The problem is one of confusing the grounds for intelligibility that experience carries with it as a marker and the things *ad extra* that are objects of experience. Fichte's overarching strategy in addressing this problem will be to assert that experience (and hence the arising of world/consciousness) is not just a matter of intellectual reflection, but also of *feeling*.

Feeling consists first in the recognition that experience is intelligible on its own grounds, containing its own norms, and second, that the knowing subject comes to terms with this by adopting a particular standpoint. Feeling will make genetic the presupposition of the externality of what is found in experience. This is achieved through the integration of feeling into reflection itself, producing a *Selbstgefühl* or "feeling of self." Here, standpoint and subjectivity come together: a broader subjectivity restrains itself (*Schauen*) to allow for the emergence of a narrower form of subjective activity (*Anschauen*). In *Selbstgefühl*, one situates oneself in light. This self-positing in light is conceptually enacted by the pair clarification [*Erklären*] and finding [*Finden*]. One clarifies what one finds; in other words, one elaborates in discourse what is already present in experience. To stand in the light implies making a world clear for oneself. Knowing is always consciousness knowing, and it is made so through the act of reflection, the conceptual counterpart to the *Selbstgefühl* where clarifying and finding take place. The reflective movement of knowledge always presupposes an I without objectifying it, meaning that knowledge implies more than it makes explicit.

We therefore begin by bracketing out the illegitimate presupposition of knowledge of externalization before anything in particular has been known. Earlier, freedom was established as the genetic middle term between the existential act and its product, concrete knowledge. Freedom is itself the power [*vermögen*] of the I, its very effectiveness. Making this relationship a genetic rather than merely factical one begins by examining freedom as absolutely external projection, apart from the power that did the projecting. This involves negating reflection itself, such that only freedom in its activity remains. Freedom here is neither act *qua* act nor act of the absolute. It is simply external activity, "*mere et simpliciter actus*."[63] This projected freedom merges with the object-oriented particular act of knowing – ultimately, with the thing, its object, and coincides with externalization. The independent, immediate subsisting of the *actus mere et simplicter* exists as feeling [*Gefühl*]. Feeling is what rests on itself without mediation. As an internal, immediate attitude, feeling contains the "pre-construction and reconstruction" carried out in discursive knowing: "And so, in the *feeling of the act*, *interior* and *exterior* being would become interpenetrated and fused, internally and without separating act and image."[64]

Feeling is a key concept for Fichte and remains consistent throughout his career. At issue is the presence of norms within the act of knowing that are not immediately derived from the object of knowledge. In encountering a particular object, the knowing subject *feels* compelled to approach it in a certain way, adopting an attitude that seems appropriate and colours the encounter with the object. At its broadest level, this is merely the "feeling of constraint" that compels one to concentrate on something in a sustained way. More determinate expressions are feelings such as obligation, guilt, disgust, awe, blessedness, and so forth. Here in the *Principles*, Fichte's goal is to clarify something that was inchoate in the expression of the WL from this period: that experience always carries with it its own sets of norms and that the subject approaches experience from a standpoint. This standpoint allows it to situate itself in the context of a particular experience. The *Principles* marks the development in Fichte's thought from feeling to standpoint.[65]

The *actus mere et simpliciter* expresses itself as feeling. This signifies that as externalization, reflection suppresses the absolute from which it comes insofar as the latter is immanence. Yet one cannot think without reflecting: reflection is thought itself, and to pretend to philosophize without it is to fall into performative contradiction. It will therefore have to be genetically re-established but without losing the consciousness of feeling we have achieved. This restoration will also be a means of making genetic the presupposition upon which lectures two to seven was based: the very externality of what is external. At work here is the attention of the philosopher, the attitude that consists in distancing oneself from the compelling nature of experience in order to see *that* it happens. Fichte's goal is to allow for the free oscillation between the principle of appearance and the very notion of principle-providing itself; their genetic link is the foundation of externalization. Together, these two constitute a self-enclosed realm of principles, a totality of discourse and its free generation that, in their reciprocal movement, comprise a world.

The genetic expression of externalization will be nothing other than the objectifying projection of principle and principle-providing. The act of projection, which posits the unity of these (and hence an interiority), also posits reflection, the external as external. In saying this, Fichte means that it is in the act of externalization that knowing comes to light, in speaking that one makes sense. The higher principle (principle-providing) according to which one orients oneself in thought (the use of principles) cannot itself be objectively brought to light, lest the discursive context that provides for the intelligibility of things in the world be reified. As was said above, the question is not only one of confusing knowing-of-knowing with knowing, but, in a derivative manner, confusing an object with its intelligibility. The concept of feeling, as a way of rationally relating to experience's accompanying interpretative key, is precisely the unity of these two worlds.[66]

In the concept of feeling, we have a unity of principle-providing and principle, that is, of a principle that, in being applied, carries with it the act of principle-providing. Our discovery of this was the result of establishing the *actus mere et simpliciter*, which, as simple act, is neither inner nor outer. Fichte calls this willful act of abstraction from antecedents and consequences "clarification" [*Erklärung*]. Clarification leads us to the conclusion that reflection is both inner and outer, oriented by feeling. In the 1804/2 WL, this function was fulfilled by description [*Beschreiben*],[67] which is a principle-providing that serves as expression of its own form. Demolishing inner and outer, it shows that reflection is a restrained shining of light. One clarifies the immediate content of what one finds in one's own lived experienced in order to make it an object of discourse – I reflect on *what is* and I know this to be both my own reflection and a true one. Here, two valences of the term reflection are at work: my outward-oriented thinking constitutes an object of thought for me (reflection's projective aspect); and what is found in discursive thought reflects the truth of what is immediately evident in experience (the more properly "reflective" aspect of reflection).[68]

One clarifies the object of reflection. The two are therefore one movement, and their fusion means that reflection is an absolute – that is, absolute reflection, or reflection of reflection, always accompanies reflection. The essence of this absolute reflection is "the existential act itself, *mere et simpliciter*, as such."[69] Absolute reflection is best called an immediate seeing, a seeing without object but one that, *qua* seeing, moves out of itself. This is the reflective pole, the standing-in-light (or simply, the truth) of experience. In order for intuition – for concrete knowing ("*Projektum des Schauens*") – to arise, something must come to light *for* me. Knowledge depends precisely on this polarity of subject and object, of intentional movement [*Schauen*] and intuition [*Anschauen*]. Clarification depends on maintaining this simultaneity in a single moment, that of seeing or knowing. Here, we find reflection repeating the unifying moment initially carried out by feeling but on a higher level: if feeling brought together principiation and principle in a simple "position" or *actus mere et simpliciter*, reflection brings together knowing and known, the totality that constitutes experience and whose bounds discursive elaboration can never leave.[70]

Hence, in knowing, reflection separates into principle and principiation. In the existential act that posits according to a principle, the provision for the generation of principles is present – intelligibility is never divorced from experience. We were able to intuit this "from below," by means of feeling. Now, "from above," we see that the existential act yields this separation. The existential act procures objects – it objectifies. What is objectified is light itself. By this, Fichte wishes to expression the polarity of reflection according to the *Schauen/Anschauen* distinction.[71] The terms are inevitably linked to the seeing metaphor. *Schauen*, or seeing in a more general sense, is the correlate of *Anschauen*, the technical term for intuition. Seeing is an intentional act, its "aboutness" is outside of itself. Seeing sees the world, and in its intentionally posits what Fichte might call in the context of WL an "absolute being" – that is, the world as realm of consciousness. Yet this intentionality is not itself an object, nor even the possibility of an object: better to call it a "feeling of confidence in intelligibility" or even "faith in reflection." It is nothing without a world of real objects, things that can come to light. To objectify light means that one knows that a particular object *stands in the light*, sustaining an encounter with reflection's discursive taking-apart of what is immediately, compellingly, and objectively present. The union of these two moments in experience is reflection-of-reflection (absolute reflection): where intentionality and intuition come together, intelligibility and understanding of something particular coincide – the immediate is made thinkable in discourse *for consciousness*. Reflection's normativity (reflection of reflection or absolute reflection) is always contained in the act of thought. Thus the middle point between principle-providing and principle, their coming-together in reflection, is nothing other than existence.[72]

"Clarification" has now reached a point where it can be identified as absolute knowing, the totality of the movement of knowing encompassed by the two poles of reflection, projection and reflection proper. Clarification is internal to the shining of light, to a "ray of light" [*Lichtstrahl*], meaning that it does not generate its own content but is simultaneously reflection-from and reflection-about experience – its boundaries are established by existence. Fichte concludes that *we* are the absolute knowing that is clarification, albeit only factically: existence manifests itself in and for consciousness.

But this affirmation is not entirely genetic. We have not yet reached the same point of view as lecture twenty-five of 1804/2, where "we are what we say, and say what we are." For if clarification is an immanent, self-closed totality that is indeed *external*, it cannot be simply intuited as a thing external to something else. Yet to say that we are clarification *qua* absolute knowing factically, and that we can articulate this in discourse, is to offer clarification of clarification, an external explanation of its activity. Clarification of clarification as factical knowing will have to be dealt with. At stake is the spontaneity of knowing; if a genetic solution is not found, a higher clarification could be construed as cause of absolute knowing, an unacceptable conclusion.

At issue is the relationship between clarification and clarification of clarification, which Fichte calls "finding" [*das Finden*]. If clarification is absolute knowing, encompassing both poles of reflection (*Schauen/Anschauen*), why does it need further clarification? When clarification is brought into discourse, the *Finden* is implied. Yet it is not a cause [*Ursache*] but rather a making-distinct [*Deutung*] that sees into clarification as it is and not as it factically appears. The *Finden* is therefore the explicit name for the act that, earlier and at a lower level, led to the *actus mere et simpliciter* – the abstraction from origins that lets us see into the essence of an act. The *Finden* clarifies clarification. In the very act of expounding on the *Finden*, we are carrying out a clarification, and in the act of clarifying, the *Finden* will reveal itself.

Moreover, this may have an impact on our conception of freedom. So far, freedom has been linked to contingency: one chooses to begin philosophizing, or ask this or that question, or begin this or that series of considerations, but what ensues is always a series of necessary consequences. Now, the disjunction in which freedom exists, that between the categorical and the problematic, is displaced to the disjunction between clarification and *Finden*. These latter terms are not removed from each other as a cause is from an effect but instead by a mere separation [*Scheidung*]. Properly defining the disjunction/separating will, proposes Fichte, changes freedom's fundamental stance from an "essence and thing [*Sache*] in itself" to a "necessary appearing."[73] In brief, it is only in reorienting the causal order that freedom can become necessary and this only in its appearing. The locus of this reorientation is the clarification/*Finden* relationship.

How, then, does one *find* clarification? Since, in asking, we are already clarifying and we *are* clarification, we are really asking: how does clarification find itself? As projecting (*Schauen*), clarification is a purely outward-oriented drive. On its own, *Schauen* is "thrown into non-being" and "is dissolved in the object."[74] Without intuition [*Anschauen*], *Schauen* is *seeing without an eye*: "The absolutely external in itself as first moment: that is the nerve of the proof. ([This idea] might be of help to you, but presupposes [an intuition into] the matter at hand: you must keep an eye on it, for in this [absolute externality] there is no eye."[75] Within the broad movement of intentionality or *seeing* that constitutes the first moment of reflection, a form of restraint will have to be posited; this, its second moment, is intuition, *Anschauen*, at once a delimitation of experience and the manifestation of subjectivity proper. As Fichte puts it, "being" as such will have to be expressly added to check the "thrownness into nothing" of intentionality. We have already established that from within the bounds of reflection, this unifying action is carried out by feeling. But precisely what kind of feeling can bring this about? It is *Selbstgefühl*, an immediate feeling of the I, the form of the I or immediate self-identity. The solidification of the I within the context of intentionality is a return of reflection upon itself, a restraining and doubling over that yields a concrete subjectivity.[76] The self is thus "the absolute ray of light of intuition … now through feeling condensed into a kernel within itself."[77] It is pure apperception, from which specific perception arises. Apperception is in one sense constrained by intentionality (*my* possible objects of knowledge constitute a field smaller than the total intentionality of thought) but in another sense beyond it and outside of it, since it constitutes real objects, while intentionality remains with the ideal of possible objects. *Anschauen* is thus constituted by a *Selbstgefühl* within *Schauen*. One might just as easily say: an eye is posited in seeing.[78]

The goal of this long argument was to arrive at the notion of *Selbstgefühl*. It is this feeling of defined subjectivity that is the root of all clarification.[79] Why is this the case? *Selbstgefühl* is a self-restraining of a broader form of subjectivity (*Schauen*) that leads to the emergence a narrower form of subjectivity *qua* activity (*Anschauen*). It is in the outward movement from the former (projection) and then back to the latter (reflection proper) that light shines. *Selbstgefühl* is inseparable from knowing in both its forms (sensible and intellectual intuition). If feeling is about establishing a stance before an event in which one already finds oneself, *Selbstgefühl* is about situating oneself in the light. Clarifying, as its name would suggest, is ultimately about bringing something to light; I can only clarify what I already know and possess, elaborating discursively what was there from the start. To answer our initial question, one *finds* clarification when one clarifies – that is, when one brings what one already carries in oneself to light; or to use Fichte's terms, clarification is clarified through the presupposition that absolute knowledge projects itself within itself.

A higher order question remains to be answered: how can we clarify the *Finden*? Clarification is the essence of the *Finden*: one clarifies what one finds already within one's own experience. The content of clarification is factical. In the *Finden*, it will be made genetic. This will occur through finding a genetic (and hence immanent) root for both internal and external. To a certain extent, a genetic *Finden* will collapse the inner/outer distinction; the outer will be through the inner and the inner through the outer, both in terms of one generating [*erzeugen*] the other and the one being understood only through the other.

Achieving this link requires us to concentrate our efforts on the *Finden* as abstracted from what is found in it; an investigation into the nature of *finding* rather than *found*. In doing this, it becomes clear that interior and exterior are together what provide principles for knowledge. That is to say, if we abstract from inner and outer, we notice that they constitute a single maxim, yet a dynamic, intelligible one that manifests itself in specific principles – there are no principles of knowing until the inner/outer distinction has been made. But this initial noticing of the highest maxim is merely factical, something found. If we were to continue in this manner, we would require a principle-providing-of-principle-providing and so forth *ad inifinitum*. The genesis above the inner/outer distinction therefore cannot be a third thing outside them. Rather, it is an externalizing, a movement from inner to outer. The form or unity of the *Finden* is this very movement. It constitutes, writes Fichte, an organic life in which inner and outer, according to form, coexist: the finding of clarification's factical content is a three- or fivefold synthesis: "In the finding of clarification as *factum* rests the well-known synthetic articulation in three or five terms [*Gliederung*]: and it constitutes an organic whole."[80] While Fichte's argument seems to have skipped a number of steps, the meaning of the difficult passage in which he makes it can be found through reconstructing the fivefold synthesis to which he has alluded:[81]

1. The external is interior to itself.
2. Yet this is a self-negation (reversal – making internal the external).
3. The external therefore externalizes what is internal (inner through outer, outer through inner).
4. The reversible terms constitute a single movement: I find what is external within myself (finding is the genetic version of the one-sided clarification).
5. The externalizing movement of finding is internal to absolute knowledge (to externalize is to reconstruct).

Fichte's argument is built on the realization that *we* are the ones who clarified clarification. Yet the basis on which we have done this, our own apperception (conceptual counterpart to *Selbstgefühl*), cannot be intuited as object for itself. Rather, one is simply aware of it, in its activity. This constitutes a non-genesis at the heart of light. In other words, when genesis is applied to itself, there is a gap, an internal hiatus.[82] In genesis a principle is given, and the result is concrete existence, which is ungenetic. Yet there is a moment of necessity built into this movement: what can be clarified must already be present, and clarification becomes clear when one finds oneself already clarifying something. Finding, then, describes the act of mediation that takes place wherever something is immediately experienced: what is found is always found in experience, and within the same realm of experience, one elaborates on its meaning. Clarification is a science of predication grounded in the intelligibility that finding makes explicit. The *Finden* is therefore made genetic by integrating clarification.

Fichte then goes over the results of the geneticization of the *Finden* in more properly epistemological terms. It is from this point of view that the promised results regarding the role of freedom appear. We have achieved a point of view between clarification and *Finden*, the space of the (ultimately genetic) gap between implicit and explicit, immediate and discursive. This unifying space is consciousness – not a particular consciousness but absolute consciousness, the very normativity of consciousness that resides in the unity of clarification and *Finden*. This absolute consciousness arises [*quellen*] from itself. This arising is but another name for freedom. To speak in the language of the WL, freedom belongs to the relationship between the categorical and problematic *Solls*, the free application of a determined structure. Moreover, freedom is always in- and for- consciousness. Consciousness is the last element in Fichte's analysis of the genetic roots of reflection; it must be integrated into this genetic whole. The last moment, then, defines the relationship between absolute consciousness and particular consciousness, the I.

The act of genetically clarifying the *Finden* (that is, inhabiting absolute consciousness, which saturates the hiatus between the two) is intelligible to us but cannot be the object of intuition. In other words, we are *aware* of absolute consciousness. This awareness [*intelligieren*] fills [*ausfüllen*] the hiatus. Reflection, which encompasses the awareness [*intelligiren*], is itself this filling in [*Ausfüllen*].[83] Reflection is therefore the form of absolute consciousness. While a constant shifting of terms obscures some of the finer points of Fichte's arguments, its conclusion, grounded in the most robustly defined of them, reflection, is clear: knowing takes place in consciousness through the act of reflection. In reflection, we clarify (discursively and mediately) what was found (immediately) in experience. That which is found in experience is always particular, and always *for me* as a particular I.[84] Wherever there is knowing, the I is always presupposed, which means that knowing is always *about* more than just what it objectively reflects.[85]

The introduction of factical content into consciousness is an imaging [*Abbilden*] or construction of an image whose image character comes from the fact that it is an image *of* the *Ausfüllen* (here nominalized into *Füllen*) that fills the hiatus. As image of activity, it unifies reflection, consolidating the interior out of which something can appear. Fichte refers to it as a "suppression [*Aufheben*] of non-being and the void."[86] As image of a *Füllen*, consciousness consists of a set of discrete particulars that could be conceived of as "a living line absolutely interior to itself."[87] This internalized succession is nothing other than the form of time and belongs inescapably to consciousness; it is linked to particularity and image in such a way that it disappears at the higher conceptual level that is absolute reflection. As the *Principles* progresses, this will present a problem: for if God (the absolute) is outside of time, thinking morality requires adopting a standpoint that can judge particular actions that take place successively in time.

Fichte's transient comments about time are not meant to demonstrate that the genetic deduction of the appearing of consciousness is incomplete (indeed, its final step was the *Ausfüllen*, the filling-in of the gap), nor that time is problematic,[88] but rather that the concept of appearing still presents us with the practical problem of application. In order to move into the realm of conscious action that is the world, an effective force [*Tatkraft*] is needed. Missing from our analysis is the weight of the particular, the concreteness that only intuition can bring. The next section, then, will mark a turn to intuition in view of establishing genesis on a practical level.

4.5 THE PRACTICAL GENESIS OF THE EXISTENTIAL ACT

The beginning of this third section, that of practical genesis (lectures fourteen to seventeen), resembles the end of the first section. There, the immanent absolute and its projective existential act seemed to constitute two self-enclosed spheres of action. In the second section, they were genetically united by means of elaborating on the notion of reflection – even if a subjective, phenomenological tool, feeling, was the means of working this out. Because of this, the problem thus far has been one of reconciling consciousness and its world with the absolute. Its solution makes religious discourse possible by allowing for the subject to indicate a necessary presence that cannot be an object like any other.

Now, Fichte turns to another kind of discourse, that which arises from the practical application of the genetic relationship found in the second section. This is the domain of moral action, where the isolated choices of a particular "I" are at issue. Here, the opposition between immanence and projection reappears, albeit in a new form: moral action takes place in time, whereas the absolute is above time. This opposition is ultimately between absolute intelligence, or the absolute's presence in the practical sphere, and absolute intuition, its immanent activity.

Reconciling these two involves establishing the "conditional presence" [*Bedingheit*] of absolute intelligence in the world.[89] Said theologically, God's transcendence must be reconciled with his presence among us.

God or the absolute will be shown to express itself through individual autonomy, or as Fichte writes, as *Soll als Soll als Soll*. Individual consciousness feels itself to belong to this construction of the absolute and hence is driven to action, to reconstruction. Since individual action occurs in succession, this individual drive yields time. In brief, the I as moral agent in time is itself the standpoint of the absolute. And that the I unites both contingent choice in that field with the necessity of action transforms the *Soll* into a *Sollen*, an imperative. Yet this imperative is also free, meaning it is better described as *Bestimmung* – at once a call and a particular determination. As with consciousness, the moral law is simultaneously within and beyond.

We begin with the claim that an in-itself always implies a not-in-itself, a for-another. This is, as Fichte himself points out, a problematic *Soll*: *If* [*Soll*] the absolute is in-itself, then consciousness must be for-another. Reconciling absolute intelligence with absolute intuition will imply clarifying this problematic *Soll*. Here, we have begun with absolute intuition, the in-itself, but one can just as easily begin from the other side: *If* consciousness arises for me, *then* I *must* be conscious of my own consciousness. Each formula appeals to a different maxim. The first, the maxim of immanence, assumes that the absolute is autonomous in relation to its *Daseyn*; the second, the maxim of projection, assumes that its *Daseyn* has a higher principle. Thinking according to either maxim implies seeking what it lacks: absolute intelligence is looking for a principle for consciousness, whereas absolute intuition already assumes it.[90] Both maxims, however, have something in common. One reasons: consciousness is, therefore the absolute must be in-itself. The other: the absolute is in-itself, therefore conscious emerges. The absolute as in-itself is common to both maxims.[91] Identifying what absolute intuition assumes and absolute intelligence cannot find consists in applying the maxim of the latter to the problem of the former, which yields: *If* the absolute is in itself, *then* it *must* itself be the principle of the appearance of conscious. Here, the terms are equal (absolute = absolute), hence we have arrived at a categorical *Soll*. The categorical *Soll* has been (analytically) expanded to an "ought-to-be-there" [*Daseynsollens*]. The absolute in-itself is therefore the genetic source of all knowing and the principle of *Daseyn*; said otherwise, the absolute (God) is the source of the facticity of intelligence. This constitutes God's mediation of his own immediacy through his own act: in brief, the divine activity's reflective return to itself (here *Rückblick*, earlier *Zurückgebogen*) gives rise to consciousness. That consciousness must [*Soll*] appear is itself a description of the activity of the absolute.[92]

It is the "divine" activity of self-return in reflection that constitutes the world of consciousness, the domain in which consciousness acts. But the agency of consciousness is more specific than this. One never merely acts; one reconciles oneself to a state of affairs. Religion, morality, and law are standpoints that a knowing subject can adopt. Since they belong to consciousness, they are not object domains but rather standpoints, ways in which a subject situates itself before a particular experience. Had we considered this point before establishing the genetic connection between immanence and projection, we might have called this act of inhabiting a standpoint *feeling* [*Gefühl*]. But having elevated the mechanisms of feeling to the level of reflection, we now know that feeling is always already reason. In order to make these standpoints really viable for subjects in a meaningful way (letting them become spaces "penetrated by light" in which subjectivity is at home), it is therefore necessary to establish the genetic root of the very notion of standpoints – in other words, the transcendental idea of a world.

The task before us is to see how such autonomous action, coloured in a very personal manner, is the genetic product of a categorical *Soll*. Knowing is an existing-outside-itself, a *Daseyn* whose principle is the categorical *Soll*. The categorical *Soll* is immediately the foundation of what knowledge mediates. Knowing is thus traced back to an immediate presence of knowledge embodied by the categorical *Soll* and which provides knowing with its norms. The structure of absolute knowing (knowing-of-knowing, awareness-of-knowing, intellectual intuition, etc.) is therefore identical to that of the categorical *Soll*. As autonomous structure, this absolute knowing negates the particular, and consciousness with it.[93] Yet such absolute existing-in-itself is merely an intellectual construct. We know that knowing and knowing-of-knowing, intelligence and intuition, immanence and projection are inseparable. If the absolute is really the source of facticity, then "the world" – at least in the restrictive sense of the standpoint to which I am committed – is always intelligible *to me*, a conscious "I." In the act of knowing, *I* mediate the various factors presented in existence, but I can only mediate what is given. The I's autonomy is dependent on something else because autonomy is always mediated and mediating.

This paradox of the dependent autonomy of the knowing subject lies at the heart of Fichte's disquisition on the world, which at its base is an exploration of the various modalities of intelligibility itself. Before the absolute, I am nothing – that is to say, there is no knowledge of particulars in the absolute itself; the absolute is the negation of the particular. Yet this somehow rests with the absolute as its own radical possibility. In one of the *Principles*'s only poetic asides, Fichte says that in this way, the I that is negated by the absolute still hovers over its own interior ruins.[94]

All of this, of course, is but a willful abstraction. The point is to bring to light the role of the categorical *Soll* in the act of knowing. Knowing relates to it as principle – no intuition can provide us with the categorical *Soll*; our knowledge of it is the product of reflection, an insight that our willful reconstruction of its mechanism has yielded. In knowing, the categorical *Soll* is always presumed. Fichte summarizes: knowledge is "the absolute *Soll* of the *Soll* as *Soll*."[95] He then explains this singular expression: "Knowledge is only there because God is present within it; that is, recognized within it: otherwise, knowledge is for nothing and is nothing in itself, hence: all knowledge outside of this is nothing and empty."[96] Even more concisely: the absolute is in every particular act of knowing.

In affirming this, Fichte has created an affinity between the autonomy of the knowing I and the activity of the *Soll*. The categorical *Soll* does not express a mechanistic necessity, the coming-into-being of something that should be. Rather, it is the expression of the possibility of projection. It carves out a space for inner experience. In this sense, projection is a project, the possibility of something coming into being and making sense in a certain context. It does not create something *ex nihilo* but rather develops a standpoint. *Should* something come into being, then it *should* present itself according to certain structures and relate contingently ("als *Soll*") to its context. This is the sense of Fichte's cryptic phrase "the absolute *Soll* of the *Soll* as *Soll*."[97] This also explains the heuristic use of the negative in the foregoing explanations. In poetically imagining consciousness as a negated particularity hovering over the ruins of its constructs, Fichte is inciting his listeners to think modally. To conceive of knowing (and more broadly, existence) as a series of causes misconstrues human experience. We clarify what we find, mediating the immediate. The question is not where something came from but how one relates to it.

We have already seen that the realization of the union of inner and outer takes place in the particular, being united by a *Selbstgefühl*. This feeling concretizes the position of an individual consciousness, operating reflection's return upon itself. What the *Selbstgefühl* accomplishes immediately can be explicated in mediation as the work of the *Soll*: the *Soll* of a *Soll* as *Soll*. The categorical *Soll* moves toward appearance through the mediation of the *Soll* structure. This movement has all the hallmarks of causality (indeed, the very if … then … of the *Soll* could easily be mistaken for a statement of cause and effect) but is not a cause. It is rather the absolute's drive to externalize itself, "causality that is not causality, drive."[98] Individual consciousness feels this drive to be something broader than its own *Selbstgefühl*; it is immediately aware of it as being the absolute's drive toward being, at once *Seynsgefühl* and *Triesbesgefühl*. The "I" *feels* that it belongs to the absolute's self-externalization. In the terms of the WL, one could say that consciousness immediately feels that if the absolute constructs itself, we are the ones who do this constructing. Because this is always achieved in the particular, it yields an immanent field of particular realizations, of successions. Hence *Trieb* yields time.[99]

The I is itself the standpoint that the absolute adopts in relating to itself. Conversely, if the I realizes that it is through the absolute and the absolute through it, it can achieve the highest of standpoints, WL, the knowledge that *we* are the ones who carry out the self-construction of the absolute. If the initial position here, the relating of the I to the absolute, is one of feeling, the reversal that places the emphasis on the absolute delves into this feeling to reveal its inner genesis, drive.

Having established the "I" as the standpoint of the absolute, Fichte now addresses the question raised earlier: to what extent is the I of consciousness determined by the categorical *Soll* – said otherwise, to what extent is the I necessary? The answer lies in the difference between the categorical *Soll* and the problematic *Soll*. Consciousness emerges as a problematic *Soll*, beginning with a contingent fact that allows for its free engagement in thought. The structure of the problematic *Soll* is derived from the categorical *Soll*; the former is defined by the latter's *Soll* structure, the *Soll als Soll*. Yet the very emergence of the I is what reveals this structure, this *Soll als Soll*. The I is therefore the principle of the emergence of the *Soll als Soll*,[100] the foundation of the representational character of representations. It is from this status as principle of *as* [*als*] that the I derives its moral agency. In its activity, the I embodies the compellingness of representations. We have already established that the *Trieb* yields a temporal field in which moral action can take place. That the I unites both contingent choice in that field with the necessity of action transforms the *Soll* into a *Sollen*; it is because the I *feels* that its actions will be effective in the world and that it is able to commit to making them. There is no moral action without a *Triebsgefühl* that allows for an immediate experience of the compellingness of one's own action. Yet *that* an I finds any situation immediately compelling is because the *Soll* structure (*Soll als Soll*) provides for intelligibility in the first place. This feeling must therefore encompass both the I's confidence in the efficaciousness of its own actions in the world but also in the higher source of this compelling structure. The moral life can therefore only be lived as a *call*, a *Bestimmung*. Fichte is playing on the double meaning of the word *Bestimmung*, which can mean either "calling" or "determination." Here, we see that in the sphere of action, they are inevitably linked – to determine something requires an inner calling, a belief that is truly inner but that one did not willfully create oneself.[101] It is a feeling of living and acting in the light.

Yet the moral *Bestimmung* does not uniformly encompass all of the I's activity. It only obtains in the intelligible, supersensible world of Kant's second critique, the "z" of 1804/2 WL. Fichte reminds us that knowing aims at something even more fundamental, sense perception. Indeed, the I is aware of the *Soll* as mechanism of a simple outward drive to know the world. Yet it is also aware of the *Soll* as form of the twofold *Bestimmung*, the moral law found at once within and beyond.[102] As it stands, then, there are two absolutes – that of the sensible world and that of the moral world. These two separate object domains will have to be placed in relation such that they are given a common genetic root. Fundamentally, both domains will have to be shown to coexist in a single world according to a shared principle.

Could one of these serve as principle for the other? It would seem that sense experience, as principle of facticity, serves as foundation for morality, which occurs in the factical world. Yet morality makes clear the *Soll* structure, the *Soll als Soll*, that gives form to all experience. The question here is what one means by principle. In this context, says Fichte, what is meant by "principle" is nothing other than the concept of an end [*Zweck*].[103] Hence the *Soll* is the end [*Zweck*] of perception. The result can be expressed according to the *Soll*: *If* [*Soll*] the moral must be (and it must, since it exists as *Sollen*, an imperative), *then* perception *must* be as well. This, says Fichte, is a teleological clarification and proves that both sensible and intelligible necessarily exist in one world. The sensible world is meaningful because it is the sphere of moral action.[104] Moral action is realized in the sensible world, in the realm of perception; through this activity, the categorical *Soll* reveals its structure, moving us from principle (the teleological orientation of action) to principle-providing (the very movement of the *Soll* itself). The movement of the *Soll* is never known as object of knowledge but reconstructed in being carried out. The *Soll* is the end of all activity, and the absolute appears in the world by means of the *Soll*.

The lesson that Fichte draws from this is that there is no sensibility without intelligibility and no intelligibility without sensibility.[105] Yet human action does not continue unbridled through the factical world. Moral action is always conditioned by the interpersonal.[106] A teleology that speaks only of "I" and not of "we" rests on a superficial level. Human action is formed, qualified, and held in check by others, each of whom is at once natural force and moral willing. But nature, the objective static moment of the WL's worldview, cannot serve as the substratum of the interaction between sensible and intelligible. This task thus falls to right insofar as it is the doctrine of the nature of the human race [*Naturlehre von der menschlichen Gattung*].[107] It is precisely this task that will be taken up in the final section of the *Principles*, which offers a genetic account of facticity itself, the static principles that govern interpersonal interaction.

4.6 THE FACTICAL AS LOCUS OF PRACTICAL GENESIS

While the *Soll* is the absolute form of human action, it only reveals itself in facticity. The factical is therefore the locus of the absolute's activity, the place where all the valences of the *Soll* come together. Since the factical world is where principles are applied and made visible, it is only in accounting for "the origin of facticity itself"[108] that the nature of principles will become clear. Fichte suggests that the path to the origins to the facticity must pass through the related concepts of end [*Zweck*] and absolute intelligence. Earlier, it was established that absolute intelligence corresponds to the projective side of reflection. The moral teleology of the previous section must therefore have some relationship to factical projection yet to be clarified. Projection is the key element in reconstruction, hence of understanding in consciousness. To understand the projective act of absolute intelligence is to understand facticity itself, and to understand facticity in its genetic totality would be to understand understanding, inhabiting the highest standpoint of Fichte's system. Here, at the end of the *Principles* (lectures eighteen to twenty-three), our ultimate goal is therefore to simultaneously inhabit the highest and lowest standpoints, WL and facticity – that is, understanding the very possibility of principles insofar as they belong to the WL.

This section is therefore aimed at the difficult task of reconciling necessity and contingency without leaving the contingent realm of discourse. To arrive at genesis, we will therefore have to learn to think modally. The natural tendency of consciousness is to think according to the relational categories of cause and effect. Shifting toward modality will allow us to conceive of something free and necessary (the absolute) that manifests itself in time, something that a simple logic of cause and effect would not allow. To initiate his listeners into modal thinking, Fichte focuses on the role of the word "as." Form of the problematic *Soll*, the *as* draws attention to the becoming of contingent being. That the factical came to appear *as* it is conveys the disjunction between immanence and projection and their union in experience. Fichte will express this according to a fivefold synthesis, the *Grundsynthesis* or foundational synthesis of the *Principles*. It concludes that intuition is a necessary product of being and that reflection is always a twofold outward-oriented movement. While this content has been stated before, it is now articulated on the broadest conceptual level, that of WL, and genetically founded. Implied in the foundational synthesis is that the I both makes time and exists in time. Time and experience are necessarily linked, meaning that succession and multiplicity are necessary parts of subjective existence. Because of this, time necessitates a multiplicity of the I itself, a *we*, allowing for external application of moral agency to interactions between individuals. These interactions lack the depth of interiority that a single "I" contains within itself – we cannot penetrate the mystery of another's interiority – but each individual can live their own engagement in the world with others according to interior morality. The external character of these interactions is the essence of right.

We begin by conceiving of projection (absolute intelligence) and then the absolute as intelligence of this absolute intelligence. Yet one cannot project one's way to the absolute – it is inaccessible to intelligence. Rather, the absolute projects itself, positing its own *Daseyn* in light.[109] While the absolute's *Daseyn* is indeed its factical product, this facticity does not alienate it from its source; the absolute's *Daseyn* carries with it its own meaning [*Deutung*]. As was made explicit in the concepts of *Finden* and clarification, experience carries with it its own interpretative key. In the case of the absolute, it *is* its own means of interpretation. This is ultimately because the absolute is neither in-itself nor for-another, interior nor exterior, but the unity of both. Nothing can exteriorize the absolute. Its *Daseyn* is instead its own mediation in the factical world. One might say: the immediately evident is brought into discourse by means of interpretation: *Daseyn* is our interpretative, mediative act of understanding, an act carried out by *Daseyn* itself. To summarize using Fichte's terms, the absolute presents itself immediately as an "as."[110]

But how do we account for this occurring *in time*? We have already seen that individual moral agency requires time. The link between the absolute and time is the heuristic concept of nothing. This nothing is to be conceived of as consciousness's conception of the ground of absolute spontaneity – that is, freedom. The absolute is what it does, and it is achieved spontaneity, absolute freedom. Yet what it factically generates, seen after the fact, are the products of necessity. The "nothing" consists precisely in the fact that spontaneity involves a free beginning. Consciousness factically reconstructs the absolute's construction, seeing its origins as something inaccessible. Time gives form to this factical reconstruction. If the factical reconstruction (of the absolute) occurs in consciousness, and the world is *for* consciousness, then time must be the factical container of freedom, the expression of modality from consciousness's point-of-view.[111] Confirming that he had modal categories in mind, Fichte asserts that freedom can only appear in the first place if it has been accorded [*vergeben*].

The absolute must [*Soll*] exist *as* externalization. Is this a categorical *Soll* that lays bare its own content (a "*Soll als Soll*") or a problematic one? More specifically, we must ask: if the absolute externalizes itself, then what it externalized is what it was as internal; the absolute externalizes itself according to internal form; what, then, is to be made of the *as*, the signifier that indicates a passage from necessity to contingency? It would seem that the necessary absolute never really achieves exterior form. Fichte proposes a dynamic solution: within the absolute and within the categorical *Soll* that is its expression, one finds the problematic *Soll*, an inward projection *per hiatum*. The pure activity that is self-thinking thought can be applied to some particular; this may or may not be undertaken. The particular, so to speak, is derived from the necessary as a "possibility of possibility." The bare possibility of possibility proves the existence of an *als* and hence the necessity of possibility.[112] This difficult argument does not present us with a new conclusion: it merely states genetically what was factically already presented – externalization is an immanent projection. Genesis itself must overcome an internal gap. We learned from the WL that the inner/outer distinction between being and appearance (or what is the same, being and becoming) is the product of idealism seeking an external cause for appearance. Thinking modally with the *als* eliminates this search for an external cause. Fichte simply means to express that the absolute is the free ground of acts of thought or, in subjective language, the (free) divine intellect is the ground of (free) thought in consciousness.[113]

Fichte concludes by transposing this exposition into a dense transcendental argument. *We* have become the essential object of WL, a *Soll als Soll* in the absolute but alienated from it and objectified. Hence WL consists (factically) in self-alienation. To posit principles from consciousness objectifies, sending WL out of itself. This self-alienation is *intuition*. Thought constitutes a movement from being to intuition to generating being [*Seynerzeugen*]. Hence thought finds being immediately and clarifies it – it moves from *Evidenz* to discourse and then back to *Evidenz*. Yet intuition must itself be the product of being; it does not generate being but instead finds it. Specifically, it finds itself *through* being. As consciousness's act, intuition is itself *Evidenz*; it is merely its own outward discursive movement. Now, if time is the product of consciousness' act, then intuition is the principle of the filling of time; intuition is the correlate of time's content.

Leaving apart the last remark on time, Fichte suggests in passing that the foregoing is an argument according to quintuplicity. His remarks can therefore be reconstructed as the fivefold synthesis of externalization:

1. Intuition posits being.
2. But intuition is being's becoming; therefore, it is being that posits intuition (*reversal*).
3. Intuition is internal to being (intuition *through* being; being *through* intuition).
4. The terms are a single movement, an immanent projection, i.e. externalization.
5. Externalization is itself reversible. Reflection is one movement with two moments, projection and return. This is a reconstruction. Hence, externalization is a reconstruction of being.[114]

This is the fivefold foundational synthesis of the *Principles*. Thought is absolute *Daseyn*. Thought moves away from itself, giving itself principles: in its activity (thinking), consciousness is a principle-providing force. Thought and the *Soll* are reciprocal: posit absolute thought, and it will take the form of a *Soll*. Posit the *Soll* as *Soll*, and thought will emerge. The hiatus is the being of thought (the factical account of intellectual intuition). While the hiatus is a fact of consciousness, it is freely posited. If it is posited (if thought is engaged), then it is certain. As an outward movement, thought cannot arrive at its own immanence; this is the role of the *Soll*. Thought is therefore aware of its immanence (intellectual or inner intuition) through knowing the structures of the *Soll*, not a particular content. Thinking is a seeing that can only be known as a directed seeing [*Absehen*]. The simple positing of seeing, to see, is to presuppose – consciousness moves outward in intuition without deciding on its content beforehand. Thinking this content then presumes a return in reflection that constitutes a re-construction.

There is, then, no thought without intuition, no consciousness without an I. And because all thought depends on intuition, which sees particulars in succession, conscious is *in* time, at once determining it and determined by it. When the foundational synthesis was presented, it was alluded to that intuition was the principle of time. Now Fichte expands on this: The I "makes time in time."[115] Time is the principle of the I's factical interaction with the world; experience happens in time, and time is constituted by the experience of I in the plural *we*. Time is the structure that allows for the very intelligibility of intuition. This means that, in the foundational synthesis itself, we see that intuition as subjective activity "makes" time. Now, we must demonstrate how the "I" lives in time – that is, in enclosed, infinite extension.

This relationship is structured by the *Soll*: If the I experiences something, then it must experience it in time. Yet the fact that time itself has come from intuition introduces yet another *Soll*: If I experience temporal succession, then it must have been produced by intuition. "The *Soll* is the *Soll* of a *Soll* as *Soll*," [116] writes Fichte, or in the language of the WL: the problematic *Soll* is from the categorical *Soll*, whose structure provides for intuition's form. Moreover, this *Soll* resides in consciousness, and if it is present in the dynamic act of thinking, consciousness is aware of its presence. One is aware of thinking when one is thinking. The factual existence of the problematic *Soll* is genetically linked to the categorical *Soll* in intellectual intuition whenever thinking occurs. This also implies a link between the two broadest categories of principles, factical principles and teleological ones, which are internal to facticity. In other words, principles can be a simple rule of application applied by consciousness (such as the maxims of realism and idealism in the WL) or as driven toward an end (as we saw with morality). While in both cases, the relationship is asymmetrical, both (problematic *Soll*, factical principles – categorical *Soll*, teleological principles) belong to the *Soll als Soll*, the *Soll* structure. Fichte's goal here is to suggest that knowing happens *in* time, and it is concrete knowing that one is aware of in the *Soll als Soll*. Time is therefore the factical substratum that hosts the binary act of intuition (knowing and knowing-of-knowing), thereby linking sense perception and moral action.

The *Soll* als *Soll* is therefore internal to consciousness and also that which provides for its determinate existence. Now, to be conscious is to exist, and consciousness's activity is itself the I. Yet the I does not create itself – it finds itself already *within* genesis. The I is the product of light's immanent movement, reflection. Yet knowledge is always knowledge of discrete particulars, which in the language of the light metaphor is the projection of light *per hiatum*, an objectification of light. Light, of course, cannot be stabilized. One can only factically schematize its mobility. To revert to the language of WL for clarity's sake: light, insofar as it is opposed to the concept (here, consciousness or thought), is akin to awareness-of-knowing. Awareness-of-knowing takes place in a particular act of knowing. Objectifying light therefore implies parcelling off the moments of awareness-of-knowing that occur with each act of knowledge. Light objectified is a continuum, a line along which "I" is a node, occurring each time knowledge and awareness of knowledge (sensible and intellectual intuition) occur in the same act.[117] The formation of these nodes is the transition from *absolute* time, an uninterrupted fluid movement, to particular time, the time of a particular act of the I. Particular time is nothing but the repetition of the I's activity in time.[118]

Hence the I is present in time. But is its presence merely a discrete section of time? This would turn subjectivity into mere spinozist attributes, factically populating experience.[119] The I is not present in the temporal realm merely as a division of it but as the free (spontaneous) expression of the *Soll* – as light. Light is absolute existence. Light factically appears *as* I. The I is therefore the factical existence of light, living principle of what appears in light. Hence the I is the principle of thought's *existence*, its concrete realization but not of thought itself. Thought is light, and we are always already in it. We do not *think* thought but rather become aware of our already thinking;[120] we cannot know the *Soll als Soll*, but we can be aware of its use in thought. Ultimately, the *Soll*'s manifestation is in the I, according to the *Soll* structure: *If* [*Soll*] the *Soll* exists, *then* it *must* exist *as* embodied in an I. In this way, necessity, the *Soll* structure, has been internalized by freedom, the activity of the I.[121]

Now, Fichte arrives at a logical foundation for the genetic relationship between the *Soll als Soll* and the particular I: the thought that the "I must" *must* come into existence.[122] To say that the I cannot come into existence in expressing its own imperative can be reduced to the statement: "I think that I don't have to think," which, if not an outright contradiction, at least provides a positive legitimation: if I must think, then I certainly do. Retorsion, then, leads to a confirmation of the I's internalization of the *Soll*. The I's activity is therefore inhabited by an imperative, a *must* or *sollen*. The I does not exist originally [*ursprünglich*] but rather *is* its coming into objective existence through activity. This *must* is a further determination of the *Selbstgefühl*. In this must as *Selbstgefühl*, spontaneity and possibility-condition are united in a single moment: no *Soll* without an I, no I without a *Soll*.

From this, Fichte is able to conclude that the world is a totality inhabited by the I. In intuition, one finds the *Soll*. It simply exists in it – it is simply there. Now, the *Soll* is the principle of temporal succession. It is also a closed, stable existence. It therefore circumscribes temporal appearance: intuition is, on a formal level, infinite repetition rather than infinite regress. Thus the infinity of time is transformed into a *totality*;[123] intuition is splintered into rays of light. This is a splintering that takes place in the conceptual *we* and not the *I think* of a particular moment.[124] The I is enclosed in the repetition of its form. This the reconciliation of the I and the world, of the I's activity as light of the world.

Yet from this, another, greater problem arises, that of reconciling particular consciousness with the totality just established. How is the I conscious of itself as being in the world? In conceptual language, we might ask, how can consciousness reconcile the immediate with the mediate?[125] At stake here is something larger than self and world: this is also a question of *Evidenz* and discourse, of the absolute on the one hand and consciousness and its world on the other.

There is therefore an opposition between the absolute as the self-enclosed repetition of intuition, self-identical and homogenous [*Gediegenheit*],[126] and the *I* whose activity is spontaneous.[127] Thus, at the end of the *Principles*, we return to the text's central problem, that of reflection. The reconciliation of the two aspects of reflection, immanence and projection, exists immediately in the absolute. The absolute is reflection's completion, at once activity and essence. Since it is outside of time, these moments exist simultaneously; the absolute is inception, effort, and achievement all at once. Fichte's expressions *Genesis* and *Tathandlung* capture this atemporal, active subsisting. Consciousness always finds itself in the act of reflection, tasked with executing what the absolute already is. The tension, then, is really one between consciousness's spontaneous becoming and its own structural completion, reason.

The gap between them will be bridged by freedom, which serves as a dynamic link between intuition and sensible intuition. Awareness of thought is, *mutatis mutandis*, awareness of the I's freedom. To be aware of my thinking is to know myself *as* thinking. The "as," the expression of the problematic *Soll*, is the ray of light that brings together two kinds of intuition in a single act.[128] The freedom of the I comes from the spontaneity of the outward movement that unites the two kinds of intuition in a single act. The I's freedom is therefore its projection. The I is free *as* intuiting, and intuiting is its activity. It is therefore free at its very root, and this freedom is limited by the particular scope of its activity, the object to be determined in consciousness.[129]

Freedom is therefore nothing other than reason's self-expression in the world. Reason always manifests itself in mediation – in discourse – for which particularity is necessity. Engagement in rational activity is the end goal of freedom, even if reason is norm-governed.[130] If there is no I without consciousness and no consciousness without an I, then there is no reason without freedom and vice-versa. The point is that the contingency that traditional metaphysics has seen as an obstacle to systematic thinking is itself the key to a sound logic: reason is at home in the world, the place of free, particular choices.[131]

5

The Way towards the Blessed Life 1806

5.1 "THE RESULT OF MY SELF-CULTIVATION": ON FICHTE'S PHILOSOPHY OF RELIGION

After spending the summer semester of 1805 in Erlangen, Fichte returned to Berlin. While the experience at the university there had not been as disastrous as that of Jena, it was undoubtedly a disappointment. After refusing chairs in St Petersburg, Landshut, and Charkow (Kharkiv, Ukraine)[1] and preparing what was perhaps his most rigorously speculative rendition of the WL to date,[2] Fichte was met with apathy in Erlangen. His lectures were poorly attended, and his relationship with his colleagues was, in the words of Fritz Medicus, "unedifying" [*unerquicklick*].[3] His peers and students were unprepared for the rigours of transcendental philosophy, as well as the scathing terms the lecturer often employed.[4] Meanwhile, in neighbouring Würzburg, Schelling's lectures were immensely popular, and Fichte's invectives against "the blind philosopher of Würzburg" became more intense. Even more devastating was the death of Schiller, who had remained an unwavering source of support. "I feel that with him, a part of my own spiritual existence has perished,"[5] declared the philosopher. Before the semester was over, Fichte was already making arrangements to return to Berlin.

What awaited him there was not the security of a university chair but the instability of his old life as a private lecturer. Berlin still had no university, and the year before, Fichte had been refused admission to its Academy of Sciences, depriving him of a permanent stipend.[6] He therefore found himself in much the same situation as when he left Berlin for Erlangen, forced to give popular lectures in view of both earning a living and obtaining a teaching position. Hoping to repeat the previous winter's success, he set about preparing a new series of lectures much as he had the *Characteristics*: he rented a lecture hall in the Berlin Academy, advertised widely, and scrupulously prepared a text that could be read aloud and published immediately. This new series, called the *Way towards the Blessed Life* [*Anweisung zum seligen Leben*],[7] would be given on Sundays at midday between 10 January and 30 March 1806. That winter, the atmosphere in Berlin was tense. The Holy Roman Empire was in a state of collapse after Napoleon's victory at Austerlitz in December 1805, and much of the Empire's territory was being reorganized into French puppet states. When unrest in Prussia led to military action later in 1806, Napoleon would cross the Rhine, deliver crushing defeats to the Prussian army at Jena and Auerstedt, and march the *grande armée* through Berlin. Given the circumstances, Fichte's lectures were, as a mutual friend reported to Goethe, well attended.[8] Once the philosopher of the French Revolution, Fichte was now heavily invested in Prussian politics and German nationalism and would follow the court into exile in Königsberg later in 1806. Yet these lectures on the *Blessed Life* were anything but a call to arms: adopting a paternal and spiritual tone, Fichte spoke of religion using vocabulary he borrowed from the Gospel of John. The rapport that these lectures had with their historical circumstances could be summarized by a verse from John's prologue, itself a central element of Fichte's text: "He was in the world … but the world did not know him."[9] The cruelties of history are passing, but the blessedness of life, in-itself and for-itself, is enduring. As Fichte wrote in his preface, these lectures were the fruit of seven years of meditation, years that had been turbulent ones that made him reflect on the very foundations of his philosophical task.[10]

In the context of Fichte's philosophical project, these lectures constitute the clearest and most rigorous of their kind, the summit of his popular philosophy. Fichte's long meditation no doubt included reflections on the relation between his popular and scientific works. The former were supposed to be a shortcut to the results of the latter, an abridged exercise for those who could not be put through the rigours of WL. Yet WL is also an exercise, an activity produced by an insight that is not itself the product of discursive reasoning. However, if one were to confine oneself to the formal results of either genre, one would find oneself confronted with two distinct philosophies: one that is a transcendental theory of the foundation of subjective knowing that abstracts from all content, the other a "life wisdom" [*Lebensweisheit*] meant to show how one lives with the knowledge that one is the appearance of an ineffable God. But such a strong separation between WL and the popular lectures is inadmissible on the WL's own terms: at the end of 1804/2, Fichte establishes an a priori link between WL and all possible particular sciences. Moreover, the WL's phenomenology, itself only a framework, requires first a mediating doctrine of principles and then a series of expositions on the a priori foundations of particular sciences in order to be complete. Fichte's philosophical project is not intended to yield an empty form, but life itself.

As particular science, religion constitutes a manner of discursively relating to the world. As discourse, its relationship to its internal, grounding truth is described by WL. But the difference between religion and other types of discourse embodied by the lower standpoints is that religion's object is the same as WL itself: God, the absolute truth internal to all forms of discourse. Religion therefore offers a kind of language through which one arrives at the same end goal as WL but through employing subjective feeling. It is therefore within the context of a doctrine of religion [*Religionslehre*] that Fichte offers a popular version of his philosophy. Ultimately, religion is discourse about the subjectively felt sense of truth contained in any kind of discourse, the science of the personal dimension of discourse – said otherwise, of how one can speak with conviction.[11]

Because of the relationship between religion and the felt efficacy of discourse, Fichte's popular lectures had a religious ethos from the beginning. In Jena, the 1795 lectures on the *Vocation of the Scholar* were given on Sunday afternoons (as would almost all subsequent popular lectures), a practice Fichte justified by calling these not academic lessons but speeches made for spiritual edification.[12] The *Vocation of Humankind* moves from doubt [*Zweifel*] to faith [*Glauben*]. The *Characteristics* link the histories of church and state in a combined eschatological vision, the culmination of which is the realization that God is already among us.

Finally, the lectures *On the Essence of the Scholar*, given in Erlangen in 1805, are something of a proto- *Blessed Life*, also sharing the same end goal as the WL. If WL elaborates discursively what religion felt intuitively, then the scholar's activity is what links the two. In the *Essence of the Scholar*, Fichte portrays the scholar as an individual who contemplates the divine idea [*göttliche Idee*] (another valence of the absolute) and seeks to communicate it to others, functioning as a conduit that helps them achieve the same contemplative act. The budding scholar will have to move through all the same standpoints described in the *Blessed Life*, an ascent that is motivated by a love greater than the individual. Ultimately, the portrait of the accomplished scholar [*vollendeter Gelehrter*] is remarkably similar to that of the Johannine Christ found in the *Blessed Life*.[13]

If the communication of the divine idea is a particular vocation, embodying it is a universal one, reaching beyond the scholarly life. Moreover, the *Essence of the Scholar* takes a descriptive approach and does not offer an account of the activity that marks the scholar's inner world, contemplation. Phenomenologically, Fichte's system has been able to accommodate free, rational, subjective experience, but the inner lives of individuals, the forum in which insight arises, remain opaque. The *Blessed Life* will contribute to the WL's phenomenology by establishing a space for authentic interiority. In Fichte's worldview, individuals are not merely hollow repetitions of the absolute but free rational subjects. This will be achieved through building on the concept of love as drive that was found in the *Essence of the Scholar*; to it will be added a mechanism taken from the WL, attention, here called *concentration*. By means of sustained attention, individuals are able to achieve increasingly broader standpoints, or subjective ways of relating to the world. Externally, the highest of these is a moral-aesthetic point-of-view [*Sittlichkeit*], that of the great individuals of history. But the inner workings of concentration move beyond mere external action and into contemplation. Still higher is the integration of the individual into a divine self-contemplation – here, Fichte will write, it is no longer I that live, but God who lives in me, contemplating himself through my act of living. At the summit of the *Blessed Life*'s progression, the imaging of the self-contemplating idea is joined to the self-sacrifice of the individual who has achieved this state; the first, perfect, image of God, the Christ, sacrifices himself in order to bring about the same state of divine living in others.

The *Blessed Life* is divided into eleven lectures. The first five are the most speculative, founded on the distinction between *Seyn* (being) and its appearance, *Daseyn*, and culminating in a description of the five standpoints. It is in these five lectures that interiority is established. The sixth lecture compares the material found in the previous lectures with the Gospel of John, with particular emphasis on John's prologue. Lectures seven to eleven are a spiritual meditation that offers complimentary material to lectures one to five. Herein, this material has been integrated into the first section.[14]

5.2 STANDPOINT AND INTERIORITY

While Fichte has promised his readers lectures on the "blessed life," he begins by affirming that the expression is superfluous. As will be conveyed in the course of this lecture series, life is always blessed, it is bliss [*Seligkeit*]. If life is blissful, it is because it is love; from the latter comes the form and force [*Form und Kraft*] of life. Love is life's twofold activity, consisting first in separating being in particular consciousness, and second, unifying consciousness in an active whole. Love, then, is the unity of unity and disjunction, the absolute as articulated from the standpoint of religion. Consequent with this duplicity, life exists according to two points of view: that of truth and that of appearance. One, however, is dependent on the other: life as it appears would not exist were it not carried [*gehalten und getragen*] by truth.[15] What appears is the appearance of truth, that which is only known in its appearing. Only truth-life (life's truth in being absolutely immanent and self-sustaining) *is*: "nothing" or, in popular language, "death" is merely a heuristic concept, the product of experience as seen from below. Yet true appearances themselves are not absolute truth, since truth itself is not a thing among others. Appearances here below, in the world, are therefore a mixture [*Vermischung*] of life and death.[16] In hearing this, Fichte's listeners may have been inclined to think that particular existence is a mere emanation of love, growing fainter as it moves farther away; to prevent this, he is quick to qualify his remarks on love as principle of the unity of unity and disjunction: love itself is the principle of particularization, its own drive toward appearance. It is in this sense that Fichte says to his audience, "tell me what you love, and I will tell you what you are."[17] More than a question of the finality of drive in general, Fichte is already orienting his listeners toward the concept of a standpoint, of investing one's attention in a particular manner.[18] This means, moreover, that the speculative and the phenomenological are linked; if theory is valid only in its execution, the WL itself finds its validity in the felt application of its theoretical content: love is, speculatively, identifiable with truth and life; yet its realization is only achieved when felt subjectively, in subjective action.

Fichte then wishes to distinguish true life from a merely "apparent" one [*von dem bloßen scheinleben*], proceeding declartively in function of the genre to which this text belongs; if the WL moves through proofs, the *Blessed Life* instead appeals to the listener's "natural sense of truth" [*dem natürlichen Wahrheitssinne*],[19] even when at its most speculative. Fichte pursues: being and living are identical – only life *is*. Being is life's activity, not some static quality that one finds in the world, an object among others. There are not many beings but rather only one act of being, life; being is absolute unity. Yet a multiplicity of things *appears to be* and so must be a mixture of being and non-being, life and death.

The one true life that *is* is commonly called God, at once source of love and its object. The goal of a blessed life is to be united to God. The alternative, the merely apparent life, is one of strife and dispersion. It is in this spirit that Fichte proposes that his listeners embark on a journey, one that cultivates interiority in view of attaining successive standpoints that culminate in WL itself – an awareness of the self-contemplation of God. While death brings dispersion, leading one on a journey of passing satisfaction that moves from one particular object to another, Fichte's proposed journey is one meant to establish a space of interiority in which authentic subjectivity can flourish, one of depth that will ultimately find interiority in *this* life, the separation between life and afterlife being death's last illusion.

This path from dispersion and misery to God is achieved through thought. Thought is the substantial form [*substantielle Form*] of life. The reason is that blessedness requires self-awareness: the living God is not an object but rather an absolute whose foundational role in one's own life can only be "seen into" (*Einsehen*, intellectual intuition) but not seen (*bloß sehen,* sensible intuition).[20] There is no path to God other than through thought. "Life in the Spirit," in God, is an inner life, and there is no means of approaching the inner life other than through thought. [21] Following the *Characteristics*' affirmation of an eternal – albeit esoteric – form of Christianity, Fichte affirms that this is what Christianity has always taught and that what the churches have called "faith" is in reality nothing other than clear and living thought [*klare und lebendige Denken*].[22] Achieving blessedness is therefore a question of concentrating one's thoughts on one thing: God, found in the inner realm. The religious attitude is therefore a question of attention, the concentration of one's mental powers in an effort of awareness. The state Fichte wishes to achieve is a passive way of being active that allows what has always been present to emerge in a new light. Ultimately, the realization accomplished in this contemplative state is a *Zurückziehung*,[23] a tracing back of all appearances to their one true foundation. Fichte will describe this movement not as an ascent but a *descent* [*in die tiefe herabzusteigen*]. This descent into the depths of truth will involve leaving behind what lies on the surface – that which is superficial and scattered – and focusing only on what is necessary.

If thought [*Denken*] is the epistemological attitude that brings on this descent toward the one truth, the attitude that corresponds to resting on the surface of things is that of mere opinion [*Meinung*]. Living according to mere opinion means simply moving from one experience to another without seeing any connection between them – it is facticity that lacks a unifying insight. While an opinion is a thought insofar as it is a mental event, it lacks any self-awareness. Such an opinion cannot be classified within the schema of the WL because it is an attitude that has not yet made any decision about philosophy; the opiniated person merely utters whatever comes into his head. If the empiricist thinks the truth of things resides in disparate appearances, those who live according to opinion have not yet considered the question of truth at all. It is therefore a non-standpoint, a total diffusion of intellectual power.

If the path toward truth is a tracing-back that descends into the depths, it is a movement that becomes more concentrated as it descends. Opinion is the purely superficial position of one who has not started yet. Phenomenologically, attitudes engender particular behaviours. How one behaves is therefore how one situates oneself in the world, a "sich verhalten"[24] that reveals an attitude and without which the attitude would not exist. The behaviour proper to every standpoint is marked by its investment in thought – that is to say, its level of concentration. If *mere opinion* is a non-standpoint, it is therefore concentration's opposite, total dispersion.

Fichte sees thought as the entryway into self-cultivation, and ultimately an activity that bridges the gap between the scientific and the popular. In thought, one achieves attention [*Aufmerksamkeit*], here better symbolized by concentration; one can conceive of this activity according to the WL's light imagery: light can shine broadly, enlightening a broad territory but only partially revealing objects, or can be concentrated, rendering a small area very bright.[25] For the philosopher, this act of concentration begins with the awareness that one is thinking when one thinks something in particular and then, through reasoning that saying and enactment, *tun* and *sagen*, must coincide in discourse, concludes that the absolute constructs itself and we are the ones who do this constructing. The non-philosopher is able to arrive at exactly the same conclusion through the use of religious imagery: beginning with one's own capacity for concentration, the religious person discovers the inner world, the inner forum of thought and finds that God is present there. Religious behaviour, its "*sich verhalten*" or comportment, does not reason through to conclusions but rather borrows established imagery and through feeling arrives at immediately evident conclusions. Fichte's definition of religion reflects this: religion consists in immediately possessing God individually, through one's own spiritual eye, one's own thoughts, and not that of another. Yet the condition for this is that one thinks for oneself – not in the sense of arriving at one's own conclusions, as the *Aufklärer* would have it, but simply (though more profoundly) in being able to say *I* and make the thought of God one's own in the interior forum. Writes Fichte:

> But religion consists precisely in the fact that one, in one's own person and not that of another, with one's own spiritual eye and not that of another, should immediately intuit, have, and possess God. This, however, is only possible through pure and independent thought, for only through this does one become one's own person; this alone is the eye through which God can be seen. Pure thought is itself God's *Daseyn*, and conversely, the divine *Daseyn*, in its immediacy, is nothing other than pure thought.[26]

Thought is what constitutes personality; pure thought itself is nothing other than God's own presence: his *Daseyn* is itself thought. Yet thoughts are always those of a particular subject, hence God's incarnation is carried out in every thinking individual. This, says Fichte, reiterating what was established in the *Characteristics*, is the essence of Christianity and is as old as God himself: thought has always thought itself, and so the single, foundational idea of Christianity is from eternity. Typical of the works that follow the 1804/2 WL, the task at hand is to bring a personal and immediate insight to discursive clarity. The test of whether or not one's discursive expression is true to its source lies in the ability to move it (simultaneously forwards and backwards, as it were) to the *Evidenz* from which it came – the first valence being embodied in the immediacy of experience, the second in the absolute life that is Fichte's God.

As discursive elaboration, Fichte's lectures on the *Blessed Life* should be, on his own terms, subjected to such scientific verification. Yet another methodological concern intervenes here, a pedagogical one that leads Fichte to frequently play on misunderstandings. "God" is Fichte's word for the absolute life that manifests itself in individual human consciousness. While this is hardly an orthodox definition, his insistence on using the word at once gives his readers a familiar idiom from which they can proceed and dismisses the accusations of atheism that had caused Fichte considerable trouble in Jena. That his audience may initially take Fichte to be more orthodox than he really is does not corrupt the exercise in which they are engaged. It is only in scientific expositions that errors in understanding are systematically eliminated; popular philosophy must cooperate however it can with the natural sense of truth of the listeners in order to elevate them to it.[27] In the *Blessed Life*, Fichte is less concerned with misrepresentations than with honing his listeners' capacity for concentration; once this is accomplished and higher standpoints are achieved, errors will appear to be what they are, and Fichte's philosophical positions about religion will no longer seem so shocking. Much the same could be said about the question of whether or not Fichte is a "mystic." If a mystic is someone who has experienced a singular, personal, and immediate insight into truth, then Fichte's insight into the cooperation between knowing and awareness-of-knowing makes him one. However, the more fantastic definition of popular imagination is to be precluded.[28]

It follows from Fichte's consideration on thought that if it is God's own *Daseyn*, the appearing of God in the phenomenal world, thought must be synonymous with life and to not think [*das Nichtdenken*] is the source of death.[29] In this way, thought has achieved the status of one of Fichte's "names of God" – along with life, love, and being. But how can thought encompass all of life, which has an evident external component, appearing outside the mind, in the world? Here, Fichte must present his epistemology in order to preclude solipsism and other charges of radical idealism.[30]

Fichte begins by articulating the relationship between outer sense perception and inner sense, or thought.[31] We perceive outer objects and are at the same time conscious of them in thought. Moreover, in inner sense, we are aware of our own act of perceiving in outer sense. These two elements coexist but do not have a categorical relationship – one is not the cause of the other, nor do they relate as substance to accident.[32] Even if one were to attempt to place them in direct rapport, one would be unable to determine which was absolutely prior to the other. Echoing the intellectual description of the third age in the *Characteristics*, Fichte asserts that his contemporaries have elevated outer sense above inner. This empiricism, however, is unwarranted and indeed illogical. As soon as one thinks in a reflective manner rather than merely being captivated by objects, one realizes that one conceives of the objective world as a state of affairs that could be otherwise. Yet taking refuge in this possibility and fabricating objects from the imaginative capacity of the mind gets one no further than the empiricist – both privilege one side of intellection without realizing that any such privilege is arbitrary.

Rather than simply flowing forth from some unbridled maxim, thought's first task is to think being sharply [*das Seyn scharf zu denken*]. Being does not proceed from non-being.[33] Thought makes no progress when it proceeds along a chain of factical causes from one object to another; rather, one must think the unity of all multiplicity if one is to really think being. Thought leads to being as unity itself, immutable from all eternity. Such a being is one, complete, and self-sufficient: it is not a thing in the world and one that therefore does not reveal itself in the world as it is in itself. It is *Seyn* and not *Daseyn*, that which is entirely in-itself. This distinction is capital: Being exists first as *Seyn*, hidden from us in its aseity, and as *Daseyn*, externalized [*geäußert*] and visible to us [*offenbar*]. *Daseyn* is the consciousness or representation of *Seyn*. External being only *is* insofar as it is being-of and image-of something.

Knowledge of objects, expressed in judgment, has an image character.[34] To be in the world is "to be outside of being,"[35] as its image. *Daseyn* is therefore *Seyn*'s image, its representation in the world. Furthermore, the only possible form of *Daseyn* is consciousness. Conversely, *Seyn* can only be God, the hidden absolute made manifest in consciousness. It is as consciousness that being exists immediately in the world. In the same way that knowledge implies awareness-of-knowledge (the intellectual and the sensible), so too does *Seyn* imply *Daseyn*: to see an image is to know that it is image-of, and this kind of knowledge is not the determinate sensible knowing of something in particular but rather an awareness-of. In sum, consciousness always manifests itself as self-consciousness in the act of knowing something in particular. The unique character of *Daseyn* is to be aware *that* it is *Daseyn* and not *Seyn*, an awareness that constantly accompanies it and beyond which it cannot go. That *Daseyn* constantly accompanies itself, and is constantly aware *that* it is *Daseyn*, is precisely what constitutes its inner life. Interiority is *Daseyn*'s mode of being, constituted by the constant interaction of knowing and awareness-of-knowing, of sensible and intellectual intuition. Interiority, then, is not spatial and static but rather an activity – it is not an inner world but an inner *life*; to use one of Fichte's preferred metaphors, this activity is a *seeing* – an activity into which an eye is inserted.[36]

Fichte's conception of interiority is meant to stress the dynamic unity of human cognition; it is in concentrating on something singular in the world, and being aware of my capacity for such attention, that a true interior life is established. The blessed life consists in turning one's attention completely over to the absolute unity that is God and away from the dispersion that distraction by multiplicity entails. Of course, God cannot be made simple object of one's thoughts, as if he were some mental content like any other; all we have of being *in se*, of God, are images. From this image character, we become aware of the grounding principle for imaging in general. It is precisely because God remains hidden that interiority is what leads to blessedness.[37]

This hiddenness must be qualified: God does indeed appear but not as he is *a se*. Rather, he appears *as image*, as *Daseyn*, and this image of God exists immediately as consciousness. As in the *Principles*, where a single movement of reflection provided for externalization as a constitutive part of God's being, so too is *Daseyn* necessary for *Seyn* and vice-versa.

That God manifests himself – remaining *a se* while becoming "incarnate" or appearing via consciousness – is part of his necessary activity. It is only from the point of view of *Daseyn* that an external *Spaltung* or scission between the two exists, a concretization of activity that leads to the constitution of a world for-consciousness.[38] While in this text, Fichte simply declares this to be the case; in the *Principles*, the necessary transcendental view of the individual "from below" is integrated into reflection by means of a *Selbstgefühl*, an immediate feeling of one's standing in light. In the *Blessed Life*, interiority, that which is "deep" and "interior," is a close correlate to this *Selbstgefühl*. The *Principles*' concept of reflection corresponds to love – both describe a movement that is at once subjective and objective, the very activity of God into which the particular subject is incorporated. All of this belongs to the exercise that is the tracing back of multiplicity to unity and feeling immediately one's participation in this unity. Such an exercise implies a certain amount of artifice on the part of the one who undertakes it, discursively reconstructing what has already been constructed. In reality, there is no *Spaltung* or scission between *Seyn* and *Daseyn*. From above, all is unified, and *Daseyn* is simply the mode according to which God makes himself present in the world. In the *Blessed Life*, Fichte describes this difference in perspective as an "as."[39] While *Seyn* exists in discourse *as Seyn* and *Daseyn as Daseyn*, their relation is genetic and internal, meaning that one must conceive of them *as* dependent on one another: *Daseyn as Daseyn* of *Seyn*, and *Seyn as Seyn* of *Daseyn*. Thus the *as* of the *Blessed Life* expresses what the technical term problematicity [*Problematicität*] did in the 1804/2 WL.[40]

Beatitude consists in complete union with the God who is *a se*, one and absolute. Yet particular consciousness – which we are – exists as knowing, representation, and image. This fundamental character of humanity cannot be abandoned in its quest for union with God. The key to understanding this relationship is to arrive at a perspective from which the particular self, consciousness, is nothing on its own, instead existing as God's *Daseyn*. In the words of the WL, consciousness cannot be eliminated, but its testimony cannot be believed when evaluating truth. Achieving this perspective is not merely a matter of logical inference but a question of commitment to a particular attitude, situating oneself subjectively in the factical world by means of feeling. As we have seen, feeling itself has a priori foundations and is able to negotiate its own act of confronting the world in a particular manner by means of a *Selbstgefühl*. One can, in other words, adopt a particular attitude that emphasizes self-awareness; this attitude integrates the subjective factor that is feeling into the broader movement that is the absolute's manifestation as subjective consciousness. All of this has been established in the *Principles*, but in purely speculative fashion. The path from a *Selbstgefühl* to union with God is one that leads not to a particular state but rather an attitude or manner of inhabiting the world; the expression "beatific vision" would be more appropriate than mere bliss or blessedness. What is lacking, then, is an active mechanism that allows for the subject's integration into the movement of reflection without losing any of its subjective qualities – without losing, in other words, its interiority, its capacity to *see* individually.

Fichte has already alluded to a solution: if the path toward God is a tracing-back, at once descent and concentration, then the mechanism required is nothing other than *attention*, already encountered at the beginning of the 1804/2 WL. Attention is the link between subjectivity and the absolute's activity, the act by which interiority is cultivated. Attention, then, is itself the phenomenological and subjective description of the unity of sight [*bloß sehen*] and insight [*Einsehen*] in activity. Yet attention, on its own, does not provide the impetus for the activity that establishes interiority; it is the phenomenological description of the path from the self to God via interiority but accordingly remains descriptive. The drive to interiority is the product of love, the "affect of *Seyn*,"[41] that is God's own *Selbstgefühl*. We are its product, and our identification with it constitutes a return to God, the achievement of interiority via a desire to be equal with oneself. Attention's specific role, then, will be to reveal that this drive is not our own worldly appetite but God's own desire to come into the world through us – to translate the speculative structure of WL into religious language, God reveals himself in the world, and we are the ones who do this revealing.

This appearing was technically expressed by means of the absolute's self-construction through us and was the transcendental conclusion of the fivefold synthesis. In the WL, the initial separation between absolute and consciousness is the initial twofold split between *Evidenz* and facticity. In the *Blessed Life*, this is the *Spaltung* or scission between

God and the world of consciousness. In the WL, this initial split is then expanded into three steps, the movement from *Evidenz* to facticity and then back to *Evidenz*. In the *Blessed Life*, this would be represented by the movement from immediate experience to God and then back to the world of experience, where one lives in a manner that embodies what one has learned – that is, the new attitude of "beatific vision" that attention has cultivated. And just as this threefold transcendental argument is expanded into the WL's fivefold deduction, so too does the *Blessed Life* qualify this journey according to five moments. On account of this, each of the five moments of the *Blessed Life*'s progression finds its place in the formula Fichte uses to describe the twofold separation of the WL: B, T, x, y, z.[42] Naturally, a parallel can also be made with the five ages of the *Characteristics*. In that text, Fichte conceives of the fivefold deduction's application to external, intersubjective relationships that unfold according to time, providing an a priori account of history. It is the application of fivefoldness to outer sense. The fivefold deduction as applied to the *Blessed Life* operates in the inner forum – more specifically, the inner forum's self-relatedness. It is therefore a history of seeing, not of being in the world with others; its five ages are ages of the soul: unquantifiable, subjective, and immediately felt. Yet they are contained by the transcendental deduction of a fivefold a priori, to which belongs a restrained and specific relationship between the valences of seeing or intuition; hence it is protected from romantic excess: attitudes cannot be separated from existence, and attention always has a material component.

A *Spaltung* or scission, as Fichte says, is not a split in the object but merely in the manner of seeing the object.[43] The further division of this scission from two to five therefore implies not five different worlds or five different people but rather five ways of seeing the world, five standpoints. In their individual journeys via attention toward God, individuals progress through different standpoints, with each higher one representing a broader point of view than the previous one. These standpoints could therefore be conceived of as a series of concentric circles, with higher ones enveloping the point of view of previous ones; using the metaphor of sight, one might say that as one grows in attention, one can occupy better vantage points allowing one to see farther. An individual whose sight is not adapted to concentrating on what lies in the distance could stand at the best vantage point but continue to observe only what is close at hand. In this way, different individuals can be the product of the same age and culture but occupy different standpoints. Some also begin their journey at an elevated standpoint that some others will never achieve. As with the ages of the world, individuality introduces an unpredictable factical element into the a priori progression.

Prior to the five standpoints resides the world of mere opinion [*Meinung*], already described above. It is not a standpoint but rather an unreflective state of dispersion that does not correspond to self-aware seeing. In other words, it does not achieve any interiority.

The first and lowest standpoint is that of the sensible world [*Sinnenwelt*]. This point of view constitutes its world out of sense experience, adopting an essentially materialist outlook. It takes pleasure in the material world and fantasizes about it, seeing humanity merely as flesh. Insofar as it is utterly arrested by what is external and incapable of conceiving of an internal life on its own, the feeling it cultivates is one of fascination, of being utterly caught up in sensation. It also corresponds to the "x" of the formula, Kant's first *Critique* as theory of knowledge of the sensible world. In Fichte's own schema it yields a philosophy of nature, a theory of the mechanisms of external necessity.[44]

The second standpoint is that of right (*Legalität*). It is a legalist worldview once removed from sense experience, supposing that laws establish equality and ground freedom. It introduces a hierarchy in which law provides for freedom, and freedom for sense experience;[45] this law *is* or exists before all other things. Born of the initial scission between the sensible and supersensible, it privileges the latter and corresponds to the "y" of 1804/2, with explicit reference to the *Critique of Practical Reason*.[46] In Fichte's system. it represents a philosophy of right [*Rechtslehre*]. While legalism represents progress over sense experience, it acts blindly, unaware of the maxim it employs in making judgments. Worse still, it is empty of any real content, a criticism of Kant's categorical imperative that Fichte has elsewhere called its *qualitas occulta*.[47] *That* one obeys the law is more important than understanding it, meaning that it lacks real affect. The feeling it elicits is that of obedience, the cold and impersonal respect for the law.

The third standpoint, the ethical life [*Sittlichkeit*],[48] is perhaps the most crucial of the five, marking the end of the material progression of standpoints. Higher levels are an inward change, not necessarily affecting the circumstances of external life. With ethical life, content is added to what was empty in the world of legalism; an authentic subjectivity is achieved, whereby one's life is ordered toward a calling or vocation, a *Bestimmung*.[49] While a life lived according to law merely orders experience according to an axiom, ethical life is creative, manifesting itself in religious art, poetry, and occasionally philosophy. Fichte portrays it as a "heroic" standpoint, one achieved by the great individuals of history: tellingly, he names Plato and Jacobi, but given the predominance of aesthetics in its articulation, Fichte certainly had Kant and Schiller in mind.[50] Here, one no longer obeys the law simply because one must, but rather embraces it personally and provides it with content. Philosophically, this involves renouncing oneself in order to embrace the empty law and then finding oneself again through supplying it with creative content. This follows the pattern of the *Soll*: *If* there is law, then *there must* be a subject who freely obeys it. The very strength of the law comes from the obedience of the free and creative individual who could have conceived of the world otherwise. This passage from legality to ethical life operated by the *Soll* is what establishes interiority: one who has achieved this third standpoint has achieved interiority. This personal investment in norms (that is, awareness of the *Soll* structure) is what constitutes freedom – reason's finality is freedom, and to become aware of this is to initiate free, rational activity. This is, moreover, the genesis of feeling, the subjective, internal, and immediate rapport with what exists abstractly and normatively. In particular, aesthetic sensibility proceeds from this new interiority. Beauty exists according to norms and conventions, but when these are internalized, a new, subjective stance toward them is possible.[51] The ethical life accordingly manifests itself through talent, and those who inhabit this standpoint are artists in the broad sense. Conscious both of their freedom and the normativity that governs its use, they make their own world inhabitable through acts of art, poetry, philosophy, politics, and jurisprudence. In this way, the third standpoint corresponds to "z" on the diagram; it is the capacity for judgment and uniting the sensible and supersensible, as does Kant's third Critique. It represents the formal study of moral philosophy but also encompasses aesthetics – a subject otherwise absent from Fichte's system. Its mood is one of inspiration, that of an artist creatively giving form to raw material.

The fourth standpoint, religion [*Religiosität*], is the inner completion of the ethical life, brought about by the realization that the content with which subjectivity supplied the empty law is not actually created by the subject but is in fact the appearance or self-revelation of God. From the religious point of view, the cultivation [*Bildung*] of the last step has become *Bild*, an image. *Seyn* alone, as we can conceive of it in consciousness, is an empty category. Its content is *Daseyn*; subjective activity in the world is itself the appearance of God.[52] To attain religiosity is to realize that we are God's life and living it out consists in adopting an attitude of reverence, treating others as appearances of God. Indeed, Fichte goes so far as to say that God *is* what the religious person *does*.[53] This attitude also corresponds to right thinking, seeing the world as it is; it represents the mental capacity for valid a posteriori judgment.

The fifth and highest standpoint is that of absolute science [*Wissenschaft*], or WL. It is here that all multiplicity can be traced back to unity, as well as the genetic procession of multiplicity from it – it is the unity of unity and disjunction and can inhabit all other points of view. This involves the integration of knowledge and awareness of knowledge; in terms of content, religion also stands at the summit, achieving the highest point that sight or conceptual knowledge can reach – the one that is God or life. WL reaches a "higher" standpoint by adding a self-reflexive element to vision, combining *bloß sehen* with *einsehen*.[54] It is only with the fifth standpoint that religion ceases to be a mere belief, a *doxa* that belongs to the individual and comes alive. It is knowledge that has been enveloped by love, a living knowledge that can be infinitely repeated – hence the inexhaustibility of *a posteriori* objects and the limited number of standpoints from which they can be assessed. Fichte puts this best in his summary of lecture ten, essentially a spiritualization of the content of lecture fifteen of 1804/2:

> This love is the creator of the abstract conception of God; the source of all certainty that the absolute, immediately and without any modification through the concept embraces in life; that reflection, whose form contains only the possibility of infinity, is extended into actual infinity; finally, the source of knowledge [*Wissenschaft*].[55]

This highest point in Fichte's progression manifests itself as absolute

Table 5.1 Quintuplicity and its standpoints

Opinion	–	–	–	Dispersion
Sensible world	*Critique of Pure Reason*	X	Philosophy of nature	Fascination
Right	*Critique of Practical Reason*	Y	Philosophy of right	Obedience
Ethical life	*Critique of the Power of Judgment*	Z	Ethics (and aesthetics)	Inspiration
Religion	*a posteriori*	T	Philosophy of religion	Reverence
Absolute science	*a priori*	B (• B)	Wissenschaftslehre	Contemplation

attention, contemplation turned toward itself and manifested in the human subject: it is attention's manifestation in activity, the accord of *tun* and *sagen* adopted knowingly as philosophical maxim. In religious language, achieving this standpoint involves knowing that one's own subjective life is actually a manifestation of God's life. Through attention, one has become aware of the a priori foundations of this manifestation.

5.3 FICHTE'S RELIGION: THE GOSPEL OF JOHN

The *Blessed Life's* philosophical exposition culminates in the description of the five standpoints. This material belongs to the genre of "popular" philosophy. Fichte's conception of the relationship between speculative and popular philosophy will take on another dimension in the sixth lecture of the *Blessed Life*, one more akin to the distinction between esoteric and exoteric meaning. There, Fichte will claim that the content exposed in the first five lectures is "as old as the world" and is contained in the Gospel of John, the imagery of which has already been integrated into Fichte's own religious language.[56] The same claim was made earlier in the *Characteristics*. But there, the context in which it was explored – the historical development of the state – did not allow for a real comparison of the WL with the Gospel of John. In the *Blessed Life*, the two are juxtaposed. Fichte does not do this in view of offering a proof, instead placing side-by-side the WL's conception of religion with his interpretation of John and letting the audience become aware of their relationship. Consistent with Fichte's pedagogy in the 1804–06 period, those who participate must actively reconstruct what they are to learn.

As was said in the *Characteristics*, John's Gospel is the only source that establishes an "inner proof" – that is, that God's revelation unfolds according to an a priori structure and not, as Paul would have it, according to the mere *a posteriori* succession of events.[57] Moreover, John's Jesus relates to God the Father as *Daseyn* does to *Seyn*: there are no proofs for the divinity of Christ in John's Gospel but rather only "signs," actions that witness to the fact that Jesus is the face of God. While the other Gospels are focused on ethical concerns, John offers a real theology, a theory of the appearance of God in the world and the spiritual role of Jesus.

In order to establish these points, Fichte will analyze at length the prologue of John's Gospel (Jn 1:1–18). This passage, writes Fichte, is the key to understanding what Jesus taught and a conceptual summary of the content of the entire Gospel of John. Indeed, the other verses that Fichte will cite later do not occasion new arguments but rather serve as proofs for what was established in the analysis of the prologue.[58] One of the main ideas Fichte finds therein is a rejection of the creation of the world *ex nihilo*. Creation out of nothing is a non-genetic conception of the origin of the world, a mere procession of factical objects that descends into infinite regress in the absence of a genetic a priori source.[59] John's Gospel does not open with God creating but rather with God already present to himself – in the beginning was the Word. This *Logos* or *Verbum* of God is God himself. They relate as *Seyn* does to *Daseyn* – the word is the being-there or presence of God, the discursive elaboration of what was always already there, as *Evidenz*. Since the world is for-consciousness, the origins of the world lie not in a creation of factical objects one after another but the manifestation of God himself as *Daseyn* – a world from God (*ex deo*) and not from nothing (*ex nihilo*).[60] If God's *Daseyn*, his Word, is consciousness, how are we to make sense of Jesus of Nazareth, in whom the Word is made flesh? Fichte is adamant that all those who achieve a vision of God – that is, those whose actions bring forth God in the world – are incarnations of God.[61] Following the fivefold movement of standpoints according to attention, this incarnation is an internal process achieved by each individual. The role of the Christ figure, then, is as "firstborn son of God." Speculatively, this means that Jesus represents a "*Daseyn* of *Daseyn*" or pure possibility of externality.[62] Phenomenologically, he is a kind of educator, an initial image of God that serves as a model for all who come after, showing them through example how to achieve mediately what he immediately possessed – that is, the fifth and highest standpoint, the vision of the absolute unity of *Seyn* and *Daseyn*. Jesus is a *Wissenschaftslehrer*, the first in history.

Aware of the difficulty that his audience would have had first understanding and then accepting this highly peculiar Christology, Fichte consecrates a *Beilage* or supplement to the sixth lecture in order to expand the claims we have just seen.[63] There, Fichte reiterates the difference between a priori foundation and a posteriori historical fact. The importance of the figure of Jesus is metaphysical and not factical, even if this metaphysical importance requires a factical incarnation. Yet Fichte is at pains to articulate how Jesus is factically necessary: how can this seemingly miraculous individual who possesses the highest standpoint (that is, divine knowledge) not through philosophical or spiritual effort but having obtained it directly from God offer only education and not grace?

This raises the question of whether Fichte's philosophy of religion can admit of a Christ figure and whether or not it needs one. If Jesus, "absolute reason become immediate self-consciousness, or what is the same: religion,"[64] as the supplement would have it, would he not have to be, in conformity with the WL, an activity that becomes incarnate in particular consciousness and not a person with factical existence? The WL does not admit of any mediation, and even if the *Principles* speaks of a pure possibility of externalization, this would seem to refer to appearance as spontaneous activity rather than an individual who existed historically. Here, Fichte's philosophy of history would seem to invalidate his philosophy of religion: in the *Characteristics*, the historical Jesus is of no importance; he is merely a symbol of a regulative state, not an educator of humankind with divine knowledge.[65] In sum, one cannot maintain the a priori theories of history and creation that Fichte does *and* claim that initiation into the standpoints began through an a posteriori event. Fichte might reply that the contradiction between history and religion is only apparent: the presence of Reason in consciousness might be through activity, but reason is also regulative – it does not disappear when unused. Moreover, it is regulative not only collectively but individually: all of *my* free actions can be oriented, as a whole, toward reason *in time*, hence continuously. Certain ways of employing reason can therefore become a habit, which allows for one to be able to inhabit a standpoint, consistently employing one's rational faculties in a certain manner. If an individual can inhabit a standpoint in time, the a posteriori actions of a particular individual can indeed incarnate or "make present" a standpoint at a particular moment in time. What occurs in time admits succession, begins, and ends. If one interprets Fichte's claim to be that Jesus is the first known instance of someone who possessed the highest standpoint (which the supplement seems to suggest), then this would be no different from claiming that a particular historical event manifests immediately the possibility of the transition to another age, as Fichte suggests was the case with the Reformation in the *Characteristics*.[66] Because historical conditions are neither causal nor philosophical, Fichte requires that we adopt a certain agnosticism when faced with a posteriori historical events: the Reformation, the French Revolution, and even the incarnation of God have a priori foundations but not discernable causes. Phenomenologically, objects are incidental – one requires an event, object, or person to awaken the possibility of a priori advancement, but the object is not the cause of advancement through the ages or through the standpoints.[67]

In accord with this, Fichte cites Jn 6:53–6:

> [53] So Jesus said to them, "Truly, truly, I say to you, unless you eat the flesh of the Son of man and drink his blood, you have no life in you; [54] he who eats my flesh and drinks my blood has eternal life, and I will raise him up at the last day. [55] For my flesh is food indeed, and my blood is drink indeed. [56] He who eats my flesh and drinks my blood abides in me, and I in him."

To eat his flesh and drink his blood is interpreted to mean to be transformed (or "transubstantiated") into what Jesus is – God's *Daseyn*. In the traditional theological doctrine, bread and wine are substantially (though not accidentally) transformed into the body and blood of

Christ; this transformation is dependent on the initial transformation that was God's incarnation. On Fichte's reading, the transformation is one of thought: God's Logos or Verbum – both could also be loosely translated as "thought" – *is* his particular manifestation, first through the person of Jesus and then through a transubstantiation operated by attention, his followers. Jesus does not ask his disciples to follow him but to become him:

> To eat his flesh and drink his blood means: to completely and thoroughly become him, and to be transformed into his person without reserve or limit – to be only a repetition of his personality – to be transubstantiated with him – just as the eternal word became flesh and blood, to become his flesh and blood, and what follows from this and is the same. to become the eternal word that was made flesh and blood: to think utterly and entirely like him, as if he himself lived in our place.[68]

CONCLUSION

The lectures on the *Blessed Life* ended in March 1806, just as the Holy Roman Empire was collapsing. Following his victory at the battle of Austerlitz in December 1805, Napoleon dissolved the Empire and reconfigured much of the German-speaking world into a group of French puppet states, called the Confederation of the Rhine. Having been neutral up until then, Prussia felt it could no longer remain indifferent to the French offensive. On his own initiative, the Prussian King Wilhelm III declared war on France in August 1806, mobilizing the Prussian population. Russia, the Prussians' main ally, was too far away to be of assistance, and that fall, the French army tore through Prussia, achieving decisive victory in Jena and Auerstädt on 14 October 1806 and marching through Berlin on 27 October. Saxony changed its allegiance and sided with France, and Napoleon continued his conquest in the northeast as the Russians finally arrived to shore up the failing Prussian forces. Wilhelm III had since fled, establishing a temporary government in Königsberg. The *Grand Armée* besieged Danzig in the spring of 1807, and the Russians continued to lose ground. Having sustained heavy losses and with no chance of victory, Prussia capitulated on 25 June 1807. A month later, the treaty of Tilsit would establish a truce between France and Russia and require Prussia to surrender half of its territory, most of which would become French client states.

Fichte was deeply invested in Prussia's plight. When war was declared in August 1806, Fichte should have returned to Erlangen, where he was still technically professor. He postponed his lectures there until Easter 1807 (these would never take place, and Fichte would never return to Erlangen) and offered his services as *Staatsredner*, a sort of secular preacher who would accompany Prussian troops, offer moral instruction, and shore up morale. The war had existential stakes for Fichte: the meaning of this war was, "whether all that the poets have sung, that the wise have thought, and that heroes have accomplished should sink into the bottomless pit of the arbitrary."[1] In such times, the scholar was called to be a "hero of the idea," encouraging all of society to defend the cultural products of which the philosopher speaks – law, morality, and religion, to employ Fichte's vocabulary – saving these from the abyss.

On 18 October, news reached Berlin that Jena and Auerstädt had fallen. Before Napoleon reached Berlin, Fichte fled, leaving his family behind. He travelled in the company of his friend Hufeland,[2] physician to the Prussian royal family, and was by extension following the government into exile. Fichte arrived in Königsberg mid-December 1806 and was quickly named temporary professor. There, at the university where Kant had spent his entire career, Fichte gave twenty-eight lectures on the WL from 5 January to 20 March 1807. Despite its enormous philosophical merit, the Königsberg WL was poorly attended, with the local intelligentsia unable to accept Fichte's criticisms of the much-admired Kant. By the twenty-eighth lecture, only three students remained.[3] As the French army drew closer, Fichte decided once again to flee, this time to Copenhagen, on 1 July 1807. But Denmark was at war with England, and it proved to be hardly safer or more comfortable than East Prussia. When word reached him that the war between Prussia and France had ended and the treaty of Tilsit had been signed, Fichte returned to Berlin in August 1807.

None of these events stopped Fichte from working on the WL, the form of which continued to evolve. For while the Königsberg WL has much in common with 1804/2 and the Erlangen WL of 1805, it is also markedly different. It serves as a turning point between the WL of the first Berlin period (1799–1806) and the second (1807–14). The casual reader of the 1807 WL will find many of the terms used in 1804/2: life, light, insight, truth, certainty, the *Soll*, and even the idea of fivefoldness are all present. The question of feeling, in particular of love and truth not merely as known but lived, is also present and in language that echoes the *Blessed Life*. Gone is the absolute – it has given way to God, or more often, simply to life, which for Fichte is the same. Light is used as it was in 1804/2, but is now complemented by its opposite, shadow [*Schatten*]. The obstacle to truth is the shadow in the hearts of humans, who live in shadow and must find the way to light, life, and God, who is love.[4] In short, the Königsberg WL seeks to integrate feeling and personal conviction into the WL itself. The absolute genesis that Fichte had been working to achieve since first moving to Berlin was now to be expressed in one stroke, with the mechanisms of WL shown to be not separate or prior to our lived experience, but within it. Philosophy is not letters on a blackboard – it is something lived, and that breathes life into the everyday. To use the terms employed in the 1807 WL, the goal of insight is not mere understanding but wisdom.[5]

But there is something radically new in 1807. In 1804/2, the passage from truth to appearance is the passage from a categorical to a problematic *Soll*, the latter emerging from the former; thought is *through* that which is *from* another. But the *from* [*Von*] remains an opaque concept in 1804/2. It is the very mechanism of genesis, the manner in which image is constructed. Now, how one gets *from* the categorical *to* the problematic is clear: projection through a gap. This, however, implies a radical autonomy; in other words, we must ask: what drives the move from the absolute truth to the world of appearances? Indeed, the very word "projection" implies someone doing the projecting. Projection, in short, must be someone's project. In the Jena versions of the WL, the question "whose project is projection?" would have a simple answer: the I [*Ich*]. After 1800, however, Fichte abandoned this term, largely because the accusations of Schelling and Jacobi, as we have seen, misinterpret the WL as placing too much emphasis on the activity or "projects" of the I. In Berlin, Fichte struggles with accounting for the *from*'s autonomy. In the *Principles*, which follows 1804/2, he abandons the use of the *from* as a technical term, looking for fresh start by redefining it in terms of principiation [*principiieren,* or as a noun, *principiat*] and the principles that arise from it. Implied is that all knowledge is the reconstruction of the absolute's construction and so the agency that makes knowledge concrete has to come from the absolute itself. In 1807, Fichte makes this move explicit. Now, God is endowed with an inner drive [*Trieb*] to externalize himself in factical being. Writes Fichte at the beginning of the twenty-eighth and last lecture:

> Presuming there is a drive in God, and given that what God is, necessarily is, that this drive would come forth as a factical being, what sort of being would it be? This is the question with whose answer we have occupied ourselves for a long time now, inasmuch as the answer to this question is itself WL.[6]

God contains within himself the drive toward externalization, and this externalization – as the rest of the compact twenty-eighth lecture explains, is as free, subjective consciousness: as in 1804/2, we are the image of God insofar as we freely engage in "reconstruction" of an original "pre-construction." Using different terms and emphasizing different aspects of the *philosophia prima,* the 1807 WL is ultimately seeking to integrate Fichte's phenomenology or theory of images, what constituted the second part of 1804/2, into the theory of truth, the first part of 1804/2.[7] In sum, what Fichte had tried to achieve in piecemeal fashion between 1804 and 1806 in Berlin was attempted in Königsberg in a more concise and synthetic manner.

The question we must ask in light of this is not: *what was lacking in 1804/2 such that a new version of WL was required?* But rather: *what were the insights that arose in 1804 that Fichte wished to continue to develop?* Put otherwise: what progress was made in 1804?

The main insight of 1804/2 is that between my thoughts and my awareness of my thoughts, no third term is admissible and this can be extended to all rational acts: therefore, a whole logic, a science of thinking, would have to be grounded in the single act of thought in which consciousness and self-consciousness coincide. The art of elaborating a presentation of WL is precisely the art of expanding this single insight containing two terms (thinking and thinking-of-thinking) into a whole system of normative rationality without ever introducing terms that stand outside of the two original ones. This is what Fichte means by the term "genetic deduction": rational forms subsist within the relationship but can never be a thing extraneous to it; indeed, even the factical products of consciousness must be integrated into the genetic relationship as non-genetic in a moment called "projection." The 1801–02 WL was unable to achieve this, treating being, knowing, and the absolute as three heterogeneous terms.[8] The improvement that 1804/2 is able to bring in order to achieve genesis is methodological: the introduction of the fivefold transcendental argument structure. The development of this structure goes hand in hand with Fichte's realization between 1802 and 1804 that language leads us away from insight but nonetheless is the only means we have of communicating it. The *through* of the fivefold deduction, the mechanism that describes the process of "preconstruction" and "reconstruction," is therefore nothing less than the "ruse of language," analogous to Hegel's "ruse of reason."[9] In this way, language is "fooled" into being of service to the *Wissenschaftslehrer*, who at the outset must realize that to talk about WL is already to be doing it.

This watershed moment in the development of the presentation of the WL required Fichte to rethink the way of presenting all the modes of thought or particular sciences that derive from WL. While it was not achieved, there is no doubt that Fichte conceived of a complete system of knowledge derived from the WL. While others have attempted to reconstruct particular sciences that Fichte did not elaborate based on the premises of the WL, this book has undertaken a different task, more historical in nature. It has sought to demonstrate that all the works produced in Berlin following the 1804/2 are dependent on it, working within a field that this version of the WL established. This book has also claimed that these works are linked by a common thread: the development of the notion of feeling [*Gefühl*] according to the principles of the WL. This development can be read as a progression. Each subsequent work further refines an aspect of Feeling. The ultimate goal of this progression is that the *we* of the WL is a human subject who comes to terms with experience in the inner forum – the progression carves out a space for subjective interiority within the overarching structure that is WL. What follows is a reconstruction of the key moments of this progression:

First, we begin with the foundational insight at the heart of WL, the necessary correlation between consciousness and self-consciousness. Since WL is foremost a practical philosophy, this is expressed as a transcendental argument. Lecture nineteen of the 1804/2 WL states this transcendental argument in its most basic form: an agreement between the enunciation of a proposition (*sagen*) and its content (*tun*). Any argument that does not conform to this basic structure is condemned to self-contradiction, such as the sceptic who affirms, "*I say it is true* that there is no objective truth." In response to the Kantian critique and its search for the possibility-conditions of experience, Fichte expands his transcendental argument into three steps: 1) experience is immediately compelling, and for the subject before it, inexorable – it is, Fichte says, *Evidenz*; 2) what was immediately experienced, what *was* (being) must then be elaborated in discourse (knowing); while the latter would seem to paradoxically move one away from the former, there is a means to test its success; 3) what was elaborated in discourse must conform to the initial experience. A transcendental argument therefore moves from *Evidenz* to the elaboration of its content in discourse, back to *Evidenz*. The argument is valid if both valences of *Evidenz* correspond. Finally, this argument can be expanded into five steps, its fullest form. The first part of this book was dedicated to articulating this fivefold deduction, which finds its ultimate expression in the twenty-sixth lecture of 1804/2:

a. Seeing sees into another, life.
b. But in so doing, it negates itself. Life is in fact the ground of seeing (reversal).
c. Seeing is part of life, life's own inwardness (life through seeing, seeing through life).
d. The terms therefore constitute a single movement, an externalization generated by the "throughness" of both terms (genetic version of seeing into life).
e. The genetic seeing into life is itself reversible; this externalization is internal to life; facticity belongs to genesis (reconstruction).

This deduction achieves, in Fichte's words, an integration of the non-genetic into the genetic. Concretely, its results are as follows: when *we* – a multitude of human subjects – decide to engage in philosophy, we do so freely and contingently. Each of us must decide where his or her own philosophical journey must begin, addressing the questions, problems, texts, and interlocutors that are informed by temperament and circumstance. Yet no matter how one embarks on the journey that is philosophy, there are two certainties: first, that one thinks freely, having made the decision to philosophize, and second, that once one has begun to think, one does so according to the structures of rational thought. Reason dwells in discourse, the world of human action. Reason itself is at once free and normative. To act freely is to act rationally, in spite of the contingency of our individual choices. *We* are therefore the reason that manifests itself in discourse. In the same manner, the WL will manifest itself not *per se* but within specific domains of knowing. The structures of reason discovered in WL remain constant, and their application and transformation to the particular is integrated into the WL. Particular factical knowledge is always "through" and "from" the WL. The one life of reason can manifest itself in many ways. Hence even if WL can, from a certain point of view, be said to subsist within particular domains of knowledge, the single movement of rational freedom has abolished inner and outer: the absolute does not "externalize" itself in an image; rather, absolute image always appears as a particular image. In sum, the free rationality that we are has no borders.

Fichte must then account for the schematization of this *philosophia prima*, connecting it to particular forms of relating to the world, called standpoints. Indeed, the 1804/2 was concerned with the structural and theoretical foundation of subjective experience as appearance of the absolute. It does not offer a full account of intersubjective interaction, nor the immediate felt desires that motivate subjective activity. The first step in reconciling activity driven by subjective desires with intersubjective interaction is establishing an a priori theory of history. This is done in the *Characteristics of the Present Age* (1804–05). This work will negotiate the a priori (that is, necessary and genetic) progression of free reason with the *a posteriori* (that is, contingent and factical) events that compose human history. Ultimately, these two elements are reconciled in time, the field in which all subjective experience occurs, and history is the external condition of subjective feeling.

Next, the *Principles of the Doctrines of God, Morals, and Right* (1805) will offer a more robust account of the concepts of time and drive found in the *Characteristics*. In the latter, these two concepts come together to give history a sense of purpose, a calling to build a fully free and rational society. The *Principles* will connect this to an element already elaborated in the WL: rationality always manifests itself as something determinate and subjective. It therefore seeks to make properly dynamic and fully subjective what still remained theoretical and structural in 1804/2 and the *Characteristics*. It does this by describing the conceptual moves of the WL subjectively (e.g., feeling, clarifying, finding, etc.). To do this, we find the dialectic of realism and idealism reiterated, this time according to the concepts of immanence and projection. Now, these must be reconciled not only theoretically but on the subjective level of lived experience. The key to this is acknowledging that feeling can be integrated into the structure of the WL as the recognition that experience is intelligible on its own grounds and that the subject grapples with experience by adopting a standpoint.

Finally, Fichte articulates the first and highest particular standpoint, religion, in the *Way towards the Blessed Life* (1806). Religion is itself a particular science, the highest of the four. Subjectively and dynamically construed, these sciences are embodied by standpoints, or manners of relating to the world motivated by an immediate engagement with experience on the level of feeling. A science, and the standpoint one must adopt to engage in it, is nothing other than what the language of the *Principles* would construe as a determination of *Selbstgefühl* – I knowingly adopt a particular manner of engaging with the world, which involves a certain level of restraint. At its most basic level, this restraint is an act of concentration, limiting my attention to a certain set of facts. Since a science is always discursively elaborated, a standpoint is therefore a certain kind of discourse. As highest standpoint, religion constitutes a reflection on the possibilities of subjective discourse. The WL is itself the science of discourse, seeking to find a common root for what is elaborated in discourse and the truth that it contains. Religion seeks the same object as WL – God or the absolute, the unity of truth and its expression in discourse – but achieves this through feeling. As the transition into the particular sciences, it is therefore a kind of subjective science of discourse, of how one can speak with immediate and felt conviction about different sets of facts. If WL seeks the unity of being and knowing in a genetic deduction, with the common root of both being internal to their relationship and not something outside, so too must the felt conviction of religion be found genetically, that is to say, internally. Cast in religious language, one arrives at truth by means of an inner proof. In sum, the human subject cannot embody its truth unless it has been found in the inner forum, and this implies attentiveness to one's own thoughts. The basic intuition of WL – that consciousness is inseparable from self-consciousness and that awareness of my own thinking provides access to this foundation truth – here receives a spiritual dimension: attention to my own thinking is the beginning of an intellectual journey.

Here, we arrive at the vocation of the WL itself: the cultivation of an interior life through which one answers the shared calling of all humans to become free and rational subjects, transforming the outer world so that it, too, might conform to the image of free rationality that one encounters within oneself both as ineffable other and intimate personal truth. Said otherwise, while WL might be first of all a guide to right thinking, it implies something more than the mere logical relationship between consciousness and self-consciousness, thinking and my awareness of my own thinking. Its end goal is life and, still more, a blessed life. The spiritual exercise twinned to the philosophical one enjoins us to pay attention, cultivating interiority in order to go deeper than the merely apparent life. This cultivation of attention – the natural piety of the soul, as Malebranche would have it – is the felt, subjective expression of a truth that Fichte had been trying to express as far back as 1793: that outer experience receives its fullest expression when it is circumscribed by inner experience and that the workings of this inner experience point to some greater self, an "absolute image."[10] Key to this theory, as we have seen, is the idea of a self-seeing, a *Sichsehen* that was one of the major metaphors of Fichte's career. To arrive at an absolute, one does not call to mind one's being but rather knowingly engages in a *seeing*, an activity that encompasses being and knowing. The *Ich*, the self, is inserted into this act of seeing, into this "eye," by means of awareness of its own activity and is integrated into the seeing that is the absolute's own act. This act is ultimately life, the dynamic expression of the absolute and all that belongs to it – it is, as Fichte will say in the 1812 *System of Ethics*, "power given an eye."[11] In the later philosophy of the second Berlin period (1807–14), the concepts of seeing and life are intimately aligned in such a convincing manner that Xavier Tilliette was prompted to say that had Fichte lived longer, he would have produced a complete system, one of absolute life.[12]

Indeed, one cannot help but wonder what would have happened if Fichte had lived as long as Schelling and produced an 1841 series of lectures on the WL. Fichte himself might retort that such further iterations of his work would not have value for their own sake – as he said in 1804, "*the same thing* is constantly repeated in the most various terms and for the most diverse purposes, so that an insight which is missed on one occasion can be produced or made good on another occasion."[13] The lecturer is only there in order to facilitate an insight, one that can't be shown on a blackboard because it is "living thinking."[14] To read the WL with one's full attention is to cultivate this insight. This book, then, has been the author's attempt at insight. His goal was to create the conditions that make such an insight possible for the reader, too, in the hopes that: "each person correctly identify with this insight, in this pure light; if each one does, then nothing will happen to extinguish this light again and to separate it from yourself."[15]

NOTES

INTRODUCTION

1 For the origins of this neologism, see Fichte's Letter to Böttinger, 1 March 1794. GA III, 2, 71–2.

2 Cf. GA III, 2, 28 (EPW 371) and GA III, 2, 32. For a synthesis, see Lauth, "Die Entstehung von Fichtes Grundlage," 155–79. Lauth is likely drawing from Willy Kabitz, *Studien zur Entwicklungsgeschichte.* Unless otherwise indicated, all translations of secondary sources, whether German, French, or Italian, are mine.

3 GA I, 4, 195. See also Fichte's letter to Reinhold, 31 March 1797, in which he states that listeners must each think through the WL on their own, each in a radically different way – hence the need to present the system in as many different ways as possible. GA III, 3, no. 354, p. 57.

4 Simon Schüz observes that all Fichte, the lecturer, can do is talk about (über) the WL, while it is up to the hearer to execute (*nachvollziehen*) it. Schüz, *Transzendentale Argumente bei Hegel und Fichte*, 283.

5 *Intelligenzblatt der Allgemeinen Literatur-Zeitung* no. 113 (1 October 1794, col. 899), cf. GA I, 2, 183.

6 Reinhard Lauth uses this term to describe the 1804 WL throughout his preface to the German edition in GA II, 8. Fichte himself will use it at 1804/2 28.195 (GA II, 8, 406–7) to describe the WL as the point from which science-of-science divides itself into particular sciences.

7 The WL *Nova Methodo* conceives of the major subdivisions of the WL in exactly the same manner as 1804/2 Cf. GA IV, 2, 262–6; 1804/2 lecture twenty-eight – i.e., from WL to nature, law, ethics [*Sittenlehre*], and religion.

8 Primary sources for the atheism controversy are to be found in *Die Schriften zu J.G. Fichtes Atheismus-Streit*, ed. Hans Lindau. Two edited translations of primary texts allow the reader to trace the development of the event: *Querelle de l'athéisme,* ed. J.C. Goddard; and *J.G. Fichte and the Atheism Dispute*, trans. and ed. Curtis Bowman and Yolanda Estes. However, the most exhaustive account remains Léon, *Fichte et son temps,* vol. 2, 518–631.

9 "Über den Grund unseres Glauben an eine göttliche Weltregierung" in *Philosophisches Journal einer Gesellschaft Teutscher Gelehrten* 7, no. 1 (Fall 1798). Translation and commentary in *Fichte and the Atheism Dispute*, 21–9 (GA I, 5, 347–57).

10 Writes George di Giovanni, "They had in common the fact that they both put 'non-knowledge' at the head of their philosophizing. They differed in that Jacobi turned immediately from the recognition of this 'non-knowledge' to a consideration of actual 'life,' that is, to a 'wisdom about life' (*Lebensweisheit*). He turned, if I may gloss, to a consideration of what it feels like to live in a world when, underlying our experiences of it, there is only 'non-knowledge.' Fichte used his reflection on 'non-knowledge' as a means, instead, for distancing himself from 'life' and dissecting it into its elements. Jacobi coped with 'non-knowledge' by filling it with his own empirical individuality; Fichte tried to fill it, instead, with ideal constructs that connect it in thought with real life experiences." Di Giovanni, "From Jacobi's Philosophical Novel to Fichte's Idealism," 96.

11 The protracted argument between Fichte and Schelling has been well documented in Vater and Wood's *Philosophical Rupture* [PR]. Write Vater-Wood on Schelling's position: "Philosophy arises only when the philosopher abstracts from the subjectivity that posited the subject-object in an ideal or psychological mode and proceeded to examine the human faculties of mind; the abstraction evidently threshes the activity found in Wissenschaftslehre from its personal hull and enables the philosopher to work with the 'pure' subject-object, the principle of theoretical or natural philosophy. Only as a result of observing and describing the self-construction of reality in nature-philosophy can the philosopher, in a separate-but-equal transcendental science, launch into the construction of consciousness on the basis of organic and animate nature." PR 16.

12 GA I, 2, 255 (FEW 200).

13 GA I, 2, 259 (FEW 203).

14 1804/2 13.106 (GA II, 8, 202–5). I have modified the translation considerably.

15 Indeed, a careful reading of the 1794 *Foundation* shows that the I was perhaps the first posited principle but never the highest: this has always been the *Tathandlung*. Cf. GA I, 2, 355 (FEW 200).

16 "Posit pure immanent being as the absolute, substance, God, as indeed it really is, and posit appearance, that is grasped here in its highest point as the absolute's internal genetic construction, as the revelation and manifestation of God, then the latter is understood as absolutely essential and grounded

in the essence of the absolute itself. I assert that this insight into absolute inward necessity is a distinguishing mark of the science of knowing as against all other systems." 1804/2 17.128 (GA II, 8, 258–61).

17 "Being and light are one. Since in the light's existence (= in ordinary consciousness) a manifold is encountered – we have initially expressed our problem empirically and we must continue to speak this way until it has been solved – a ground for this manifold must let itself appear in the light itself as absolute oneness and in its [*Evidenz*] a ground that will explain this entire manifold as it occurs empirically. 'In the light and its [*Evidenz*].'" 1804/2 20.147 (GA II, 8, 300–1). Translation modified.

18 Cf. 1804/2 26.187 (GA II, 8, 388–91).

19 1804/2 WL 6.60 (GA II, 8, 94–5).

PART ONE

1 GA III, 5, n. 642. Cited in Lauth, "Fichtes Lehrtätigkeit," 201. The translation above is mine.

2 As Daniel Breazeale points out, Fichte insists on the importance of the subtitle of the 1794 *Foundation,* "a manuscript for the use of my students." IWL, *Editor's Introduction*, xi. The *Wissenschaftslehre* is not a book, still less a series of books, but an exercise in laying the conditions for becoming aware of the finality of reflection.

3 Concerning the 1804/2 version, Lauth and Gliwitzky write, "The second lecture from the 1804 WL, like the first, does not provide a presentation of the WL as a whole, but rather only its highest part." GA, II, 8, xxix–xxx. For Isabelle Thomas-Fogiel, the WL's various incarnations are concerned with: representation (the *Meditationen* of 1793), finitude (1794 *Foundation*), the infinite (*Nova Methodo* 1796–99), the absolute (1804/2 WL), the knowing of being (1805 WL), and appearing (1812). Cf. Thomas-Fogiel, *Présentation*, in Fichte, *La Doctrine de la Science de 1805*, 9–37. See also Tilliette's sympathetic meditation on the "curious beginning of the Wissenschaftslehre." Tilliette, "Fichtes Erfindung der Wissenschaftslehre." This position is to be contrasted with that of Julius Drechsler and Martial Gueroult, who see the WL as developing in three "moments" (though they differ on the dates for these), with these moments corresponding to the three positions of the 1794 *Foundation*. In this way, they see Fichte as historically rehearsing the whole of WL over the course of his life.

4 Fichte will write of his own strategy in 1804, "As I like to repeat frequently so no one will lose heart, in the nature of our science the same thing is constantly repeated in the most various terms and for the most diverse purposes, so that an insight which is missed on one occasion can be produced or made good on another occasion." 1804/2 5.48 (GA II, 8, 68–9).

5 "'But,' one asks oneself, 'do you really know what you are saying: can you clarify it to yourself to the extent of providing a lucid and transparent construction of it? Has it been described? [22–3] How has it been described? With such and such words. All right, the lecturer said this: and these are words! I will construct it.'" 1804/2 II.28 (GA II, 8, 20–3).

6 1804/2 VI.60 (GA II, 8, 94–5). It is no coincidence that these remarks are one lecture after a justification of the proliferation of metaphors in Fichte's presentation.

7 "The year 1804 represents a summit in the development of the Wissenschaftslehre. In that year, Fichte succeeded in presenting the highest part of the Wissenschaftslehre in one movement, that is to say, in the unity of the principle." Lauth, *Hegel critique de la doctrine de la science*, 145. Lauth also uses the term, of which he is fond, in both the *Einleitung* and *Vorwart* to GA, II, 8. As Fichte will make clear in the twenty-eighth and last lecture of 1804/2, a *Philosophia Prima* is a philosophy of the principles of the division of knowledge.

8 Xavier Léon is no doubt one of the first advocates of this myth: "From 1801 to 1804, for three years, Fichte lived in Berlin in absolute philosophical silence." Leon, *Fichte et son temps*, vol. 2, 377. Fichte's correspondence and Frau Fichte's assertion that her husband was shut up in his study "from the earliest dawn until four o'clock in the afternoon" certainly aggravated this misconception. Cf. Lauth, "Fichtes Lehrtätigkeit," 196–9.

9 Not to be confused with the street of the same name in Berlin-Kreuzberg. The place where Fichte's house once stood is now the Hackescher Markt S-Bahn station. In 1840, the street was renamed Neue Promenade. In 1862, a formal request was made to rename it Fichtestraße, which was refused. That year, a bronze commemorative plaque was placed on the house instead. With the construction of the city railway (*Stadtbahn*), the house was demolished in 1878 to make room for what would initially be called the Börse station.

10 The third WL was presented from 5 November to 31 December. The *Characteristics* began on 4 November 1804 and ended on 17 March 1805.

Fichte had initially planned lecturing on the *Principles of the Doctrines of God, Morals, and Right* at that time, but these would be postponed until later in 1805. Lauth, "Fichtes Lehrtätigkeit," 218.

11 Lauth, "Fichtes Lehrtätigkeit," 209–10. The official reason was that a number of people had hoped to attend the first series but were prevented from doing so. The two reasons are not mutually exclusive. The fact that a number of people who attended the first series also attended the second speaks to their difficulty.

12 Lauth, "Fichtes Lehrtätigkeit," 214.

13 I.e., "in vollständiger Ausarbeitung," GA II, 8, xv. There is textual evidence that Fichte would have produced this final MS while lecturing on the *Characteristics* in the Fall of 1804. GA, II, 8, xix.

14 I.e., SW XI, xii.

15 *Johann Gottlieb Fichtes Werke*, ed. Fritz Medicus, vol. 7, 627.

16 GA, II, 8, xvii.

17 "So then, on a particular occasion I divided the science of knowing into two main parts; one, that it is a doctrine of reason and truth, and second, that it is a doctrine of appearance and illusion, but one that is *indeed true* and is grounded in truth." 1804/2 15.115 (GA II, 8, 228–9).

18 Cf. 1804/2 19.141 (GA II, 8, 288–9). While Fichte himself very clearly makes this distinction, Fichte scholarship owes an enormous debt to Isabel Thomas-Fogiel for identifying this as Fichte's fundamental argument. For Thomas-Fogiel, the agreement between *tun* and *sagen* is the bedrock of Fichte's transcendental philosophy. She summarizes this argument in the simple interrogation, "How do you know this? [*D'où le savez-vous?*]" Fichte continually asks his interlocutors on what grounds they say what they say. "The first principle of reflexivity therefore consists in assuring congruence between the content of what is said and the very act of saying it." Thomas-Fogiel, *Fichte*, 94.

19 "Hence, there are four basic factors in each standpoint (five if you also add the unifying principle). Together these yield twenty main factors and primordial fundamental determinations of knowing; and, if you add the science of knowing's indicated fivefold synthesis, which we have just completed, this becomes twenty-five. It has already been proved that this division into twenty-five forms coincides with the absolute breakdown of the real [420–1] or [with the breakdown] into absolute multiplicity of that effect of reason, which is immediately inaccessible in its oneness.

This follows because multiplicity in general arises out of the genetic nature of reflection on oneness. However, this reflection on oneness immediately breaks down into fivefoldness. Therefore, the manifold from which it is necessary to abstract breaks down in the form of fivefoldness, by the same rule of reason." 1804/2 28.200 (GA II, 8, 418–21).

20 Cf. 1804/2 1.22 (GA II, 8, 4–5).

21 The main positions on the structure of the 1804/2 WL found in the secondary literature are as follows: For Wolfgang Janke (*Einleitung und Kommentar*), the text is divided into two parts: the ascent toward truth (lectures 1–15) and the phenomenology of knowing, or descent (lectures 16–28). Joachim Widmann (*Die Grundstruktur*) divides it into six moments: lectures 1–3, 4–8, 9–15, 16–20, 21–5, 26–8. Christoph Asmuth (*Das Begreifen des Unbegreiflichen*) divides it in four: prolegomena (1–3), propaedeutic (4–14), the doctrine of truth (15), and the phenomenology (15–28). Didier Julia (*La Question de l'homme*) follows Martial Gueroult, identifying 25 syntheses. Julia will later revise his position (in *Fichte 1804*), proposing the following: prolegomena, methodology, analysis of what we are (1–8); the theory of truth (9–14); opening of the phenomenology, the unity of thought (15–20); transcendental phenomenology, the theory of the image as a new language (21–5); the process of maturation of thought, the realization of experience (26–8). Andreas Schmidt (*Der Grund des Wissens*) proposes: the prologemena (1–3); the theory of truth (4–15) subdivided into 4–7, 8–10, 11–15; the theory of appearances, or the immanence of concepts within the absolute (16–28) subdivided into 16–18; 18–20; 21–3; 24–5; 26–7; 28 and the *Way Towards the Blessed Life*. Ulrich Schlösser (*Das Erfassen des Einleuchtens*) follows a different methodology, in many ways the opposite of Gueroult's. Rather than focus on the structure of the 1804 WL, he concentrates on what he considers to be the key arguments, whether those be about the *durch* and *Urbegriff* (fluid in the text), the failure of the idealist-realist dialectic (12–14), the rejection of false forms of transcendental argumentation (15–21), or the theory of certainty (23). Certainty is for Schlösser the key to understanding the WL, the epistemological goal to which it aspires. Simon Schüz (*Transzendentale Argumente bei Hegel und Fichte*) offers a historical reconstruction of 1804/2, consisting of propaedeutic and prolegomena (1–3, 1–8); realism and idealism (9–14); the theory of truth (15); and the theory appearances (16–28). But Schüz's main intention is to establish the form and function of transcendental arguments in Fichte as opposed to

Hegel's *Phenomenology of Spirit*. He therefore pays particular attention to the dialectic between light and concept as the products of meta-theoretical considerations (4–10); Light as the transcendental possibility-condition of the concept (11–13); knowledge as the originary meaning of reality (14–15); certainty (23); and law as certainty's self-representation (24–5). For an overview, see Thomas-Fogiel, *Fichte*, 191n3.

22 On this reading, the merit of ES is that Gueroult has followed Fichte's advice to *understand* the WL for oneself and then reconstruct it as one can. As *Wissenschaftslehrer*, Gueroult's work is impressive; he reproduces every major moment of Fichte's argumentation and brings them together in such a way that his reconstruction traces the same path as Fichte's construction. Yet it is unmistakably Gueroult's (at times problematic) interpretation and not an exegesis. Still, its importance is such that throughout this text, Gueroult's syntheses will be identified in the footnotes.

CHAPTER ONE

1 For Gueroult, these three lectures constitute the first of the twenty-five syntheses (Synthesis A^1). ES II.109–11.

2 The Port Royal logic was the inescapable foundation for German Idealist "logics," cf. Tonelli, "L'origine della tavola dei giudizi," 129–38; Finocchiaro, "The Port-Royal Logic," 393–410; Thomas-Fogiel, *Fichte*, 150–5.

3 In this, there is affinity between Fichte's *Wissenschaftslehre* and Hegel's *Wissenschaft der Logik*. For the "logical" dimension of Hegel's *Logic*, see Redding, "The Role of Logic Commonly So Called," 281–301. For an examination of Fichte's contribution to this development, see di Giovanni, "'Das Logische' of Hegel's Logic," 71–87. For a more general comparison of the 1804 WL and Hegel, see Ludwig Siep, *Hegels Fichtekritik*.

4 Thomas-Fogiel, *Fichte*, 192–6; cf. The three "fundamental principles" of WL, §1, §2, and §3. GA I, 2, 255–82 (FEW 200–23).

5 1804/2 5.48 (GA II, 8, 68–9).

6 The most important of these are in italics.

7 1804/2 1.22 (GA II, 8, 4–5).

8 1804/2 10.82 (GA II, 8, 148–9).

9 1804/2 1.23 (GA II, 8, 8–9).

10 For Thomas-Fogiel (*Fichte*, 45–59), Kant's (and subsequently Fichte's) transcendental philosophy is meant as a bulwark against scepticism.

For Fichte, this is undoubtedly the scepticism of first principles that he encounters in *Aenesidemus*: "in philosophy nothing can be decided on the basis of incontestably certain and universally valid principles concerning the existence or nonexistence of things in themselves and their properties nor concerning the limits of man's capacity for knowledge," English translation in Breazeale, *Thinking Through*, 29; op. cit. Schulze, *Aenesidemus* ed. Manfred Frank, 26.

11 1804/2 19.141 (GA II, 8, 288–9).

12 The twentieth century saw a rich development in retorsive arguments that would have been impossible without Fichte. Joseph Maréchal uses the same argument in exactly the same context as Fichte: correcting Kant's "static" transcendental arguments in favour of a "dynamic" version. Maréchal first develops his retorsive arguments in *Le Point de depart* (I.46–8). It will reappear in his "transcendental deduction of ontological affirmation" (V.97–8; V.491–504). Both the term and the method will be explicity developed by Maréchal's disciples. See, in particular, Isaye, "La Justification critique par retorsion"; and Weissmahr, *Die Wirklichkeit des Geistes*. One also finds the term in contemporary analytic philosophy, most notably in Karl-Otto Apel's Transcendental Pragmatics, e.g., Apel, "Das Problem einer philosophischen Theorie der Rationalitätstypen." Behind all modern forms of retorsive argument lurks Aristotle, who first theorized that a demonstration could be made by refutation (*elegktikos apodeixai*), cf. Aristotle, *Metaphysics*, Book Gamma, 1006[a] 11.

13 1804/2 1.25 (GA II, 8, 10–11).

14 Similarly, in the Jena WL, "I" and "not-I" are posited simultaneously. Cf. GA I, 2, 258–60 (FEW 202–4).

15 1804/2 2.31 (GA II, 8, 26–7).

16 The criticism was already raised by Maimon in *Kritische Untersuchungen*, 259.

17 1804/2 2.31 (GA II, 8, 28–9).

18 Ibid.

19 1804/2 2.32 (GA II, 8, 30–1). One reads in Kant's introduction to CPJ: "Now although there is an incalculable gulf fixed between the domain of the concept of nature, as the sensible, and the domain of the concept of freedom, as the supersensible, so that from the former to the latter (thus by means of the theoretical use of reason) no transition is possible, just as if there were so many different worlds, the first of which can have no influence on

the second: yet the latter should have an influence on the former, namely the concept of freedom should make the end that is imposed by its laws real in the sensible world; and nature must consequently also be able to be conceived in such a way that the lawfulness of its form is at least in agreement with the possibility of the ends that are to be realized in it in accordance with the laws of freedom. – Thus there must still be a ground of the unity of the supersensible that grounds nature with that which the concept of freedom contains practically, the concept of which, even if it does not suffice for cognition of it either theoretically or practically, and thus has no proper domain of its own, nevertheless makes possible the transition from the manner of thinking in accordance with the principles of the one to that in accordance with the principles of the other." CPJ 63 (AA 5, 176).

20 For Thomas-Fogiel, Kant sought to move beyond the division between being and thinking implicit in dogmatism and thus posited a division between the sensible and the intelligible. He attempted to produce a synthesis of these in the *Critique of Judgment*, but it is external to its terms, or as she says, "post factum." How so? In CPJ, Kant claims that in art and the living organism, everything takes place *as if* sensibility and intelligibility were unified. Yet his only proof for this is the result of the synthesis. How, then, does Kant know that there is a real shared ground beyond the affirmation that the synthesis is produced "as if" this were the case? Kant would need to produce another form of discourse that qualifies judgment as a uniting factor and so on *ad infinitum*. This grounding unity depends on its effects – one must presume the first two critiques for it to make sense. Thomas-Fogiel, *Fichte*, 201.

21 1804/2 3.34–5 (GA II, 8, 36–9).

22 Compare the above quotation from 1804/2 3.34–5 to the well-known thought experiment from the *Wissenschaftslehre Nova Methodo* (1796–99): "Think the concept 'I' and think of yourself as you do this. Everyone understands what this means. Everyone thinks of something thereby; one feels one's consciousness to be determined in a particular manner, and it is by virtue of this that one is conscious of something specific. Now one must observe what one does when one thinks of this concept. Think of any object at all – the wall, for example, or the stove. The thinking subject is a rational being; but, in thinking of this object, this freely thinking subject forgets about itself and pays no attention to its own free activity

… With the same freedom with which I think about the wall, I now think about the I. I am also thinking about something when I think about the I; but in this case the thinking subject and the object of thought cannot be distinguished from each other in the way they could be while I was still thinking about the wall. The thinking subject and the object one is thinking of, the thinker and the thought, are here one and the same." FTP, 110–11. The same example – this time using a stove – will be used in the 1813 WL (lecture three), GA II, 15, 140–1.

23 There is much debate in the literature about Fichte's use of the term intellectual intuition. The clearest expression in the Fichtean corpus is found in the *Second Introduction to the Wissenschaftslehre* (1797): "'Intellectual intuition' is the name I give to the act required of the philosopher: an act of intuiting himself while simultaneously performing the act by means of which the I originates for him. Intellectual intuition is the immediate consciousness that I act and of what I do when I act. It is because of this that it is possible for me to know something because I do it … This is something everyone has to discover immediately within himself; otherwise, he will never become acquainted with it at all." IWL 46 (GA I, 4, 216–17). While this term is used in a number of ways throughout Fichte's career, there is a "strict sense" of the term which is present through Fichte's work. Daniel Breazeale writes: "When it is employed in this strictly methodological sense, intellectual intuition [*intellektuelle Anschauung*] is simply a synonym for a number of other terms that Fichte employs in these same texts, including 'observation' [*Zuschauen, Zusehen, Beobachtung*], 'attentiveness' [*Aufmerksamkeit*], and 'reflection' [*Reflexion*]. This, however, is by no means the only sense that is assigned to 'intellectual intuition' in Fichte's later Jena writings, in which he continues to describe the I itself – more specifically, its immediate presence to itself in original self-consciousness, conceived of as a 'fact/act' or *Tathandlung* – as an intellectual intuition. But now we also find him applying this same term to the philosopher's immediate consciousness of this *Tathandlung*, as a 'fact of consciousness' for him, as well as to our practical, extraphilosophical awareness of our own freedom and our concurrent recognition of the commanding authority of the moral law." Breazeale, *Thinking Through*, 200. See also Stolzenberg, *Fichtes Begriff der intellektuellen Anschauung*, and Xavier Tilliette, *L'intuition intellectuelle*. In the final analysis, the consistency of the logical foundation of the concept through Fichte's career seems to preclude a myriad of

contradictory meanings designed to invalidate latter acceptions (Breazeale) or a "metaphysical turn" (Stolzenberg). If anything, the (unnamed) use of intellectual intuition in 1804 is much more circumspect than that of the later Jena period. Note that the term is also absent from the 1794 *Foundation of the Entire Wissenschaftslehre*; both Breazeale and Tilliette see it implicitly present. Much the same can be said of 1804.

24 1804/2 3.35 (GA II, 8, 38–9).

25 In 1804/2, Walter Wright translates it as "manifestness." This is a gloss and a confusing one, since he also uses manifestness for a very different term, *Aeusserung*. Herein, I keep *Evidenz* in the original in order to highlight its importance as a technical term and render *Aeusserung* as "externalization."

26 1804/2 3.37 (GA II, 8, 42–3).

27 For Gueroult, syntheses 2, 3, 4, and 5 (B^1, C^1, D^1 and E^1) are all contained *in nuce* in lecture four and are expounded almost simultaneously in the non-linear development that constitutes lectures five to eight. These first eight lectures therefore constitute Gueroult's "first point of view of reflection: the construction of the factical being of knowing: prolegomena." ES II.109–12. The reader wishing to reconstruct Gueroult's syntheses should consistently refer to the diagram on II.136–7.

28 "When I presented it, I already suspected that my last talk might seem too rigorous and deep for a fourth lecture." 1804/2 5.51 (GA II, 8, 74–5). At the beginning of lecture five, we read "Nächsten Mittwoch dürfte es sich, des allgemeinen Bettages willen, geziemen, die Vorlesung auszusetzen. Ich würde daher schon deßwegen heute mich noch mit Prolegomenen beschäftigen, wenn ich nicht noch [copia: auch] überdies die Nothwendigkeit, mit der stärksten Speise dermalen noch zu verschonen, in Erfahrung gebrachte hätte." GA II, 8, 66–7. Wright mistranslates this as "It might be appropriate to cancel the lecture this Wednesday, because of the general day of prayer. I would have taken up preliminary matters again today had I not also seen the necessity, because of this, for sparing you the strongest nourishment." The German says the opposite: we will remain with preliminaries in this lecture ("Ich würde mich noch mit Prolegomenen beschäftigen").

29 SW and *Copia* reproduce this diagram differently. My version is based on 1804/2 4.40 (GA II, 8, 52).

30 Initially, writes Fichte, it would seem that consciousness's mere positing of A furnishes an absolute principle. But it is merely a working principle and must be recognized as such in order to function: "We only seem to

have [posited an absolute], but it is an empty seeming. We see merely *that* it is so, but we have no insight into what this qualitive oneness in fact is." 1804/2 3.36 (GA II, 8, 40–1). Translation modified.

31 "All transcendental philosophy, such as Kant's (and in this respect the science of knowing is not yet different from his philosophy), posits the absolute neither in being nor in consciousness but in the union of both." 1804/2 2.30 (GA, II, 8, 24–5).

32 "[A] must actually be a *purely self-sustaining substance*," 1804/2 3.34 (GA II, 8, 36–7). Also, "I claim that this much is evident from all philosophies prior to Kant, the absolute was located in being, that is, in the dead thing as thing," 1804/2 1.25 (GA II, 8, 10–11). For the Spinoza connection, see di Giovanni, "The Spinozism of Fichte's Transcendental Argument."

33 1804/2 4.40 (GA II, 8, 52–3). Fichte would have made this affirmation earlier, since he begins "sagte ich …" This was either an aside or a remark made during a question period, and subsequent questions about this aside guide the content of lecture four. Note that interspersed among Fichte's lectures are discussion periods of which there is no written record other than Fichte's own allusions to them in the lectures.

34 This will become explicit in 1804/2 13.106 (GA II, 8, 202–5): Genesis is successor to the earlier WL's *Tathandlung*, with A's facticity forming the "Tat" and mere Genesis the "Handlung."

35 1804/2 4.43 (GA II, 8, 58–9).

36 Wright omits this expression altogether, and his translation at 1804/2 4.43 is a gloss. In the German (at GA II, 8, 58–9), we read, "Soll es zur Auesserung und Realisation des absoluten Lichtes kommen, so muss der Begriff gesetzt sein, um durch das unmittelbare Licht vernichtet zu werden: denn darin eben besteht die Aeusserung des reinen Lichtes; das Resultat aber, und gleichsam der todte Absatz dieser Auesserung ist das Sein an sich, welches darum, weil das reine Licht zugleich Vernichtung des Begriffes ist, ein Unbegreifliches wird." Here, the German language alchemical tradition is invoked: *Absatz* is a translation of *caput mortuum*, or the neutralized remainder of alchemical operation, a precipitate. See Figala, "Der alchemische Begriff."

37 1804/2 4.45 (GA II, 8, 64–5).

38 Kant's well-known phrase, "Ich denke, muss alle meine Vorstellungen begleiten können" (CPR B 132; AA III 108) contains two expressions of subjectivity: the *Ich* of conditions and the "mine" of determinate existence.

Kant's claim about their relationship will be that that *when* experience is constructed within the space of subjectivity, *then* a unified concrete subject appears. This, too, is a movement from experience to conditions and back and does not in itself create any new content, instead making a meta-empirical claim: *I am* this *Ich* who is thinking. Here, time (*when … then …*) constitutes the movement from consciousness in general to consciousness in particular. Time as form of inner sense is meant to demonstrate whose *I* is being talked about (cf. Refutation of idealism, CPR B 277; AA III, 192). Yet objects intuited in time are appearances, not things-in-themselves, which are "incognizable" (CPR A 239 / B 298; AA III, 204). Yet if things-in-themselves *cause* appearances, then Kant has given us a Cartesian-style ontological argument in spite of himself. Even on the most generous reading, Kant's problematic thing-in-itself creates a gap between lived and reflected experience. Ultimately, Kant provides no account of why we find experience meaningful in the first place – no account of *Evidenz.*

39 1804/2 4.45 (GA II, 8, 64–5).

40 Principles [*Principien*] are not proven but rather provided or generated – that is, "principiated" [*principiieren*]. Cf. lecture twenty-three.

41 Wolfgang Janke writes of an *Urrealität* as the goal of lecture eight, distinct from the *Urbegriff*. In the context of the overarching argument that Janke is making, this peculiarity proves to be merely semantic. Janke, *Einleitung und Kommentar*, 112–19.

42 1804/2 7.63 (GA II, 8, 100–1).

43 The introduction of image here marks the beginning of a major motif in Fichte's later philosophy. For Julius Drechsler, whose is the first major survey of all of Fichte's thought (especially the late philosophy), image is what characterizes Fichtean philosophy, its development continuing until it reaches its summit in the WL of 1812. Cf. Drechsler, *Fichtes Lehre vom Bild.*

44 1804/2 7.63 (GA II, 8, 102–3).

45 "Now, the something imaged in the concept's content should be the light: therefore our principle (i.e., we, ourselves) rests no longer either in the light or in the light's representative but rather in the oneness in and through the two, a oneness realized in our act of thinking. Therefore, I have called the concept situated here the primordial concept [*Urbegriff*]." 1804/2 7.64 (GA II, 8, 103–4) translation modified.

46 1804/2 7.64 (GA II, 8, 104–5).

47 As Fichte will write later, the concept is the "absolute relation of the imaged to the image and vice-versa." 1804/2 9.74 (GA II, 8, 128–9).

48 1804/2 8.69 (GA II, 8, 116–17).

49 1804/2 8.71 (GA II, 8,120–2).

50 1804/2 9.74 (GA II, 8, 128–9).

51 1804/2 9.76 (GA II, 8, 132–3).

52 Lecture nine is an introductory lecture that announces the conflict between realism and idealism. Gueroult therefore sees it and the first position, realism (the first part of lecture ten), as constituting the sixth synthesis (A^2: immediacy, realism. The being of light, antecedent of the concept). ES II.113–16.

53 1804/2 10.80 (GA II, 8, 142–3).

54 Ibid.

55 Janke calls this "the interiorly separating or immanently externalizing light." Janke, *Einleitung und Kommentar*, 122.

56 Fichte puts this somewhat obscurely: "In the previously discussed point, L was taken up as a starting point, as things stood then; if so, the concept proceeds genetically from this L, since L has transformed itself into the concept. Or said more exactly: our own observing – which was not then visible, which we lived, and into which we merged – divided itself beyond the then regnant L, and in this division negated the L (light) into o/C; thus creating both out of itself." 1804/2 10.83 (GA II, 8, 150–3).

57 Throughout the idealism-realism dialectic, Fichte's focus will be on the insufficiencies of one position and its corrective in its successor. This moment often occurs in the middle of the lecture. Hence, idealism begins in the last pages of lecture ten and is carried over into lecture eleven. For Gueroult, the idealist position of ten and eleven is synthesis seven (B^2: mediacy, idealism. – Concept: B. T. unity). ES II.214–16.

58 1804/2 10.85 (GA II, 8, 154–5).

59 1804/2 11.87 (GA II, 8, 160–1).

60 1804/2 11.88 (GA II, 8, 162–3).

61 1804/2 11.89 (GA II, 8, 164–5).

62 1804/2 11.90 (GA II, 8, 166–7).

63 This conclusion is Fichte's portrayal of Jacobi's position. Because philosophy is bound to consciousness and consciousness is caught in a vicious circle wherein its own grounds are an illegitimate external presupposition, the

only way to arrive at *life* is to renounce philosophy and simply to *live*. Jacobi is not, according to Fichte, an idealist. Rather, it is he who has understood the basic problem of idealism and proposed the only viable solution one finds within the idealist framework. The point is that Jacobi still thinks according to an idealist maxim or principle. In rejecting transcendental philosophy, Jacobi offers a summary of its procedure and a diagnostic of where it goes wrong in practice. Hence, Fichte owes as much to Jacobi as he does to Kant. Cf. Zöller, "Das Element aller Gewissheit," 34. See also Lauth, "Fichtes Verhältnis zu Jacobi"; Hammacher, "Fichte, Maimon und Jacobi"; di Giovanni, "The Early Fichte as Disciple of Jacobi"; and Ivaldo, "Leben und Philosophie." Fichte will deal with Jacobi explicitly in lecture eighteen.

64 1804/2 11:90–1 (GA II, 8, 168–9). The = 0 represents "the lowest conceivable level of reality." Janke, *Einleitung und Kommentar*, 122.

65 1804/2 11.91 (GA II, 8, 168–9).

66 For Gueroult, this is synthesis eight (C^2 – immediacy, realism. – Justified negation of idealism by realism by means of the realization of the in-itself.). Cf. lectures 11–13, ES II.116–17.

67 1804/2 11.91 (GA II, 8, 168–71).

68 Cf. 1804/2 12.95, point 4 (GA II, 8, 178–81).

69 1804/2 12.97 (GA II, 8, 182–3).

70 1804/2 12.98 (GA II, 8, 184–5).

71 Ibid.

72 Ibid., 186–7).

73 For Gueroult, synthesis nine (D^2 – Mediacy, idealism. – The energy of reflection, the condition of the realization in us of the in-itself, posited as abolute = pure I, absolute I.). Cf. Lecture thirteen, ES II.117–18.

74 1804/2 13.105–6 (GA II, 8, 202–6). Writes Daniel Breazeale, "In the spring of 1799, following a brief flirtation with the standpoint of the Wissenschaftslehre, K.L. Reinhold became enamored of C.B. Bardili's conception of philosophy as a system of 'rational realism,' based purely upon 'thinking qua thinking' with no need whatsoever to make any appeal to intuition. In embracing this new conception of philosophy, Reinhold publicly announced that the Wissenschaftslehre had been superseded by Bardili's system, which he described as occupying a standpoint 'between Fichte's philosophy and Jacobi's.'" Breazeale, *Thinking through*, 388n84. By 1800, Reinhold considered Bardili's *Denken als Denken* to be an alternative

formulation of the foundations of transcendental philosophy found in the *Foundation*. Moreover, this new foundation is an improvement, since it replaces the "psychological" aspects of WL with formal logic (GA III, 4, 199). Fichte replied that this was a return to dogmatism (GA III, 4, 271–3). Fichte cannot articulate a definitive answer to Reinhold and Bardili in 1800 any more than he could answer Schelling or Jacobi at that time: indeed, even in the 1801–02 WL, Fichte has not made explicit the common genetic root of thought and being. In 1804, the answer is clear: thinking always has a material component: Bardili's thinking *qua* thinking cannot exist without thinking something in particular. The absence of factical content means that Bardili ultimately confuses thinking-of-thinking and thinking itself, since otherwise, he would not be able to account for our access to thinking-of-thinking. As we shall soon see, Jacobi commits a similar error, though on a much more sophisticated level. For further details, see Zöller, "The Unpopularity of Transcendental Philosophy."

75 1804/2 13.105 (GA II, 8, 200–1).

76 Ibid., 202–3. Here, Fichte has made explicit what we surmised already in the prologemena: genesis is the *Tathandlung* of the early philosophy. We read in the *Aenesidemus Review*, "The initial incorrect presupposition, and the one that caused the principle of consciousness to be proposed as the first principle of all philosophy was precisely the presupposition that one must begin with a fact. We certainly do require a first principle that is material and not merely formal. But such a principle does not have to express a fact [*Tat*]; it can also express an Act [*Tathandlung*]." EPW 64 (GA I, 2, 46). In a seminal essay, Paul Franks charts the origins of this expression, calling its imperative tone a "summons" that has a necessarily intersubjective dimension. Franks, "Freedom, *Tatsache* and *Tathandlung*."

77 For Gueroult, synthesis ten (E^2 – Immediacy, realism. – Being as in-itself, posited as absolute, suppressing the relation in-itself/not-in-itself, independent of subjective energy.). ES II.118–19. Cf. lecture fourteen.

78 1804/2 13.107 (GA II, 8, 204–5).

79 Fichte has in mind Schelling's *Darstellung meines Systems der Philosophie* (1801), the work which stands at the centre of the heated correspondence between Schelling and Fichte in the years 1800–02. This debate opened with the question of the place of nature in a transcendental system and would have largely been invited by Schelling's use of Fichtean vocabulary in the *System des Transcendentalen Idealismus* of 1800. Yet the debate about

nature quickly morphed into a debate about transcendental philosophy itself, forcing both parties to consider what their own writings meant to express in using terms such as "being," and "intuition." Schelling's *Darstellung* marks the transformation of their conflict into a stalemate in which each would radically revise the presentation of his system in function of the criticisms of the other. Fichte's answer to the *Darstellung* in the 1804/2 WL is the last word in a debate that Schelling had long since abandoned. See PR 1–15; and Lauth, "Die zweite philosophische Auseinandersetzung."

80 This declaration would seem to be the clarification of a cryptic phrase from Fichte's *Ankündigung* of 1800: "I will not discuss here the extent to which my talented collaborator, Professor Schelling, has been more successful at paving the way for the transcendental standpoint in his natural scientific writings and in his recently published *System of Transcendental Idealism,*" PR 86. Schelling was much troubled by it. Caroline Schlegel encouraged him to write to Goethe to inquire as to its meaning. Goethe, who always held himself above the fray of academic disputes, wrote back facetiously: "Even I was occupied and entertained by the Fichtean 'Announcement' in the *Allgemeine Zeitung*" (letter to Schelling, 1 February 1801). It was only much later that Schelling came to understand the inside joke shared by Fichte and Goethe (to whom the 1800 *Wissenschaftslehre Neue Bearbeitung* was – or would have been, had it reached the press – dedicated): Schelling couldn't philosophize on his own. For a translation of the *Ankündigung* (Announcement) and its historical context, including correspondence, see PR 77–92.

81 1804/2 14.109–10 (GA II, 8, 214–17).

82 Vater-Wood summarize: "Commenting on Schelling's new standpoint, Fichte maintains that the new system has being or an absolute real ground as its principle, even if that principle is given the lofty name 'reason.' Philosophy, he argues, must proceed from a seeing, not a being. If it starts from anything other than a living intuition of self-activity ('intellectual intuition'), it is simply realism, a greater or lesser sketch of Spinozism, and is quite unable to account for freedom or spontaneous activity and the consciousness that derives from it" PR 15.

83 Letter from Fichte to Schelling, 31 May 1801. [*Es kann nicht von einem Seyn … sondern es muss von einem Sehen ausgegangen werden*]. "One cannot proceed from a *being* (everything to which mere *thinking* refers, and what would follow from this, to which the *real-ground* applies, is being; granted, it

might also be called reason); but one has to proceed from a *seeing*; it is also necessary to establish the identity of the ideal-[ground] *and* real-ground, [which] = the identity of intuition and thought" PR 56. This is Fichte's first letter to Schelling since he received the *Darstellung* and contains *in nuce* his critique of that text. Telling is Fichte's geometric example of the line and the point, which immediately follows: "For instance, grasp in consciousness that there can only be one straight line between two points. First and foremost, here you precisely have your conceiving and penetrating of the act of self-evidence itself, and this [is] my *fundamental point*. You presuppose and assert absolutely that this proposition is valid *for* all possible lines, as well as *for* all possible intelligences; and you do it in the following manner: you posit in the first instance, i.e., the form of *grasping* itself, as something *determined* (material); in the second [instance], as something *determinable*. The first gives you in time as an *individual* itself; the second, where you precisely posit it merely as something *determinable*, positing the empty form of egoity, subsequently gives you the spirit world. Universal (finite) consciousness is therefore the absolute union of the consciousness of the spirit world and that of the individual. The latter is the ideal ground of the former; the former ([which] can never, however, be *cognized* and *penetrated* by self-evidence) is the *real ground* of the latter" PR 56 (GA III, 5, 46). Here, the points stand for objects of sensible intuition, and the line for intellectual intuition. Schelling's error lies precisely in the need to speak of an "empty form of egoity," as if the ground of knowing were some physical container. It is, rather, light, that which enlightens, and about which one is aware but cannot know as object. As Fichte repeatedly articulates, when one thinks, one *always already* knows that one is thinking, aware of one's own act as *fait accompli*.

84 In spite of bitter disagreement, Fichte is deeply indebted to Schelling. Indeed, the Berlin WL as a whole (what Gueroult and Drechsler call the "second and third moments of the *Wissenschaftslehre*") would not have taken on the form it did were it not for Schelling's critique. In a seminal article, Hartmut Traub identifies three ways in which the 1804/2 WL is influenced by Schelling: "a) the elevation of seeing to the level of absolute being, above the opposition of real and ideal; b) the positing of the result of this ascent not only as last synthesis, but also as starting point and first principle; c) the supplementation of the genesis of seeing through a genesis of being, which the idealist construction and its principle of

evidence [*Evidenzprinzip*] ground through the agility and productivity of the absolute, i.e., its self-construction." Traub, "Schellings Einfluß," 136.

85 1804/2 14.110 (GA II, 8, 216–17).

86 1804/2 14.111 (GA II, 8, 218–19). Fichte claims that this maxim announces a "new idealism" that has validity only insofar as appearances are concerned – in other words, a phenomenology, which is a "transcendental idealism," or transcendental theory of appearances. In contrast, Janke sees lecture fifteen as a "higher" (i.e., absolute) idealism. Janke, *Einleitung und Kommentar*, 132. This, I suggest, reifies the position of lecture fifteen, which is knowing-of-knowing, the structural gathering-together of truth (in lectures one to fourteen) and appearance-of-truth (in lectures sixteen to twenty-eight). Proof for this is that the WL is not an idealism – indeed, Fichte sees it as being closer to realism. Moreover, the second half, as we shall see, will repeatedly make use of idealism's methodology, ultimately purifying it in lecture twenty-five.

87 1804/2 14.111–12 (GA II, 8, 220–1).

88 The *Lager des Todes* belongs to same metaphorical constellation as the *todter Absatz*. Both speak in the same way of the non-genetic nature of the contents of consciousness and imply that through an alchemy of thought, they will be integrated into a genetic deduction of truth and consciousness. It is likely that in crafting these metaphors, Fichte had in mind Lessing's ditch, the gap between historical fact and (eternal) reason, the place that Jacobi said on principle couldn't be traversed philosophically. Cf. *Über den Beweis des Geistes und der Kraft* (1777), *Lessing: Werke,* 8:13.

89 1804/2 14.112 (GA II, 8, 220–1).

90 1804/2 14.113 (GA II, 8, 224–5).

91 For Gueroult, lecture fifteen stands at the juncture between the two parts of the 1804/2 WL, between the second and third points of reflection. He incorporates it into the same synthesis as lecture sixteen, the eleventh (A^2 – Immediacy, realism = synthesis E^2). Note that the last synthesis of the theory of truth and the first of the theory of appearances are the same – this is precisely where the "basic proposition" stands. ES II.120.

92 1804/2 15.115 (GA II, 8, 228–9).

93 1804/2 15.116 (GA II, 8, 230–1).

94 Philosophy of language becomes an explicit concern for Fichte in the *Reden an die Deutsche Nation* (1809). Yet the theoretical antecedents of a Fichtean philosophy of language go much deeper, back to the very

beginnings of his philosophy. See Jergius, *Philosophische Sprache*; and Barbarić, "Fichtes Gedanken vom Wesen der Sprache."

95 1804/2 15.116 (GA II, 8, 230–1).

96 Ibid.

97 1804/2 15.117 (GA II, 8, 234–5).

98 1804/2 15.118 (GA II, 8, 234–5).

CHAPTER TWO

1 1804/2 21.156 (GA II, 8, 320–1). "Wir lassen es daher, als bloßes Mittel des Heraufsteigens fallen, bis es im Herabsteigen sich wieder findet."

2 1804/2 16.121 (GA II, 8, 242–3).

3 For Gueroult, "this whole first part [i.e., lectures one to fifteen] can be considered an 'understanding' of being. The second is an 'understanding of this understanding.' [cf. *Tatsachen des Bewusstseins* (1813). *Nachgelassene Werke*, II, 457]." If the *understanding* is the phenomenon of being, this second part [i.e., lectures sixteen to twenty-eight] will explicitly posit this *understanding* as phenomenal, i.e., as the necessary manifestation of the absolute. ES II.119. Didier Julia expands on this: "The second part of the WL begins by reminding us that it is always human consciousness that is the subject of philosophy, and thereby its ultimate concern, that according to which philosophical reflection distinguishes itself from logical analysis. The sixteenth lecture formulates this demand very clearly, and the dissatisfaction of real consciousness in regards to a logically absolute knowing. This dissatisfaction is made manifest because, for us, absolute knowing is not an initial affirmation, but the philosophical culmination of the genesis of consciousness ... There is only absolute knowing *if* someone makes the concrete decision to think." Julia, *La question de l'homme*, 249.

4 1804/2 15.115 (GA II, 8, 228–9); Wolfgang Janke renders this into a helpful aphorism: "Being means being-present [*Anwesendsein*], a constant resting." Janke, *Fichte: Sein und Reflexion*, 394.

5 The genealogy of Fichte's use of the term *Phänomenologie* goes back to Johann Heinrich Lambert (1728–1777), who uses it in his *Neues Organon* vol. I, vi. [1764]; *op. cit.* Piché, "Der Phänomenologiebegriff bei Kant und Reinhold." Kant, in a letter to Lambert dated 2 September 1770, considers calling his investigation into the conditions of the possibility of sensible knowing a *Phänomenologia generalis* (AA 10, 98). See also Orth, "Der

Terminus Phänomenologie bei Kant und Lambert"; and Irrlitz, "Die Dissertation von 1770" in *Kant Handbuck*, 48–9.

6 Fichte himself offers an account of the structure of his phenomenology in lecture twenty-two, stating it is divided into three sections: a theory of transcendental knowing, a theory of ordinary knowing, and their unity, in which "the two extreme sections come together in the *middle*." (1804/2 22.163; GA II, 8, 336–7). This third section, which is meant to accomplish for the WL itself what the other two did for appearance and knowledge, is announced as being co-terminus with becoming what we say and saying what we are, a task accomplished at the end of lecture twenty-five. At the beginning of lecture twenty-six, Fichte announces that he wishes to spend the three remaining lectures exploring how it is that *we* became WL. Answering this question will provide not only a summary of the threefold transcendental deduction that preceded it (in lectures sixteen to twenty-five) but also account for the appearance of particular sciences.

7 For Gueroult, synthesis twelve (B^3) deals with the question of the "*Soll als Soll*," encompassing material found in lectures sixteen and eventeen, its result appearing at the beginning at eighteen. Note that seventeen is largely a review of sixteen. Cf. ES II.120–2.

8 1804/2 16.122 (GA II, 8, 244–5).

9 1804/2 16.124–5 (GA II, 8, 250–1).

10 "Soll es zu der absoluten Einsicht kommen, daß u.s.w., so muss eine solche ideale Sichconstruction absolut faktisch gesetzt werden. – Die Erklärung in unmittelbarer Einsicht ist bedingt durch die absolut faktische Voraussetzung des zu Erklärenden." GA II, 9, 250 (1804/2 16.125).

11 The pair *Categorisch-Categorizität* [categorical] and *Problematisch-Problematizität* expresses, within the content of the *Soll*, necessity and contingency. Wright translates the latter as "hypothetical."

12 1804/2 16.125 (GA II, 8, 252–3).

13 1804/2 16.126 (GA II, 8, 252–3).

14 The *Soll* made its first clandestine appearance at 1804/2 1.24 (GA II, 8, 8–11), where Fichte declares that *if* one philosophizes, *then* one *must* do so according to a principle (maxim).

15 In a parenthetical remark, Fichte shifts terminology, speaking of God and his externalization. This is the first brief hint of Fichte's move towards calling the absolute (or *esse in mero actu*) "God." This terminology will be more consistently pursued in the *Principles of the Doctrines of God, Morals,*

and Right (1805) and *The Way Towards the Blessed Life* (1806). "Posit pure immanent being as the absolute, *subsisting* [*Substante*] God, as indeed it really is, and posit appearance, that is grasped here in its highest point as the absolute's internal genetic construction, as the revelation and *externalization [Auesserung]* of God, then the latter is understood as absolutely essential and grounded in the essence of the absolute itself." 1804/2 17.128 (GA II, 8, 258–61). Translation modified.

16 1804/2 17.131–2 (GA II, 8, 266–7). Compare this synthesis with the first deduction of the *Soll* at 14.124–5 (GA II, 8, 248–53).

17 1804/2 18.134 (GA II, 8, 272–3).

18 As Fichte will forcefully argue in the 1805 WL, "God is creator of the world: No! For there is no world. Only the absolute *is*. The absolute, however, cannot *realiter* and in truth go out of itself. From nothing comes nothing. Nothing remains eternally nothing." GA II, 9, 288. Luigi Pareyson explains Fichte's attitude toward the idea of creation and creationism: "The refutation of creationism in Fichte is made from the point of view of the finite. In fact, creationism and idealism both assume the transformation of pure concepts into material: both God and the I are pure intelligence, and as such have pure concepts, which in turn are transformed into a material world. The difference is that while the God of the dogmatist is an infinite intelligence, the I of the idealist is finite intelligence. And while the becoming-material [*sensibilizzazione*] of the concepts of a finite intelligence contains no difficulty, the materialization of an infinite intelligence is incomprehensible. The materialization of a world resulting from finite intelligence exists for finite intelligence, and only for it; but it is incomprehensible as to how a world resulting from the materialization of infinite intelligence could also hold for a finite intelligence. 'The philosopher can and must show that the concept of a finite intelligence is transformed, under a certain valence, into a material world'" (Fichte, *Nachgelassene Schriften*, II, 569). Fichte writes elsewhere: "Do not take refuge in the lazy argument that supposes an intelligence created the world, because it is absolutely unthinkable that an intelligence has created matter [Massolo, *Fichte e la filosofia*, 513.]" Pareyson, *Fichte: Il sistema della libertà*, 361–2.

19 1804/2 18.136 (GA II, 8, 276–7).

20 Gueroult's synthesis thirteen (C^3). ES II.122–3.

21 1804/2 18.138–9 (GA II, 8, 282–5).

22 1804/2 18.139 (GA II, 8, 284–5).

23 See Breazeale, *Thinking Through*, 32; cf. GA, I, 2, 55. There is no passage from interior to exterior. In this sense, Fichte's reply to Aenesidemus also works for Jacobi, whose philosophy could be considered a kind of scepticism, albeit a more sophisticated one than Schulze's.

24 1804/2 18.139 (GA II, 8, 284–5).

25 1804/2 19.141 (GA II, 8, 288–9): "Ich sage: schlechthin in allem abgeleiteten Wissen, oder in der Erscheinung ist ein Widerspruch zwsichen dem Thun, und dem Sagen: propositio facto contraria."

26 1804/2 19.142 (GA II, 8, 288–9).

27 Ibid., 290–1.

28 The following is my reconstruction, more or less corresponding to Gueroult's D^3, although Fichte would seem to invite this by introducing the *von* according to two premises and a conclusion (these two premises are themselves the conclusions of "B^3" and "C^3." Moreover, it is common throughout the phenomenology for Fichte skip over sections of his arguments by merely subjecting them to performative contradiction in order to save time; since the *tun-sagen* accord is at the heart of the fivefold synthesis, presumably, one could expand every use of performative contradiction into a fivefold argument.

29 1804/2 19.145 (GA II, 8, 296–7).

30 1804/2 19.146 (GA II, 8, 298–9).

31 Gueroult divides the phenomenology into three syntheses, each of which has five syntheses in turn. "C" is 16–20; "D" is 20–5; "E" is 25–8. Lecture twenty therefore is his conclusion of the *Soll*, both synthesis fifteen (E^3) and sixteen $A^4 = E^3$.

32 1804/2 20.149 (GA II, 304–5).

33 1804/2 20.150 (GA II, 306–7).

34 1804/2 20.152 (GA II, 8, 310–11).

35 1804/2 21.154 (GA II, 8, 316–17).

36 This duality is inherited from Kant and finds only tentative solutions in CPR. See Lachièze-Rey, *L'Idéalisme kantien*, 149ff. See also Maréchal, *Le Point de depart*, IV, 92–101. Cf. CPR B 154 (AA III, 121).

37 1804/2 21.154 (GA II, 8, 316–17).

38 The metaphor is not a random one; indeed, it would seem to be one that Fichte encourages his readers to find, since this "second part of the second part" is preparing the terrain for a logic of discourse, or hermeneutics. Consciousness is discursivity itself. Discourse always

presupposes something unsaid. From within any given proposition, the unsaid must remain inchoate, otherwise the proposition will sink into tautology. It is, in other words, in speaking that one "makes sense," not in giving preambles to what one will say. In this spirit, Didier Julia uses similarly imagery. Cf. Julia, *La Question de l'homme,* 273.

39 1804/2 21.154 (GA II, 8, 316–17).

40 1804/2 21.155 (GA II, 8, 318–19).

41 1804/2 21.156 (GA II, 8, 320–1).

42 For Gueroult, the self-application of genesis in lecture twenty-one is synthesis seventeen (B^4). ES II.127.

43 1804/2 21.159 (GA II, 8, 326–7).

44 1804/2 22.160 (GA II, 8, 330–1).

45 1804/2 22.161 (GA II, 8, 332–3). The German reads: "Absolute Sichgenesis, und derselben ein Princip gegeben, im Wissen versteht sich, welches da eben ein Principiieren ist[.]"

46 1804/2 22.162 (GA II, 8, 334–5). In Kantian terms, this is meant to eliminate the heterogeneity between the sensible and intelligible, the task Fichte first set for his listeners at 1804/2 2.31 (GA II, 8, 26–9).

47 Lecture twenty-two, which opens the theory of principles, is a transitional lecture, providing an overview of the phenomenology as a whole. Its main contribution to the content of the WL is to assert that the factical is genetic. Gueroult groups it with lecture twenty-three in synthesis (C^4) as "first aspect" at ES II.127–8.

48 1804/2 22.164 (GA II, 8, 338–9).

49 Lecture twenty-three, which begins with this point, constitutes synthesis eighteen (C^4) along with lecture twenty-two but bears the brunt of the weight. Here, "the content of this knowledge [of the absolute principle of this absolute fact] is the internal necessity or certainty of the rapport between genesis and non-genesis." ES II.128.

50 1804/2 23.166 (GA II, 8, 344–5).

51 For Gueroult, certainty revisits the work done on the genesis of genesis in lecture twenty-one. Both lectures twenty-one and twenty-three describe movements that are born of the internal structure (that is, the internal necessity) of the *Soll.* Both also speak of the need for discourse. Yet in lecture twenty-one, discourse seemed to be a logical incongruity, an internal gap in genesis. In lecture twenty-three, it belongs to the whole movement of internal necessity, becoming internal when the inner/outer

distinction is reconfigured. Cf. ES II.128, "We discover in a new way what was produced in synthesis B^4 …"

52 1804/II 23.167 (GA II, 8, 346–7).

53 Ibid. This is the key passage on certainty, from which the whole lecture can be reconstructed.

54 1804/II 23.168 (GA II, 8, 348–9).

55 Ibid.

56 1804/2 23.169 (GA II, 8, 350–1).

57 Didier Julia offers an extensive analysis of lecture twenty-three, which he sees as the completion of Fichte's phenomenology and the move toward a logic. "In the twenty-third lecture, reflection achieves [*réalise*] absolute knowing through the feeling of certainty, but does not yet prove it; certainty is a fact that does not explain itself. Yet this demonstration or explanation is required by the essence of knowing itself: in phenomenological reality, the feeling of certainty coincides with the act of describing, with an intuition, i.e., with the projection through words or propositions. Certainty is only real ground insofar as it grounds the actual moment of discourse by means of concepts." Julia, *La Question de l'homme*, 285.

58 Lecture twenty-three is for Ulrich Schlösser the heart of the WL. He offers an extensive reconstruction of its arguments. Writes Schlösser in conclusion, "Certainty is thought of not just as a process, but as a self-regulating process, not just according to the blueprint of being-oneself [*Selbstsein*], but of self-determination – in such a way that there is no mere knowledge of determination. Rather, the original knowledge itself is the determining factor. Fichte thus posits the thesis that the process depicted is not only to be identified with life in the sense of living things, but with reason itself." Schlösser, *Das Erfassen des Einleuchtens*, 152–3; his full reconstruction is found at 137–53.

59 1804/2 23.170 (GA II, 8, 352–3). Here, light is directly identified with the transcendental *we*.

60 This metaphor is crucial in Fichte's reconfiguration of inner/outer in lectures twenty-two to twenty-five, one of the main aspects of certainty. Gueroult's concise definition of the term is helpful here. It is "An objective projection that constitutes the description (*Aussage, sprechen*) of being intuited in its qualitative unity." ES II.129.

61 See Aquinas, *Summa Theologiae, Tertia Pars*, qq. 75 and 78. For Aquinas, the transformation is accomplished in language (q. 78 art. 1.) and is likened

to God's creation of the world through the Verb (q. 75 art. 7). Yet in the becoming of the sacarament, nothing new is actually created. It is this "creative speech act" (to adopt contemporary language) as repetition and not creation that leads Fichte to use transubstantiation as metaphor.

62 1804/2 23.170 (GA II, 8, 354–5).

63 1804/2 23.171 (GA II, 8, 354–5).

64 Ibid., 356–7.

65 1804/2 24.172 (GA II, 8, 358–9).

66 Ibid. Translation modified.

67 1804/2 24.174 (GA II, 8, 362–3).

68 A law is "a principle that, in order to provide a principle factically, presupposes yet another absolutely self-producing principle" 1804/2 24.174 (GA 8, II, 263). "ein Prinzip, welches zu seinem faktischen Principiieren noch ein anderes, absolut sich selber erzeugendes Princip voraussetzt[.]" For Gueroult, the introduction of law is the key move in synthesis nineteen (D^4), ES II.130–1. Writes Didier Julia: "Projection, which constitutes the essence of knowing and which corresponded in lecture twenty-three to the word, is objectified in lecture twenty-four as language-structure: from an objective point of view, it corresponds to the act of predication." Julia, *La Question de l'homme*, 293.

69 1804/2 24.175 (GA II, 8, 364–5).

70 Ibid.

71 This is the clarification of what was only foreshadowed in lecture fifteen: "this content [i.e., of the *we*] brings only the mere repetition and repeated supposition of one and the same I, or We, which is entirely self-enclosed." 1804/2 15.117 (GA II, 8, 232–3).

72 1804/2 24.176 (GA II, 8, 366–7).

73 Ibid., 368–9.

74 1804/2 25.179 (GA II, 8, 372–3).

75 1804/2 25.180 (GA II, 8, 374–5). For Gueroult, this total removal of the material is the contribution of lecture twenty-five, synthesis twenty (E^4), and the completion of the fourth "point of view of reflection." ES II.131–2.

76 1804/2 25.180 (GA II, 8, 374–5).

77 The results of the WL are essentially the same as those of Jacobi's system. At the end of the WL, nothing new has been achieved, no concrete result can be claimed. Fichte's *philosophia prima* has given us an awareness of life, a consciousness of what we are and what we have done all along, though

inchoately. Particular truths may be fleeting, but one always lives the moment of truth *sub specie aeternitatis* (cf. Julia, *La Question de l'homme,* 312). Fichte is thus able to arrive rationally at the *Gefühl* [Feeling] that Jacobi was seeking. This *Gefühl* was reason all along, only Jacobi could not see it. See, for example, the preface to Jacobi's 1799 open letter to Fichte: "It would not be any reproach to Transcendental Philosophy that it does not know anything about God, for it is universally acknowledged that God cannot be *known,* but only *believed in.* A God who could be *known* would be no God at all." MPW 500 (*Jacobi an Fichte* [1799], ix).

78 1804/2 26.184 (GA II, 8, 382–3).

79 1804/2 26.184–5 (GA II, 8, 382–3).

80 1804/2 23.167 (GA II, 8, 346–7).

81 1804/2 26.185 (GA II, 8, 384–5).

82 1804/2 24.174 (GA II, 8, 362–3).

83 1804/2 26.185 (GA II, 8, 384–5).

84 Ibid.

85 1804/2 26.185–6 (GA II, 8, 386–7).

86 One should follow the summary on 187 (GA II, 8, 388–9) rather than the enumerated list on 186. Martial Gueroult does not condense this description of fivefoldness into a deduction, as I have done above, though he does recognize it as the "realization of the synthesis" that is at the core of lecture twenty-six (synthesis twenty-two, A^5 was, of course, equal to E^4, the transition from the fourth to the fifth "point of view of reflection"). ES II.133–5.

87 1804/2 26.188 (GA II, 8, 392–3).

88 Ibid.

89 1804/2 27.190 (GA II, 8, 396–7).

90 Indeed, this is the reason why "intuition" is never qualified in 1804; it is described as neither intellectual nor sensible but simply as intuition. This is what seeing, as metaphor for intuition, is meant to capture. On this matter, Dieter Henrich offers a helpful description. In commenting on the phrase from the 1801–02 WL "self-consciousness is an activity in which an eye is inserted," Henrich writes, "An eye *is* inserted into the activity. This nuance sharpens the sense of [Fichte's] new formula. It emphasizes that the activity can never be found unless the eye is also present: If the eye *comes to be inserted,* then activity takes place before it contains the eye. If the eye *is* inserted, then activity and eye together form a single essence. The eye is

related to the act not as an ornament is to a body, but as the heart is to life." Henrich, "Fichte's Original Insight," 31. A marginal note such as this one is not the place to address the fact that Henrich sees that formulation as wanting and that it will eventually slip back into the "problem of reflection." In this context, it suffices to say, with Daniel Breazeale, that the problem of reflection is inherent to the problem of thought and that because thought is always embodied, reflection has already been integrated into the WL. Self-conscious is always already consciousness and vice-versa. Fichte solved Henrich's problem at the outset – if it can be called a problem at all (cf. Breazeale, *Thinking Through*, 166). Here, in lecture twenty-seven's discourse on formal seeing, Fichte reaffirms in 1804 what was already established in 1794. The most basic logical structure of the WL, the "unity theory of intuition," never changes.

91 While Gueroult adopts a markedly cartesian tack, he still identifies the basic structure of this argument: "Vision necessarily sees, we necessarily posit its existence (Seeing = appearance, existence, knowing, *Verbum*)" (ES II.138). This is synthesis twenty-three (C^5) found in the first part of lecture twenty-seven. ES II.137–8.

92 1804/2 27.191 (GA II, 8, 398–9).

93 1804/2 27.193 (GA II, 8, 402–3).

94 This is Gueroult's synthesis twenty-four, found in the second half of lecture twenty-seven. ES II.138–9.

95 Julius Drechsler offers the following commentary: "Appearance as expression and revelation of the absolute has in itself the character of necessity. The true manifestation of an absolute no longer acts from itself, but has its existence from something higher, which supports it and from which it lives. Seen from this point of view, the problem of freedom receives a completely new illumination in the second period of the *Wissenschaftslehre*. For Fichte, true freedom can only be found in action that comes from being moved by the absolute. Without this relatedness to the absolute and boundness to the absolute, there is no real freedom." Drechsler, *Fichtes Lehre vom Bild*, 133. The "new illumination" of which Drechsler speaks is a clarification and change in presentation, brought about by the explicit foundation of freedom in the absolute named as such, not a new idea of freedom.

96 1804/2 27.194 (GA II, 8, 404–5).

97 1804/2 27.195 (GA II, 8, 406–7).

98 This continuation of the WL, moving from *principiieren* to the principles

of specific forms of appearance, is a task that Fichte will undertake in the *The Principles of the Doctrines of God, Morals, and Right* (1805). This text can legitimately be called part of Fichte's *Philosophia Prima* – yet not on its own. If principles are always *from principiieren*, then the very generation of principles, the aseity of principledness, is the beating heart of first philosophy, and that can only be the WL.

99 Here, in lecture twenty-eight, is Gueroult's synthesis twenty-five (E^5), ES II.139–43. He is transitioning toward the *Way towards the Blessed Life*, which expands on the content of this lecture and is the next step in his extensive commentary.

100 1804/2 28.201 (GA II, 8, 420–1).

PART TWO

1 Unlike in part one, the works treated in part two cannot rely on a contemporary scholarly translation with which to work; the English versions of two of the texts dealt with herein, the *Characteristics of the Present Age* and *The Way towards the Blessed Life* are outdated, having appeared between 1848 and 1899. They can be found in *The Popular Works of Johann Gottlieb Fichte*, trans. William Smith, ed. Daniel Breazeale. In the case of the *Principles of the Doctrines of God, Morals, and Right*, no English version is available. From here on, all translations are those of the author. Readers of French should consult *Le Caractère de l'époque actuelle*, trans. Ives Radrizzani; *Principes de la doctrine de Dieu, de la morale et du droit*, trans. Grégoire Lazare, and *L'Initiation à la vie bienheureuse*, trans. Patrick Cerutti et al.

Reinhard Lauth has attempted to reconstruct a Fichtean philosophy of nature in *Die transzendentale Naturlehre Fichtes*. For his part, as late as 1812, Fichte still expressed the desire to write a philosophy of nature. Cf. GA III, 8, 6.

2 GA I, 9, 71–2. There is a similar, if shorter, declaration on methodology in the *Characteristics*, GA I, 8, 235–6.

3 Fichte's definition of religion confirms this. In lecture two of the *Blessed Life*, he claims that religion is the possession and vision of God by one's self, with one's own eyes, and not those of another. It is this personal conviction (*my* possessing, *my* seeing) that allows one to speak of the absolute with felt conviction as God. Cf. GA I, 9, 69.

CHAPTER THREE

1 *Zufällige Gedanken in einer schlaflosen Nacht*, GA II, 1, 104–5.

2 *Beitrag zur Berichtigung der Urtheile des Publicums über die französische Revolution*, GA I, 1, 203–404; *Contribution to the Correction of the Public's Judgments on the French Revolution*, trans. and ed. Jeffrey Church and Anna Maria Schön.

3 This projected second part is documented in Marco Ivaldo, "L'approche pratique et éthique de l'histoire," 50.

4 Rousseau writes in the *Discourse* (1755): "O Man, whatever land you may be from, whatever may be your opinions, listen; Here is your history such as I believe I read it, not in the books by your kind, who are liars, but in Nature, which never lies." Rousseau, *The Discourses*, 133. Kant's *Idea of a Universal History on a Cosmopolitan Plan* [*Idee zu einer allgemeinen Geschichte in weltbürgerlicher Absicht*] (1784) will be addressed in the course of this chapter's exposition.

5 The *Letters* were published as *The Philosophy of Freemasony* [*Philosophie der Mauerei*] in 1802–03. GA I, 8.

6 This claim is made in Hammacher, "Comment Fichte accède à l'histoire," 401.

7 Cf. 1804/2 28.195 (GA II, 8, 406–9).

8 FiG I, n. 446, 375.

9 In lecture nine of the *Characteristics*, Fichte declares that physics is the first part of empiricism and history the second. GA I, 8, 295.

10 This is Wolfgang Janke's hypothesis. He sees the *Characteristics* as a primarily political text, the ancestor of the *Speeches to the German Nation* (1808) and the *Staatslehre* (1813). *Die dreifache Vollendung*, 221–2.

11 This was a source of disappointment for a number of Fichte's more dedicated students, who followed both the lectures on the WL and the popular lectures from the same period. Cf., FiG III, no. 1533, 274.

12 FNR 40 (GA I, 3, 349).

13 Radrizzani provides an authoritative account: "If one examines more closely the act by which the I enters history, it turns out that the process of individuation that the summons makes possible is simultaneously free and determined, both formally and materially. This apparent paradox results from the fact that the foundation of my causality lies, at the same time, both outside and inside of me. It lies outside of me because, if a being outside of

me did not act causally on me and did not address a summons to me, in a general way, I would not be able to undertake an action. Moreover, my action is also determined materially, for through the summons, the general sphere of my action is indicated to me." Radrizzani, "Fichte's Philosophy of History," 279.

14 Cf. 1804/2 16.121–3 (GA II, 8, 242–9).

15 *Resignation* [1784], in SWN 2/1, 401–3. Fichte offered a rebuttal as early as the *franzözische Revolution* text of 1793, writing there that it is too late to evaluate Socrates's virtue after he has been executed. GA I, 1, 210–11. Cf. Radrizzani, "L'engagement historique," 30–1.

16 Schiller died before the defeat of the Holy Roman Empire at the Battle of Austerlitz in December 1805. His friends – Goethe chief among them – found his silence about Napoleon irresponsible. Cf. Müller-Seidel, *Schiller und die Politik,* esp. chapter 5, "Napoleon ante portas: Das Verschweigen einer Gegnerschaft."

17 In this respect, Fichte is much indebted to Kant, who was also looking for an a priori that governs the progression of history in his *Idea of a Universal History on a Cosmpolitan Plan* (1784). Yet Kant seeks to ground this a priori in nature, which Fichte would find incongruous: "One can regard the history of the human species in the large as the completion of a hidden plan of nature to bring about an inwardly and, to this end, also an externally perfect state constitution, as the only condition in which it can fully develop all its predispositions in humanity." Kant, *Idea for a Universal History with a Cosmopolitan Aim*, trans. Allen W. Wood, 116 (AA 8, 27). Aside from the insistence on nature, Fichte would also object to the lack of subjectivity in Kant's account. The "hidden plan of nature" allows neither for moral agency nor religious sentiment to develop socially in time. "A natural plan" that somehow secretly aligns with the moral calling of human subjects is also irreconcilable with the mechanistic concept of nature found in the first Critique. For discussion and commentary, see di Giovanni, *Freedom and Religion*, 22–4.

18 Marco Ivaldo comments on the singular role of history in Fichte's system: "The doctrine of history, however, also presupposes and intersects with other doctrines. We can conceive the system of human activity in time only if we possess the concept of time and if we know what action and interaction are; on the other hand, time, action, and interaction manifest themselves in lived experience always according to an historical dimension

that qualifies them and makes them concrete … History is not a sphere that stands next to the other four. It rather is a horizon in which religion, morality, society, and nature manifest themselves." DM 40.

19 See bibliography. Immanuel Hermann Fichte reproduces this text exactly in SW VII. The first and the twelfth lectures were first published separately, as journal articles in the reviews *Eunomia* and *Geschichte und Politik*, respectively, in 1805.

20 GA I, 8, 245. Cf. Lauth, "Fichtes Lehrtätigkeit," 222.

21 Quoted in Lauth, "Fichtes Lehrtätigkeit," 223. Lauth describes the extraordinary public response to Fichte's popular lectures at 219–24.

22 Xavier Léon offers a detailed account in *Fichte et son Temps,* vol. 2, 464–9.

23 At GA I, 8, 193–4.

24 GA I, 8, 196.

25 Cf. 1804/2 1.23 (GA II, 8, 8–9).

26 As Ives Radrizziani writes, "If philosophy must be able to be completed, the philosophy of history, insofar as it belongs to philosophy, must also be apt to be completed; that is to say, it must be possible to exhaust the a priori structure of factical events, bracketing their factical content, which, on its own, does not belong to philosophy. In other words, it must be possible to present an exhaustive deduction of the transcendental structure of history." Radrizzani, "L'Engagement historique," 26.

27 GA I, 8, 196–7.

28 Ibid., 198.

29 Ibid., 199.

30 Ibid., 200.

31 For Radrizzani, this is a meta-historical end: "Its function [i.e., the meta-historical end] is to provide a key to reading history, a meta-historical standard of interpretation that can judge the progress accomplished in the course of history, as well as guide to rational construction of the future." Radrizzani, "L'Engagement historique," 32. Elsewhere, he writes that the progression that is the *Weltplan* gives meaning to historical events: "Independent of the course of history and of the part of rationality guiding man in his actions, the universal plan gives a 'synoptic view' of the possible progress of humanity, and serves as a standard for evaluating the respective contribution of each age. It is only in the light of such a plan that events take on meaning, as an illustration of the progress or retreat of humanity in relation to the pursuit of its ends," Radrizzani, "Fichte's Philosophy of History," 285.

32 On this reading, the *Characteristics*' main goal is to provide Fichte's theory of intersubjectivity, elaborated at the end of the Jena Period in the WL *Nova Methodo*, with a phenomenological dimension. This interpretation is made possible by the work of Ives Radrizzani ("L'Engagement historique"; also, his French translation of the *Characteristics, Le Caractère de l'époque actuelle*; and in particular, his groundbreaking work, *Vers la fondation de l'intersubjectivité chez Fichte*). Such an interpretation, however, traces its origins back to Philonenko, *La Liberté humaine dans la philosophie de Fichte*. Therein, one finds a strong justification of the lynchpin argument: freedom is reason's becoming.

33 In this sense, the third age can be compared to the *Lager des Todes* of 1804/2 lecture fifteen. Its goal is to contain a historical *projectum*. Fichte affirms that the third age is a unique transitional space in the fifth lecture. GA I, 8, 244.

34 GA I, 8, 221.

35 Ibid., 209. Note the WL's realism-idealism dialectic begins with the same position: the search for an *Urbegriff*.

36 This is the criticism of "empty formalism" (Hegel) or "*qualitas occulta*" (Fichte) levelled against Kant's Categorical Imperative by his successors. Cf. Hegel, *Elements of the Philosophy of Right*, § 135; Fichte, SE 52 (SW IV, 50). Kant, it would seem, is the philosopher of the third age. And while Kantianism has shortcomings, it represents the movement forward from the second to the third age, reason's initial emancipation.

37 Here, Fichte is not claiming that reason is the absolute but rather that there is one life, the life of reason. This is a popular rendition of the more subtle conclusion found at 1804/2 lecture fourteen. GA I, 8, 210.

38 GA I, 8, 213.

39 This is contrary to the case of animals, who possess a bodily a priori in the form of instinct. Cf. GA I, 8, 214.

40 This is the position of higher idealism, cf. WL 1804/2 lecture thirteen.

41 GA I, 8, 220. Cf. Mt. 16:24.

42 Fichte explains the notion of a Summons at §16 of the *Nova Methodo*: "How is the act of reflection we have just described possible? It is possible only in such a way that the cognition involved in a limitation brought about by a concept, that is, the cognition of a concept of individuality, which limits me, is itself impossible apart from an act of willing – and vice versa. The latter point, that willing is possible only by means of cognition, is clear and is valid for all consciousness But the first half of this statement, that

cognition is impossible without willing, can be thought of only as follows: An act of willing would have to be contained within the cognition in question, and all that would be grasped within such cognition would be the given determinability of the act of willing. That is, we are not free to choose whether we will view the matter in this particular manner or not; willing could not be understood in any other way. Expressed differently, the concept that is here involved is that of a summons to willing, a summons to free activity … The entire determinate act that is involved here is a summons to engage in free activity. Self-consciousness originates with my act of selection from a general mass of rational beings as such. This is the deepest point of consciousness: As soon as anyone achieves consciousness, he perceives himself. This perception of oneself is impossible without a concept of a mass of rational beings. Therefore, the concept of selfhood is a concept constructed from the concept of a mass of rational beings. This concept of selfhood as a 'person' is impossible without a concept of a rational being outside of us. Accordingly, this concept too is constructed by an act in which something is selected from a higher and more encompassing sphere. The first representation I can have is that of being summoned, as an individual, to engage in an act of free willing.)" FPT, 350–1. Translation modified. See also FNR 53–84. For commentary, see Breazeale, *Thinking Through*, 175–82. The reader should also consult Radrizzani's *Vers la fondation de l'intersubjectivité chez Fichte*.

43 GA I, 8, 221. In the 1805 *Essence of the Scholar* [*Wesen des Gelehrten*], Christ is compared to a scholar and the sacrifices of the scholarly life described as Christlike, cf. GA I, 8, 125–31.

44 Cf. GA I, 8, 223. The criticism would seem to be directed both at the *philosophes* whose thought culminated in the reign of terror and the more Leibnizian Enlightenment thinkers of Germany, such as J.J. Spalding and Moses Mendelssohn, whose Panglossian worldview was countered in Fichte's *The Vocation of Humankind* (1800). If Kant is the philosopher who brings us forward into the third age, the *Aufklärer* are a regression back to the second. For a fuller account, see Radrizzani, "La Doctrine de la science et l'Aufklärung."

45 This is Hegel's opinion as well. Cf. *The Phenomenology of Spirit* [1807], §584–95. In the Hegelian perspective, Fichte's third age is that of self-alienated spirit. What Hegel sees as its successor, romanticism, was largely generated by the reception of Fichte's work. The *Characteristics* is, on this

reading, a corrective to the historical moment that Fichte had set in motion. Xavier Léon expounds at length on this interpretation, detailing Fichte's position against "the evolution of romanticism towards Catholicism," cf. Léon, *Fichte et son temps*, vol. 2, 394–422.

46 GA I, 8, 234. Fichte will explore this line of thought more fully in the *Blessed Life*.

47 Ibid., 235.

48 Cf. Jn. 6:63; GA I, 8, 236.

49 GA I, 8, 269.

50 Ibid., 275. This third phase of Christianity bears much resemblance to the third age of Joachim de Fiore. Here, Fichte is in agreement with Schelling, who calls this phase of Christianity the age of "The Church of Saint John," an age of the Spirit that is successor to the Church of Peter (Catholicism) and the Church of Paul (Protestantism). See F.W.J. Schelling, *Urfassung der Philosophie der Offenbarung*. For an overview of Fiore and his role in the German Idealist conception of salvation history, see Sean McGrath, "The Tyranny of Consumer-Capitalism."

51 "*Was da nur wirklich nothwendig da ist, ist schlechthin nothwendig also da, wie es da ist; es könnte nicht auch nicht da seyn, noch könnte es auch anders da seyn, als es da ist.*" GA I, 8, 296. The italics are Fichte's.

52 GA I, 8, 298. While Fichte first achieves a deduction of the separation [*Spaltung*] of knowledge into self-consciousness in the WL *Nova Methodo* (FTP § 13), it is only in the 1804/2 WL that it becomes clear that the realm of particular consciousness is language, as is made clear in the concept of principle-providing [*principiieren*], cf. 1804/2 lecture twenty-three.

53 GA I, 8, 300.

54 Ibid., 312.

55 These five periods of the state also correspond to the five standpoints of the *Blessed Life*.

56 GA I, 8, 343–4.

57 Ibid., 365.

58 Ibid., 375.

59 Cf. WL 1804/2 lecture twenty-five.

60 Cf. GA I, 8, 377–8. Xavier Léon observes that after Novalis's *Europa* speech (1799; first printed 1802), German intellectual life took a distinctly Catholic turn; A.G. Schlegel and Ludwig Tieck introduced Catholic baroque thought into the German language through translations of Calderón and Cervantes,

and Friedreich Schlegel would convert to Catholicism in 1808. Cf. Léon, *Fichte et son temps*, vol. II, 410–15.

61 GA I, 8, 380.

62 Ibid., 382.

63 Ibid., 386–7.

CHAPTER FOUR

1 *Jenaische Allgemeine Literaturzeitung, Intelligenzblatt* 126, op. cit. Lauth, "Fichtes Lehrtätigkeit," 218.

2 Cf. 1804/2 3.38 (GA II, 8, 44–7) and 23.170 (GA II, 8, 352–5).

3 GA II, 7, 316.

4 Ibid., 311.

5 These have been published in ibid., 289–368.

6 It is Lauth's opinion (ibid., 299) that Fichte knew this by the fifth lecture (cf. ibid., 316). One can only presume that, having taken a *louis d'or* from every listener, he felt compelled to give the twenty-four planned lectures. Fichte's own stubbornness surely played a role in the decision.

7 Spalding's Father, Johann Joachim Spalding, was himself author of an important philosophical work that went through many editions, called *Die Bestimmung des Menschen*, a title Fichte would also use in 1800, though it prefaced a very different work. The elder Spalding died in Berlin in May of 1804. See di Giovanni, *Freedom and Religion*, 1–33.

8 "So ist es, wenn populär, gemein; wenn nicht gemein, unverständlich." GA II, 7, 299.

9 For example, at GA II, 7, 350.

10 GA II, 7, 371.

11 Johann Gottlieb Fichte, *Die Principien der Gottes- Sitten- und Rechtslehre: Februar und März 1805*, ed. Reinhard Lauth (Hamburg: Felix Meiner Verlag, 1986); GA II, 7, 370–489. While GA is canonical and used here throughout, the Meiner edition has the advantage of filling in a number of elliptical expressions; Fichte often made use of the abbreviation pp, i.e., "*perge perge*" (latin for "go on, go on …") whenever a previously used formulation was to be pronounced. It is not always obvious to the reader what pp stands for; that it is made explicit in the Meiner edition makes the text more readable.

12 GA II, 7, 376.

13 Both because of its recent publication and the difficulties of interpretation,

little has been published on the *Principles*. The most important work to date is Marco Ivaldo's article "The Doctrine of Manifestation in Fichte's *Principien* (1805)," here abbreviated as DM. The divisions made herein largely follow Ivaldo, who posits the following: 1. Prolegomena; 2–7. Knowledge as *Daseyn*, external or existential act of the absolute (with lectures 2–3, 4–5, and 6–7 each containing seven "moments"); 8–13. Making genetic the absolute's existential act; 14–17. Practical aspect of the genetic existential act; 18–23. The passage from a practical imperative to absolute knowledge (DM 42, 47). Wolfgang Janke dedicates some twenty pages to the *Principles* but does not offer a structural commentary. He considers the *Principles* to be a series of *Solls*, linking the various standpoints and subsuming them under WL, and focuses on what he considers to be the transitions from God to world-consciousness in lecture fourteen and from subjectivity to morality in lecture seventeen. These transition points are compatible with Ivaldo's division (Janke, *Die dreifache Vollendung*, 318–37). The only monograph written about the *Principles,* Matthias Müller's *Theologie im Transzensus*, does not offer an extended commentary on the *Principles*. Rather, it follows Ivaldo's analysis and uses it as a springboard for elaborating a systematic theology.

14 GA II, 7, 378. In the 1804 WL, what is simultaneously synthetic and analytic is light as immanent self-projection. Cf. 1804/2 23.170 (GA II, 8, 352–5).

15 Fichte adds here, "with prudence, however" [*mit Bedacht, also*]. This phrase must be understood in terms of the WL, not simply an indwelling of the Holy Spirit.

16 GA II, 7, 378.

17 Cf. GA I, 8, 365–6 (fifteenth lecture).

18 GA II, 7, 379.

19 Throughout, I render *Recht* as right and *Gesetz* as law.

20 1804/2 28.199–200 (GA II, 8, 416–21).

21 Notably missing from this lecture series is objective factical thinking, *Naturphilosophie*. As was just said, Fichte considers its basic elements to have been covered here through the inclusion of its subjective corollary, right. Nature, in sum, is not a kind of discourse but that which allows for the possibility of discourse.

22 GA II, 7, 380. Throughout, *Daseyn* is treated as a technical term and left in German.

23 Ibid.

24 Ibid., 381.

25 On the relationship between these five standpoints, Wolfgang Janke writes, "These follow a dialectic of sublation, since the lower level of rational science is negated in its independence, but in its rationality preserved and through a higher world-standpoint elevated." Janke, *Die dreifache Vollendung*, 318.

26 Lectures two and three constitute an argumentative whole, with enumerated points begun in two continuing in three. This is also the case for lectures four and five. Moreover, the two latter retrace the steps of two and three.

27 This shift back to pre-Berlin vocabulary (indeed, as we saw in 1804/2, intellectual intuition had largely been replaced by *Einsicht*) signals Fichte's desire to reincorporate the Jena apparatus into this work.

28 Marco Ivaldo highlights this consistency of vocabulary in the 1805 texts: "Knowledge is 'external,' the existence of the absolute. This principle is derived from intellectual intuition; 'one has understood correctly if one understands that knowledge and … the existent (*Daseyn*) stand in an immediate unity, and that their immediate identity yields at one and the same time the being-for-itself of knowledge [Cf. GA II, 7, 384]. In the Erlangen Wissenschaftslehre, written only a few months earlier, in Summer 1805, we find the formula: '… in itself, knowledge is the absolute [existence] … or the existence of the absolute …' [GA II, 9, 185]." DM 48. As Isabelle Thomas-Fogiel will note in the preface to her French translation of the 1805 WL, here, Fichte is approaching the split between being and thought as the knowing of being; 1804/2 approached the same from the other side, as the being of knowing. Cf. Thomas-Fogiel, *Présentation*, in Fichte, *La Doctrine de la Science de 1805*, 9–37.

29 GA II, 7, 384.

30 The *from* is a key concept in the WL's phenomenology, and its absence here – as we shall see in detail later – complicates the *Principles*'s presentation. Hoping to develop the concept of *Erscheinung* or appearance in accord with the ideas of "principle" and "principle-providing" (here nominalized into "*Principiat*" where the WL had the more accurate verbal form, "*principiieren*"), Fichte leaves the *from* out of his presentation. He could have only stood to gain from its inclusion. Not only was the *from* in need of development in the WL, expressing a radical autonomy, it could have highlighted more clearly the dynamic link between the categorical *Soll* and knowing, equivalent to immanence and projection. The *from* could

have made explicit that projection, as we will see in the practical genesis of knowing, is *someone's project.*

31 GA II, 7, 384.

32 Ibid., 385.

33 Ibid.

34 A reference to §1, 2, and 3 of the 1794 *Foundation*. The "I" that became a "we" in the being of knowing of 1804 is now, under the aegis of the knowing of being, "*Daseyn*."

35 Ivaldo summarizes, "If, on this basis, one were to extract an initial synthetic result with respect to the *Was* of the existence of the absolute, one would obtain a structure with four elements. The first three elements – identity, difference, relation – concern the *Daseyn* of the absolute. The fourth is the absolute as such, in itself. Let us examine this last [element]. First, *Daseyn* is self-position, absolute genesis, immanent power, the identity of self with self. Second, it is such 'insofar as' it 'externalizes' itself. Third, in its 'self-externalizing,' it depicts itself externally, and in doing so it connects, through 'an external activity,' the external and the internal. Fourth, it is all of this as *Daseyn* of the absolute; in this way (as an 'internal external') it is the existence of the absolute, relation to pure being (cf. WL 1805, 16) [GA II, 9, p. 190]." DM 48.

36 In the 1804/2 WL, the fivefold synthesis is presented in detail twice: first with the introduction of the *Soll* at lecture sixteen and again in lecture twenty-six, where it shows the completeness of Fichte's system. Here in the *Principles*, a similar strategy using strikingly familiar deductions is at work: the synthesis of *Daseyn* found here in lecture two will be completed by the foundational synthesis in lectures nineteen and twenty.

37 GA II, 7, 387.

38 Ibid., 391.

39 Fichte's theory of the image does not, in the first instance, refer to the visual arts. But the analogy is helpful. In this spirit, Thomas-Fogiel writes the following: "In the figurative painting of the classical age, the work of art refers us to an external object – a face, a landscape, a *historia* – that it is meant to represent. To use Alberti's metaphor in *Della Pittura*, the painting is a 'window unto the world.' Still, the painting defines itself as painting, otherwise it would be neither painting, nor window, but instead itself the world. It therefore contains indices that designate it as a painting, i.e., as

the product of a painter and not an object found in nature. These indices prevent the distracted spectator from mistaking the painting for the thing it represents. The painting, while indicating something other than itself, also indicates that it is something that 'indicates something else.' It ultimately therefore refers to itself. 'A window unto the world,' the painting is at the same time and in the same context *index sui*." Thomas-Fogiel, *Fichte*, 135. This twofold character of the image is precisely the viewer's capacity for *Einsehen*. Similarly, if one requires light to see *that* there is a painting at all, so too is light *qua* representation required within the painting – one says that the painter rendered the lighting beautifully, even if one cannot see the light within the painting as an object. The light in the world is analogous to awareness-of-knowing and the light in the painting to the constructed nature of art, to *Daseyn-of-Daseyn*.

40 GA II, 7, 392–3.

41 A law is "a principle that, in order to provide a principle factically, presupposes yet another absolutely self-producing principle." 1804/2 24.174 (GA II, 8, 362–3). Let us recall that one of the conclusions of lecture twenty-four was that knowing produces an image, or what is the same, seeing is principle-providing. In other words, projection and predication go hand in hand.

42 Writing about both the 1805 Erlangen WL and the *Principles*, J-C. Goddard suggests that: "Originary vision, seeing itself, cannot be seen by anyone. No seeing subject precedes it, and it is only through seeing that seeing subjects come into being. That is why the correlative seeing that is the discursive articulation of the seen is itself necessarily vision. Seeing cannot be seen but through folding over onto itself [*moyennant un pli sur soi*]. Said otherwise: ob-jective existence is not seen because it appears before the eyes of the subject, but because it is the necessary existence of existence – because its being-there [être-là] is itself there for itself. The very meaning of ob-jectivity is here radically changed: the ob-ject is fundamentally subject, that is, reflection. The singularity of Fichtean idealism is that reflexivity does not consist in a subject facing the objective world and experiencing itself as a determinate self, but rather the facticity of the world itself, i.e., the differentiated existence of being. It is a fold [*pli*] in existence. A fold in the externality of being [*du dehors de l'être*]." Goddard, "Réflexivité, affectivité et anéantissement de soi," 224–5. "*Le pli*" would seem to be his translation of *zurückgebogen*. The latter term is first found here, and then developed

in Erlangen. Fichte himself says that this sheds new light on the WL.

43 Ivaldo expresses the contradiction as follows: "Knowledge, then, is an emergence from itself (according to its principle), but it is an emergence that (according to its content) is not an emergence from itself. In its being, a sequence (a self-exteriorization) is included that is not a self-exteriorization. Once again the 'contradiction' appears between form and content, the 'exterior' and the 'interior.'" DM 50–1.

44 Fichte uses the Greek letters alpha, beta, gamma.

45 GA II, 7, 396.

46 For Wolfgang Janke, the *Principles* is an extended application of the *Soll* that was conceptually defined in 1804/2, with each standpoint finding its link to its superior and inferior neighbour via a *Soll*, cf. Janke, *Die dreifache Vollendung*, 319.

47 Fichte is essentially repeating the argument that secures rational projection in 1804/2 lecture twenty-three, called projection *per transsubstantionem*. Now, his intentions in coining this expression become clearer: consciousness (as free rational being) is the sacrament of the absolute.

48 In the 1804/2 WL, the same results were achieved through certainty.

49 GA II, 7, 397.

50 Ivaldo summarizes: "The solution of the 'contradiction' can be explicated as follows: if the existential act is to be [*soll*] exterior, insofar as it is interior, there must [*muss*] be an exterior expression of the same existential act. This exterior expression includes within itself a duplicity: it contains the projection of pure being, and contains its 'vitality'; the 'exterior' and the 'interior', the act and the light, all at once. This exterior expression is the I, freedom, because it is never the pure being-there of the existential act, but it is being-there as being-there, reflexivity. Freedom makes possible an internal exteriority, an internal that exteriorizes itself without losing itself. The I is the 'site' in which the 'existing' exists as such, and such that the interior and exterior do not exclude the other reciprocally, but rather reveal themselves as two sides of the same act: the 'existential act of the existential act.' We should observe finally that: 1. freedom is nothing in itself, as absolute, but is a 'modification of the light,' the expression of the existence of the absolute; 2. nonetheless, we have seen that if the light should [*soll*] appear, it must [*muss*] contain [*esservi*] freedom: freedom belongs to the structure of original manifestation, as the position of an absolute *Soll*." DM 51.

51 GA II, 7, 398.
52 Ibid., 399.
53 Ibid., 400.
54 Fichte had tried to express this idea in 1804 through the *we*, a plurality meant to encompass the I–world poles of experience. The change in vocabulary in the *Principles* portrays the role of consciousness as true manifestation of the absolute. Writes Ivaldo, "Now, 'I = world' – not in the subjectivistic sense that the world would be a product of the I, but in the sense that an ordered context of experience appears only 'in' the figure that is the I (beginning, as we will see, from an absolute *Soll*)." DM 52.
55 1804/2 14, 110 (GA II, 8, 216–17).
56 GA, II, 7, 403.
57 Ivaldo offers a concise conclusion to lectures two to seven: "Through the clarification of the 'existence' of the absolute (= doctrine of God) as 'existential act,' insofar as light and freedom in the light, we are able to describe the essence of the I as image, projection of the light and figurative power of the substantial light in effectuations, forms." DM 50.
58 Cf. 1804/2 13.102–4 (GA II, 8, 192–9).
59 Writes Thomas-Fogiel, "The epitome of the change operated by the notion of reflection, the question '*how does one know that*?' [*d'où il le sait*?] is a formal notice to philosophy that it must account for the conditions of its own discourse … If the philosopher cannot establish the conditions of the validity of their own discourse, then the ensuing propositions, like those of kantianism, remain indemonstrable." Thomas-Fogiel, *Fichte*, 79. The question "*d'où il le sait*?" is the investigative correlate to the performative *tun-sagen*; both describe the same transcendental argument structure.
60 GA II, 7, 407.
61 For Ivaldo, "We have attempted to 'describe' absolute knowledge (the explicit moment [as above], the 'saying'). But absolute knowledge is not the result of our 'description.' It lies rather at its origin, and is active within it (the foundational moment, the 'acting'). We have a 'contradiction' between the 'saying' and the 'acting' … that the Doctrine of Science, insofar as transcendental, has to resolve. We must 'say' explicitly the effective action, and the effective action needs to be said, 'explained.'" DM 53.
62 Here, as per Fichte's usage, absolute knowing = knowing-of-knowing.
63 GA II, 7, 410.
64 Ibid. Pages 408–10 are particularly obscure. The account herein follows

Ivaldo's summary: "If there is freedom (and there should [*soll*] be freedom, as we will consider below) it is the 'capacity,' the 'potency' to create effects. If we abstract from this 'capacity,' and consider freedom in its projection, as absolutely 'external,' we have the projection simply 'as such,' as 'qualitatively determined,' in which the 'external' is simply coincident with the 'thing.' This 'external' point is called in the *Principien* an *actus mere et simpliciter* – neither the act of the absolute, nor the act as act (a reflective act), but simply as the position of freedom. The 'subjective' expression of this simple '[to be] as such' is 'feeling.' Feeling is the unity of a duality, a unity of projecting and projected." DM 54–5.

65 In a footnote, Ivaldo traces this conception of feeling back to the *Nova Methodo*. FTP, 177; GA IV, 3, 377–8; cf. DM 55. George di Giovanni traces it back to the contemporaneous *Second Introduction to the Wissenschaftslehre,* writing, "At issue in feeling is not simply how one spontaneously stands with respect to a sense-given material (as is the case with impulse), but how one stands with respect to one's original stand before that material. Or again, at issue is not whether one finds some sense material pleasant or unpleasant, but how one finds oneself in thus finding that material, that is, how one feels about one's otherwise purely impulsive reaction to it. One can feel good or bad about it, elated or depressed, guilty or innocent. In other words, in feeling, though this feeling still is very much part of the sense economy of the mind, and is therefore a suitable object of consciousness, a first abstraction has already been made from the given content of sensations. Feeling presupposes a norm that is not necessarily derived from the senses. In principle, therefore, it already constitutes a self-directed experience. As such, it exhibits in inchoate form the reflective properties that define reason. All this is in line with Fichte's general intention of establishing a gradation between rationality and sensibility." di Giovanni, *Freedom and Religion*, 219–20. In the *Foundations of Natural Right,* it is used to establish a gradation between rationality and sensibility. Cf. FNR 5.

66 GA II, 7, 413.

67 Cf. 1804/2 24.175 (GA II, 8, 366–7).

68 GA II, 7, 417. Note that this is an elaboration of material that was presented in lectures eight and nine. Ivaldo refers to projective and reflective poles of genetic explanation, cf. DM 55.

69 GA II, 7, 417.

70 Ibid., 418.

71 This is only implied in the text. Ivaldo alludes to it at DM 55. He may have in mind 1804/2 27.190 (GA II, 8, 396–7).

72 GA II, 7, 419.

73 Ibid., 421.

74 Ibid., 421–2.

75 GA II, 7, 422. The material in brackets is taken from the three sentences that precede this. This is one of many sentences in the *Principles* that must be reconstructed in order to be read.

76 The feeling of constraint already alluded to in the *Foundations of Natural Right* (FNR 5) is the same feeling, seen from the other side – that is, starting from intuition.

77 GA II, 7, 423.

78 Cf.1801–02 WL, GA II, 6, 150. The same image returns in Fichte's 1804 sonnet, "*Was meinem Auge diese kraft gegeben.*" SW 11, 347.

79 GA II, 7, 423.

80 Ibid., 427.

81 Lecture twelve is particularly telegraphic. Extemporaneous elaboration would have counted for much in rendering it intelligible. This is perhaps why Ivaldo avoids the *Finden* in his analysis in favour of a broader overview of the role of apperception.

82 Here we see a condensed version of the argument found in 1804/2 lecture twenty-one, where a problematic remainder arose when genesis was applied to itself and its solution in lecture twenty-three with the concept of certainty.

83 GA II, 7, 430.

84 Ibid., 431.

85 Summarizing lecture thirteen, Ivaldo writes, "The overcoming of the hiatus between absolute reflection and consciousness, as posited by reflection, is the form of absolute consciousness. Again, and now more clearly; no knowledge without consciousness, no consciousness without knowledge, by means of reflection. Reflection posits the active root of absolute consciousness in its factical being." DM 57.

86 GA II, 7, 431.

87 Ibid.

88 Indeed, Fichte already attempted a deduction of time in the 1795 *Grundriß des Eigenthümlichen der Wissenschaftslehre* (at EPW 291–306) that is perhaps

one of the most brilliant moments of his early days in Jena. On the *Grundriß*, see Green, "Fichte's Critique."

89 GA II, 7, 433.

90 These two maxims are, of course, idealism and realism. Here, Fichte is rehearsing the argument found in lectures thirteen and fourteen of 1804/2 but in the opposite direction: there, Fichte's concern was to achieve an internally coherent maxim, that of WL, an "upward" movement. Here, his concern is establishing a genetic principle for the appearance of the absolute in the world, a "downward" movement of application.

91 As was seen in the WL, *Evidenz* can be approached either as the absolute or as immediately compelling experience.

92 GA II, 7, 435.

93 Throughout this discourse, Fichte uses *Intelligenz* to stress that he has adopted the point of view of immanence, bracketing out or negating the projective side of knowing.

94 GA II, 7, 439.

95 Ibid., 440.

96 Ibid.

97 Fichte would have saved himself and his readers much trouble had he simply described this as a problematic *Soll from* [*von*] a categorical *Soll* and then developed the principle of the *from*, making it robust enough to encompass what in the WL required absolute law and *principiieren* to communicate. Fichte might object that his concern in the WL was establishing certainty from a categorical *Soll*, while here, the opposite, the presupposition of a principle for the contingent, is what is at hand. One might have pressed him on this, too, conjecturing that the *Washeit* that established certainty, in conjunction with the *from*, could have filled this role and maintained a consistent set of terms. But as we have seen, Fichte's pedagogy is linguistically polyvalent. In the *Principles*, the price for this is the lack of development of certain key terms.

98 GA II, 7, 443. *Trieb* or *drive* is one of the central ideas of the 1798 *System of Ethics*, where it stands for the practical self-determination of the subject. Fichte explains this using the example of a spring: "Imagine a compressed steel spring. Within this spring there is undoubtedly a striving to push back against what presses upon it; hence this striving within the spring is directed outward. This would be an image of actual willing, as the state of

a rational being; but this is not what we are talking about here. Now what is the proximate ground (not the condition) of this striving, understood as an actually determined manifestation of the steel spring? The proximate ground in question is undoubtedly an inner effect [*Wirkung*] of the spring upon itself, a self-determination." SE 32. Later, he concludes, "[*Drive*] is what one might call the ground of the elasticity in the steel spring that served as our example; for a drive operates necessarily and in a materially determined manner, so long as the conditions of its efficacy are present[.]" SE 34. As Günter Zöller points out (with specific reference to the 1812 WL), the concept of *Trieb* will be retrieved in the later philosophy. With the 1812 WL in mind, Günter Zöller describes the reintegration of the concept of *Trieb*. Zöller, "A Philosophy of Freedom," 298.

99 GA, II, 7, 444–5.

100 This is what Fichte means when he refers to it as "the principle for the as, as, as" [*sic*]. Ibid., 445.

101 Ibid., 446.

102 Ivaldo summarizes, "We can distinguish two dimensions of the I and, correlatively, two valences of the [*Soll*]. The first dimension is of the I as a principle of representation, which comes to consciousness from impulse in the form of a [*Soll*] as a pure tendency. The second dimension is that of the I, as the principle of the position of free intentions, which comes to consciousness of 'duty as duty' as a categorical imperative. The first dimension is placed within the second, in the sense that the position of the impulse (of the I as a tendency, and as a principle of representation) is made possible, as a principle, by the position of the categorical [*Soll*] in the I." DM 60.

103 GA II, 449. This use of *Zweckbegriff* or "concept of an end" harkens back to the 1798 *System of Ethics*. There, it is related to the uniting of subject and object in efficacious act [*Wirkung*], practical philosophy's rendition of what theoretical philosophy performed in the act of cognition. Writes Fichte, "In this case, the two [i.e., subject and object] are viewed as harmonizing in such a way that what is objective is supposed to follow from what is subjective; a being is supposed to result from my concept (the concept of an end [*Zweckbegriff*]). Practical philosophy has to investigate the origin of the assumption of such a harmony." SE 8

104 GA II, 7, 450.

105 Ibid., 452.

106 For a critical examination of this issue, see one of Reinhard Lauth's most important essays, "Le Problème de l'interpersonnalité."

107 "In this connection, the doctrine of right functions as the articulation between nature and moral-being; in fact, nature is not immediately apt as the context for morality; this is particularly visible in the case of the relation between human beings (as both free beings and natural forces), who can prevent each other, reciprocally, from the actualization of moral ends. Right (and the doctrine of right) – as a determination and limitation of the reciprocal action of finite rational beings – functions as an indispensable mediation by which to organize nature so that it could be a context [*ambiente*] for morality." DM 61. Cf. GA II, 7, 450.

108 GA II, 7, 453.

109 Ibid., 454.

110 Ibid., 455.

111 Ibid., 456. Ivaldo interprets: "[The] divine scheme is absolute thought; the scheme of nothing is time, as a tendency to nothing held in check by the divine – and therefore 'empty' – scheme, a pure temporality absolutely receptive to its fulfillment." DM 62.

112 GA II, 7, 461.

113 Ivaldo interprets Fichte's point thus: "[The] absolute manifests itself, and it manifests itself as 'pure thought,' divine thought, the divine idea. Pure thought is a unity; the expression of unity, the manifestation of the idea in reflection, the point of genesis of categorical disjunctions (being, not being, becoming are articulation of a single pure thought – of light – in the 'insofar as' of reflection)." DM 62.

114 I have reconstructed this based on the end of lecture nineteen, from p. 461 at "Nun zufördest den Gedanken …" until the end of the lecture on the next page. All the moments reoccur in lecture twenty, which is largely a review.

115 GA II, 7, 469.

116 Ibid., 470.

117 Ibid., 472.

118 Hence the three forms of time distinguished in the text: absolute time, the particularization time with the I (second time), and the repetition of particular moments, which ultimately constitute absolute time (third time).

119 Fichte alludes to this at the bottom of GA II, 7, 467, where Spinoza is named, this time derogatively.

120 GA II, 7, 472–3.

121 Ibid., 476.

122 Ibid., 477.

123 Ibid., 480.

124 Hence the "second" and not the "third" time.

125 Fichte pre-emptively answers a sceptical objection: we already know that we all inhabit the same world, since intuition proceeds from consciousness, which is grounded in the *Soll*. The *Soll* is necessarily the same for all of us, and to say otherwise would be to fall into self-contradiction. We all inhabit the same world, which is for *us*. Cf. GA II, 7, 481.

126 One would normally translate the word as *purity*, as in the purity of metals. This is a continuation of the alchemical metaphor seen in 1804/2 lectures four and fourteen, where this purity of the absolute generates a precipitate, a *todter Absatz* that is the neutralized remainder left over after purity has been achieved. Here, the emphasis shifts: *prima facie*, there is no place for subjective freedom in a world governed by the necessity generated by the absolute.

127 Ivaldo frames the question in this way: "A problem arises; what is the relationship between the system of the I in time (as manifold) and the single law of reason, between the multiplicity of actions in the world and the absolute 'must'? In other words; which is the sense of the unity of the world, with regard to the absolute?" DM 63–4.

128 GA II, 7, 484.

129 Ibid.

130 Notice the shift in perspective: in the WL, reason is free *in spite of* facticity; here, consciousness is free *in spite of* normativity. Both perspectives integrate the contingency of existence into the norm-governed life of reason. Cf. WL 1804/2 lecture seventeen.

131 Ivaldo summarizes this concluding point: "Consciousness 'must' raise itself from projection to absolute reflection (as philosophy, too, must do); consciousness (in its manifoldness) 'must' become the unity-of-reason. This, therefore, is the end of factical existence, an end that is not a necessary destiny, but instead a law of freedom." DM 64.

CHAPTER FIVE

1 The University of Kharkiv (modern German: *Charkiw*), located in modern-day eastern Ukraine, was founded in 1804 in what was at the time the Russian Empire. The city was a hub for Russian romanticism, and at the

beginning of the nineteenth century was remarkably cosmopolitan with a significant German-speaking population. University authorities had asked for Goethe's help in recruiting German intellectuals. Seen from Weimar, Charkow's request would have been an excellent opportunity to lure unruly academics into voluntary exile.

2 The 1805 WL, which Fichte called the "The fourth presentation of the Wissenschaftslehre," is the culmination of the series begun with 1804/1. Fichte's notes, not published until 1984, are the most intensely speculative – and also the most telegraphic – of this series. In all the renditions of the WL from 1801–05, knowledge is the appearance of the absolute. And while it stands to reason that knowledge is always manifested in activity, the link between particular subjectivity and appearance is only implied up to 1804 and, as we have seen, is worked out arduously in companion texts. In 1805, Fichte attempts to make an explicit link between his theories of subjectivity and appearance, first by means of a concept of absolute reflection and second by the use of *Existenz* as term of art, describing a standing-out distinct from the more abstract *Seyn*. For further analysis, see Zöller, "Einsicht im Glauben"; Janke, *Die dreifache Vollendung*, 339–48; and Thomas-Fogiel, *Présentation*, in *La Doctrine de la Science de 1805*.

3 Medicus provides an account of Fichte's time in Erlangen in *Fichtes Leben*, 213–15.

4 This is Manfred Kühn's account in *Ein deutscher Philosoph*, 477–87.

5 I.H. Fichte, *Johann Gottlieb Fichtes Leben*, 410.

6 This was a political rather than academic decision. Fichte's old enemy Nicolaï – who had also thwarted Kant's election to the Berlin Academy in favour of Moses Mendelssohn – waged a campaign against him. Fichte's candidacy lost by two votes. See Léon, *Fichte et son temps*, II.466.

7 Established convention translates this title as I have above. Fichte's German is much more nuanced, with "*Anweisung*" standing for something that combines "instruction" and "initiation."

8 FiG III, 411–12.

9 Jn. 1:10.

10 "These [lectures] amount to the result of my self-cultivation [*Selbstbildung*], continued assiduously for the past six or seven years, with more leisure and in mature age, pursuing the philosophical insight I had thirteen years ago and which may have changed something in me (or so I hope), has not itself changed in any way since then." GA I, 9, 47.

11 The difference between WL and religion is tenuous and remains aporetic. Here, the difficulties of distinguishing the WL and the derivative sciences on the one hand and the popular lectures on the other comes to a head. Is *Wissenschaftslehre* already religion? Fichte is not clear on the matter. He is clear that religion is a separate science and the text of the *Blessed Life* a theory of subjective feeling, of "standpoints" that cultivate the subject's interior life. This is not WL. But the *Blessed Life* is not a "scientific" text in the same sense as the WL or Jena *Ethics* or *Doctrine or Right*. Yet precisely because of its relationship to felt subjectivity, it would seem inappropriate to elaborate religion scientifically; indeed, given that it has the same object as WL (and is driven forward by the same mechanism: attention), to do so would be simply to offer an iteration of the WL – and indeed, later articulations of the WL will explicitly speak of "God" as "absolute" (something 1804/2 allows but does not pursue). Moreover, to call religion a "science" is an anomaly, even in Fichte's day. What sort of science could religion be, if not a speculative exploration of the absolute? Yet the *Blessed Life* is not a popular presentation of the WL – indeed, as Alexis Philonenko points out, its use of the term "being" and its epistemology are incommensurate with the WL (Philonenko, "Vie et spéculation," 244–5). The problem, then, remains intractable.

12 Cf. Lauth, "Fichtes Gesamtidee der Philosophie," 254–5.

13 Cf. GA I, 8, 111–17. This seventh lecture describes the total self-sacrifice that the "holiness of the learned profession [*Heiligkeit des Gelehrten-Berufs*]" (113) requires.

14 In his extensive commentary on the *Anweisung*, Frédéric Seyler considers lectures seven to eleven to be a "Theorie lebendiger Besitz," an instruction on taking possession of virtue. Seyler, *Fichtes » Anweisung zum Seligen Leben «*.

15 GA I, 9, 56.

16 This "mixture" is the popular expression of the genetic integration of the factical *qua* factical; this means that in the language of the WL, "truth" would be the categorical *Soll* and appearances in the world the problematic *Soll* that is *from* the categorical.

17 GA I, 9, 57.

18 In the WL Nova Methodo, Fichte uses the term standpoint as a heuristic one, beginning with a division between the standpoints of ordinary thought and philosophy. Cf. FTP § 13, 19. For more on its use in this context, see Breazeale, "The 'Standpoint of Life.'"

19 GA I, 9, 58. For Alexis Philonenko, Fichte's goal here is not to prove but rather to cultivate understanding. This *Verstanden* is akin to Pascal's "feeling of truth [*sentiment du vrai*]." Philonenko, "Vie et spéculation," 245.

20 GA I, 9, 62.

21 Fichte here reiterates an idea formulated in the *Characteristics*. There, Fichte argued that since "humanity" requires an a priori concept, sacrificing oneself for the betterment of humanity is essentially living a life dedicated to ideas. Cf. GA I, 8, 221.

22 GA I, 9, 63.

23 This is the "*zurückführen*" of the 1804/2 WL.

24 Heideggerian jargon renders this expression as "comportment." The use of *sich verhalten* in Fichte must be distinguished from that of Heidegger, whose phenomenological goals are radically different. For Robert Formisano, Fichte's *Anweisung* is a major source for Michel Henry's response to Heidegger. See Formisano, "Michel Henry et le problème de l'ontologie."

25 In the seventh lecture, Fichte calls this a gathering and contraction of the self [*Erfassen und Kontrahieren*]. Cf. GA I, 9, 130. This is in keeping with the geometrical imagery that remained dear to Fichte throughout his career. Cf. Wood, *Mathesis of the Mind*.

26 GA I, 9, 69.

27 Cf. Ibid., 71–3.

28 For a strong refutation of mysticism in Fichte, see Zanelotti, "How Not to Read Fichte's *Anweisung zum Seligen Leben*."

29 GA I, 9, 80.

30 These remarks, which occupy much of the *Blessed Life*'s third lecture, echo the presentations on intellectual intuition found in the second lecture of the *Principles* and the *Nova Methodo* – indeed, the same thought experiment with the wall is also found at FTP 110–11. In the 1804/2 WL, this content is expressed according to the division between insight and seeing at 3.34–5 (GA II, 8, 36–41).

31 The question of inner sense and its relationship to outer sense is a major problem in Kant, taken up by Fichte. On this point, see Nabert, "L'Expérience interne chez Kant"; and Green, *The Aporia of Inner Sense*, esp. pp. 223–89. Green also provides an impressive bibliography on the subject.

32 GA I, 9, 82.

33 Here (ibid., 86), Fichte offers as justification a classic argument from infinite regress. This differs somewhat from the argument of the genetic deduction

found in the WL. One can only presume that Fichte hopes to eventually elevate his audience to realizing the infinite regress of factical deductions of which Kant is accused in 1804/2 lectures one to three.

34 Fichte dispenses with rigorous philosophical explanation in these popular lectures. The rigorous proof for *Daseyn's* relation to *Seyn* is made in the 1804/2 WL through the *Bild/Abbilden* first established in the idealist position and then finalized through the concept of certainty in lectures twenty-two to twenty-five.

35 GA I, 9, 86–7.

36 "Eine tätigkeit, der ein Auge eingesetzt ist." We have already seen the importance of such phrases in both letters to Schelling (May 1801) and Fichte's 1801–02 WL, as well as Dieter Henrich's analysis (*infra*, chapters 1 and 2, esp. notes 123, 124, and 229). Now, the activity that is seeing, and life itself, are being brought into dialogue. Fichte will describe their relationship in two striking phrases from his diary in 1808: "Sehendes Leben: Leben dem Auge eingesetzt ist [*A seeing life: life into which an eye is inserted*]" and "im Sehen aufgehendes Leben [*a life that arises in {or: from} sight*]." GA II, 11, 185–6. For analysis, see Zöller, "« Life into Which an Eye Is Inserted »"; and Gloy, "Selbstbewusstsein als Prinzip des neuzeitlichen Selbstverständnisses."

37 GA I, 9, 92.

38 It is easy to misconstrue the God-world relationship in this paragraph (ibid., 97). There are indeed objects that are not consciousness, and the world is not merely some emanation of God, still less the product of consciousness. As was made clear in the *Principles*, the point is that *if* there is a world, *then* it is for free consciousness. Cf. GA II, 7, 403

39 GA I, 9, 96.

40 Cf. 1804/2 22.163 (GA II, 8, 336–9). There, this shift in attitude is embodied the concept of *Soll als Soll*.

41 GA I, 9, 134.

42 Cf. 1804/2 4.40 (GA II, 8, 52–3).

43 GA I, 9, 105.

44 Ibid., 106.

45 Ibid., 107.

46 Ibid., 108.

47 Cf. SE 52.

48 The English translation uses the term "higher morality." Fichte sometimes

uses the term to qualify the *Sittlichkeit*, cf. GA I, 9, 110: "*durch höherer Moralität*."

49 GA I, 9, 109.

50 Philonenko suggests that the latter's idea of *Erziehung* is crucial to the elaboration of the *Sittlichkeit*. Philonenko, "Vie et spécualtion," 245.

51 GA I, 9, 156.

52 Ibid., 110.

53 Ibid., 111–12. This is hardly as heterodox as its rhetorical presentation makes it seem – the first two commandments, love of God and love of neighbor, form a unity and are really only one commandment. Cf. Mk. 12:28–34.

54 GA I, 9, 112.

55 Ibid., 53.

56 Ibid., 115.

57 Ibid., 116. Cf. GA I, 8, 269–70.

58 To that end, Fichte will cite Jn 5:19–26; Jn 10:28–3; the encounter with Nicodemus at Jn 3:1–22; the bread of life discourse at Jn 6:53–6; Jn 5:24–5; and the encounter with Mary and Martha at Jn 8:51.

59 This is a point that Fichte makes consistently throughout his career. In *On the Basis of Our Belief in a Divine Governance of the World* (1798), Fichte writes, "The world is, simply because it is; and it is the way it is, simply because that is the way it is. Within this standpoint, one begins with an absolute being, and this absolute being is precisely the world: these two concepts are identical. The world becomes a self-grounding whole, complete within itself; and, precisely for this reason, it becomes an organized and organizing whole which possesses within itself and within its own immanent laws the ground of all the phenomena that occur within it. Insofar as it is our task to provide an actual explanation of *the world and its forms*, and thus to the extent that we find ourselves within the realm of pure – note that I said *pure* – natural science, it is complete nonsense to offer an explanation of the world and of its forms in terms of the goals or purposes of any intellect. Furthermore, to assert that an intellect is the creator of the sensible world provides us with no assistance whatsoever and does not advance our inquiries in the least, for such an assertion possesses not the least intelligibility and furnishes us with nothing but a few empty words rather than with an answer to a question that should never have been raised in the first place. The determinations of an intellect are undoubtedly concepts. But the first intelligible word still remains to be

uttered in explanation of how such concepts either manage to transform themselves into matter (which is what must occur within the monstrous system of creation from nothing) or else are able to modify whatever matter is already present (which is what must occur within the scarcely more rational system that posits the mere operation of concepts upon an independent, eternal matter)." IWL 144–5.

60 GA I, 9, 119–20.

61 Ibid., 120.

62 As found in the *Principles*, cf. GA II, 7, 135.

63 At GA I, 9, 188–93.

64 Ibid., 191.

65 Cf. GA I, 8, 275.

66 GA I, 8, 272–3.

67 While such a conception invites comparison with Kant, there would also seem to be a strong influence from Schiller. In Über die ästhetische Erziehung des Menschen (1794), being and becoming are reconciled in time via a *Spieltrieb*, or drive for play. For Schiller, the *Spieltrieb*, like all forms of drive, has an object. In this case it is *lebende Gestalt*, living form. Concretely, the contemplation of something beautiful inspires free action, and while human nature is incomplete beforehand, the activity that such contemplation inspires is what best characterizes humanity. Cf. SWN 20, 353–73.

68 GA I, 9, 125. The image of transubstantiation also occurs at 1804/2 lecture twenty-three.

CONCLUSION

1 GA II, 10, 71, quoted in Kühn, *Ein deutscher Philosoph*, 487.

2 Christoph Wilhelm Hufeland (1762–1836) was a medical doctor, public intellectual, and proponent of vitalism. In addition to being professor of medicine and director of Berlin's Charité hospital, he was royal physician, much trusted by Queen Luise, Wilhelm III's wife. It was the Queen, whose health was fragile, who insisted that Hufeland follow the government to Königsberg.

3 Kühn, *Ein deutscher Philosoph*, 489–90. Lauth and Gliwitzky describe the situation in their preface to the text in GA II, 10, 105–10.

4 See especially the (presumed) ninth lecture, ibid., 133–7.

5 Lecture one, ibid., 115.

6 Ibid., 201. See also ibid., 172.

7 This is Gaetano Rametta's conclusion about the goal of the speculative structures of the 1807 WL. See Rametta, "The Speculative Structures," 490.

8 I follow Gueroult's critique at ES 96–7. He reiterates it again at ES 105 as "the fluidity [*flottement*] between being and freedom."

9 I borrow this term from Ives Radrizzani, who coins it in Radrizzani, "The Ambivalence of Language," 367. He uses to it to refer to something slightly different – the manner in which Fichte adopted the rhetoric of his opponents as a means of outwitting them, as was done in the *Vocation of Man* in regard to Jacobi's *Letter to Fichte* (1799). For Jean Paul, the *Vocation* was destructive cipher [*vernichtende Chiffre*]: for the exoteric reader, the text means the contrary to those who actually know the WL. Cf. FiG 2, 303.

10 A well-known passage from the Aenesidemus Review expresses this in purely transcendental terms, putting emphasis on the inner circumscribing the outer: "This passage from the external to the internal or vice versa is precisely what is in question. It is precisely the task of the Critical philosophy to show that no such passage is required, that everything that occurs in our mind can be completely explained and comprehended on the basis of the mind itself. The Critical philosophy does not even dream of trying to answer a question that it considers to be contradictory to reason. This philosophy points out to us that circle from which we cannot escape. Within this circle, on the other hand, it furnishes us with the greatest coherence in all our knowledge." EPW 69.

11 GA II, 13, 317.

12 Xavier Tilliette, "La Théorie de l'image chez Fichte," 542–3.

13 1804/2 5.48 (GA II, 8, 68–9).

14 1804/2 6.60 (GA II, 8, 94–5).

15 1804/2 6.60 (GA II, 8, 96–7).

BIBLIOGRAPHY

FICHTE IN GERMAN

Fichte, Immanuel Hermann. *Johann Gottlieb Fichtes Leben und litterarischer Briefwechsel.* 2 vols. Sulzbach: Seidelsche Buchhandlung, 1830–31. Second edition published in Leipzig: Brockhaus, 1862.

Fichte, Johann Gottlieb. *Briefwechsel: Kritische Gesamtausgabe.* Edited by Hans Schulz. 2 vols. Second edition. Leipzig: Haessel, 1930.

– *Fichtes Werke.* Edited by I.H. Fichte. 11 vols. Berlin: de Gruyter, 1971.

– *Die Grundzüge des gegenwärtigen Zeitalters. Dargestellt von Johann Gottlieb Fichte, in Vorlesungen, gehalten zu Berlin, im Jahre 1804–5.* Berlin: Im Verlage der Realschulbuchhandlung (Reimer), 1806.

– *J.G. Fichte-Gesamtausgabe der Bayerischen Akademie der Wissenschaften.* Edited by Erich Fuchs, Reinhard Lauth, and Hans Gliwitzky. Stuttgart and Bad Cannstatt: Frommann-Holzboog, 1964–.

– *J.G. Fichte im Gespräch. Berichte der Zeitgenossen.* Edited by Erich Fuchs, in cooperation with Reinhard Lauth and Walter Schieche. 8 vols. Stuttgart and Bad Cannstatt: Frommann-Holzboog, 1978–2012.

– *Johann Gottlieb Fichtes nachgelassene Werke.* Edited by I.H. Fichte. 3 vols. Bonn: Adolphus-Marcus, 1834–35.

– *Johann Gottlieb Fichtes sämmtliche Werke.* Edited by I.H. Fichte. 8 vols. Berlin: Viet and Co., 1845–46.

– *Nachgelassene Schriften.* Vol. 2: *Schriften aus den Jahren 1790–1800.* Edited by Hans Jacob. Berlin: Junker und Dünnhaupt, 1937.

– *Die Principien der Gottes- Sitten- und Rechtslehre: Februar und März 1805.* Edited by Reinhard Lauth. Hamburg: Felix Meiner Verlag, 1986.

– *Werke. Auswahl in sechs Bänden.* Edited by Fritz Medicus. Leipzig: Felix Meiner Verlag, 1908–12.

– *Die Wissenschaftslehre Nova Methodo.* Edited by Erich Fuchs. Hamburg: Felix Meiner Verlag, 1982.

Fichte, Johann Gottlieb, et al. *Die Schriften zu J. G. Fichte's Atheismus-Streit, 1798–1800*. Edited by Hans Lindau. Munich: Georg Müller, 1913.

FICHTE IN TRANSLATION

Fichte, J.G., and Schelling, F.W.J. *The Philosophical Rupture between Fichte and Schelling: Selected Texts and Correspondence (1800–1802)*. Edited and translated by Michael G. Vater and David W. Wood. Albany: SUNY, 2012.

Fichte, Johann Gottlieb. *Le Caractère de l'époque actuelle*. Translated and edited by Ives Radrizzani. Paris: Vrin, 1990.

– *Contribution to the Correction of the Public's Judgments on the French Revolution*. Translated and edited by Jeffrey Church and Anna Maria Schön. Albany: SUNY, 2021.

– *Doctrine de la science 1801–1802 et textes annexes*. 2 vols. Edited, translated, and with commentary by Alexis Philonenko. Paris: Vrin, 1987.

– *La doctrine de la science de 1805. Traduction de l'allemand, notes et présentation par Isabelle Thomas-Fogiel*. Paris: Cerf, 2006.

– *La doctrine de la science: Exposé de 1804*. Translated by Didier Julia. Paris: Aubier-Montaigne, 1984.

– *Early Philosophical Writings*. Edited and translated by Daniel Breazeale. Ithaca: Cornell University Press, 1988.

– *Foundation of the Entire Wissenschaftslehre and Related Writings (1794–95)*. Edited and translated by Daniel Breazeale. Oxford: Oxford University Press, 2021.

– *Foundations of Natural Right*. Edited by Frederick Neuhouser. Translated by Michael Baur. Cambridge: Cambridge University Press, 2000.

– *Foundations of Transcendental Philosophy (Wissenschaftslehre) Nova Methodo*. Edited and translated by Daniel Breazeale. Ithaca: Cornell University Press, 1992.

– *L'initiation à la vie bienheureuse, ou encore la doctrine de la religion*. Translated by Patrick Cerutti et al. Introduction by Alexander Schnell. Paris: Vrin, 2012.

– *Introductions to the Wissenschaftslehre and Other Writings*. Edited and translated by Daniel Breazeale. Indianapolis: Hackett, 1994.

– *The Popular Works of Johann Gottlieb Fichte*. Translated by William Smith. Edited and introduced by Daniel Breazeale. Bristol: Thoemmes Press, 1999.

– *The Science of Knowing: J.G. Fichte's 1804 Lectures on the Wissenschaftslehre*. Translated by Walter E. Wright. Albany: SUNY, 2005.
– *The Science of Knowledge with the First and Second Introductions*. Edited and translated by Peter Heath and John Lachs. Cambridge: Cambridge University Press, 1970.
Fichte, Johann Gottlieb, et al. *J.G. Fichte and the Atheism Dispute (1798–1800)*. Translated by Curtis Bowman. Commentary by Yolanda Estes. London: Ashgate, 2010.
Fichte, Johann Gottlieb, et al. *Querelle de l'athéisme, suivie de divers textes*. Introduction, translations, and notes by J.C. Goddard. Paris: Vrin, 1993.
Schelling, F.W.J., and Fichte, J.G. *Philosophie et Religion et Principes de la doctrine de Dieu, de la morale et du droit*. Translated, introduced, and annotated by Grégoire Lazare. Hildesheim: Georg Olms Verlag, 2009.

OTHER SOURCES

Apel, Karl-Otto. "Das Problem einer philosophischen Theorie der Rationalitätstypen." In *Rationalität*, edited by Herbert Schnädelbach, 15–31. Frankfurt: Philosophische Beiträge, 1984.
Aquinas, Thomas. *Summa Theologiae*. Vols. 4–12 (1888–1906) in *Opera omnia*. Leonine edition. 26 vols to date. Rome: Typographia Polyglotta, 1882–.
Aristotle. *Aristotelis Metaphysica*. Edited by Werner Jaeger. Oxford: Oxford University Press, 1957.
– *Metaphysics*. Translated by W.D. Ross. Oxford: Clarendon Press, 1908.
Asmuth, Christoph. *Das Begreifen des Unbegreiflichen. Philosophie und Religion bei Johann Gottlieb Fichte 1800–1806*. Stuttgart and Bad Cannstatt: Frommann-Holzboog, 1999.
Barbarić, Damir. "Fichtes Gedanken vom Wesen der Sprache." *Fichte-Studien* 19 (2002): 213–22.
Breazeale, Daniel. "The 'Standpoint of Life' and the 'Standpoint of Philosophy' in the Context of the Jena Wissenschaftslehre (1794–1801)." In *Transzendentalphilosophie als System: Die Auseinandersetzung zwischen 1794 und 1806*, edited by Albert Mues, 81–104. Hamburg: Felix Meiner Verlag, 1989.
– *Thinking through the Wissenschaftslehre: Themes from Fichte's Early Philosophy*. Oxford: Oxford University Press, 2013.

Drechsler, Julius. *Fichtes Lehre vom Bild*. Stuttgart: W. Kohlhammer Verlag, 1955.

di Giovanni, George. "The Early Fichte as Disciple of Jacobi." *Fichte-Studien* 14 (1998): 63–86.

– *Freedom and Religion in Kant and His Immediate Successors: The Vocation of Humankind 1774–1800*. Cambridge: Cambridge University Press, 2005.

– "From Jacobi's Philosophical Novel to Fichte's Idealism: Some Comments on the 1798–99 'Atheism Dispute.'" *Journal of the History of Philosophy* 27 (1989): 75–100.

– "'Das Logische' of Hegel's Logic, in the Context of Reinhold's and Fichte's Late Theories of Knowledge." In *Von der Logik zur Sprache: Stuttgarter Hegel-Kongress 2005*, edited by Rüdiger Bubner and Gunnar Hindrichs, 71–87. Stuttgart: Klett-Cotta, 2007.

– "The Spinozism of Fichte's Transcendental Argument in the Lecture Notes of 1804." *Fichte-Studien* 44 (2016): 49–63.

Figala, Karin, "Der alchemische Begriff des Caput Mortuum in der symbolischen Terminologie Hegels." In *Stuttgarter Hegel-Tage 1970: Internationaler Hegel-Jubiläum Kongress: Hegel 1770–1970. Gesellschaft, Wissenschaft, Philosophie*, edited by H.G. Gadamer, 141–52. Heidelberg: Bouvier Verlag Herbert Grundmann, 1974.

Finocchiaro, Maurice. "The Port-Royal Logic's Theory of Argument." *Argumentation* 11 (1997): 393–410.

Formisano, Roberto. "Michel Henry et le problème de l'ontologie, entre Heidegger et Fichte." *Laval Théologique et Philosophique* 72 (2016): 65–82.

Franks, Paul. "Freedom, *Tatsache* and *Tathandlung* in the Development of Fichte's Jena *Wissenschaftslehre*." *Archiv für Geschichte der Philosophie* 79 (1997): 310–23.

Gloy, Karen. "Selbstbewusstsein als Prinzip des neuzeitlichen Selbstverständnisses: Seine Grundstruktur und seine Schwierigkeiten." *Fichte-Studien* 1 (1990): 41–72.

Goddard, Jean-Christophe. "Réflexivité, affectivité et anéantissement de soi. De la Wissenschaftslehre de 1805 à l'Anweisung zum seligen Leben de 1806." *Fichte-Studien* 34 (2009): 221–33.

Green, Garth W. *The Aporia of Inner Sense: The Self-Knowledge of Reason and the Critique of Metaphysics in Kant*. Leiden: Brill, 2010.

– "Fichte's Critique of Kant's Doctrine of Inner Sense." *Idealistic Studies* 37 (2007): 157–78.

Gueroult, Martial. *L'évolution et la structure de la doctrine de la science chez Fichte.* 2 vols. Paris: Belles Lettres, 1930.
Hammacher, Klaus. "Comment Fichte accède à l'histoire." *Archives de Philosophie* 25 (1962): 388–440.
– "Fichte, Maimon und Jacobi: Transzendentaler Idealismus und Realismus." In *Transzendentalphilosophie als System. Die Auseinandersetzung zwischen 1794 und 1806*, edited by Albert Mues, 243–63. Hamburg: Felix Meiner Verlag, 1989.
Hegel, G.W.F. *Elements of the Philosophy of Right.* Edited by Allen Wood. Translated by H.B. Nisbet. Cambridge: Cambridge University Press, 1991.
– *The Phenomenology of Spirit.* Translated by Terry Pinkard. Cambridge: Cambridge University Press, 2018.
Henrich, Dieter. "Fichte's Original Insight." In *Contemporary German Philosophy*, vol. 1, 15–52. University Park and London: Pennsylvania State University Press, 1982.
Irrlitz, Gert. "Die Dissertation von 1770." In *Kant Handbuck: Leben und Werk*, 48–9. Stuttgart: J.B. Metzler Verlag, 2015.
Isaye, Gaston. "La justification critique par retorsion." *Revue philosophique de Louvain* 52 (1954): 204–33.
Ivaldo, Marco. "L'approche pratique et éthique de l'histoire dans la philosophie transcendantale de Fichte." *Revue de Métaphysique et de Morale* 101 (1996): 49–70.
– "The Doctrine of Manifestation in Fichte's Principien (1805)." Translated by Garth Green. *Laval Philosophique et Théologique* 72 (2016): 35–64.
– "Leben und Philosophie: Die Anweisung zum seeligen Leben als Antwort auf Jacobis Nihilismus-Vorwurf." *Fichte-Studien* 43 (2016): 172–85.
Jacobi, Friedrich Heinrich. *Briefwechsel, Nachlass, Dokumente.* Edited by Walter Jaeschke, Birgit Sandkaulen et al. 33 vols to date. Stuttgart and Bad Cannstatt: Froomann-Holzboog, 1981–.
– *The Main Philosophical Writings and the Novel Allwill.* Edited and translated by George di Giovanni. Montreal and Kingston: McGill-Queen's University Press, 1994.
Janke, Wolfgang. *Die dreifache Vollendung des Deutschen Idealismus: Schelling, Hegel und Fichtes ungeschriebene Lehre.* Amsterdam and New York: Rodopi, 2009.
– *Einleitung und Kommentar zu J.G. Fichte: Wissenschaftslehre 1804. Wahrheits- und Vernunftlehre, I.-XV. Vortrag.* Edited by Wolfgang Janke. Frankfurt: Klostermann, 1966.

– *Fichte. Sein und Reflexion – Grundlagen der kritischen Vernunft*. Berlin: de Gruyter, 1970.

Jergius, Holger. *Philosophische Sprache und analytische Sprachkritik. Bemerkungen zu Fichtes Wissenschaftslehren*. Freiburg and Munich: Karl Alber, 1975.

Julia, Didier. *Fichte 1804: La recherche de l'absolu et la phénoménologie de la conscience*. Paris: Hermann, 2015.

– *La question de l'homme et le fondement de la philosophie: réflexions sur la philosophie pratique de Kant et la philosophie spéculative de Fichte*. Paris: Aubier, 1964.

Kabitz, Willy. *Studien zur Entwicklungsgeschichte der Fichteschen Wissenschaftslehre aus der Kantischen Philosophie*. Berlin: Reuter und Reichard, 1902.

Kant, Immanuel. *Critique of Pure Reason*. Edited and translated by Paul Guyer and Allen W. Wood. Cambridge: Cambridge University Press, 1998.

– *Critique of the Power of Judgment*. Edited by Paul Guyer. Translated by Paul Guyer and Eric Matthews. Cambridge: Cambridge University Press, 2000.

– *Idea for a Universal History with a Cosmopolitan Aim*. Translated by Allen W. Wood. In *Anthropology, History, and Education*, edited by Günter Zöller, 107–20. Cambridge: Cambridge University Press, 2007.

– *Immanuel Kants gesammelte Schriften (Akademieausgabe)*. 22 vols to date. Berlin: de Gruyter, 1902–.

Kühn, Manfred. *Johann Gottlieb Fichte: Ein deutscher Philosoph*. Munich: Beck, 2014.

Lachièze-Rey, Pierre. *L'Idéalisme kantien*. Paris: Vrin, 1950.

Lambert, J. H. *Neues Organon*. 2 vols. Leipzig: Wendler, 1764.

Lauth, Reinhard. "Die Entstehung von Fichtes 'Grundlage der gesammten Wissenschaftslehre' nach den 'Eignen Meditationen über ElementarPhilosophie.'" In *Transzendentale Entwicklungslinien von Descartes bis zu Marx und Dostojewski*, 155–79. Hamburg: Felix Meiner Verlag, 1989.

– "Fichtes Gesamtidee der Philosophie." *Philosophisches Jahrbuch* 71 (1964): 253–85.

– "Fichtes Verhältnis zu Jacobi unter besonderer Berücksichtigung der Rolle Friedrich Schlegels in dieser Sache." In *Transzendentale*

Entwicklungslinien von Descartes bis zu Marx und Dostojewski, 266–96. Hamburg: Felix Meiner Verlag, 1989.
– *Hegel critique de la doctrine de la science*. Paris: Vrin, 1987.
– "Le problème de l'interpersonnalité chez Fichte" *Archives de Philosophie* 25 (1962): 325–44.
– *Die transzendentale Naturlehre Fichtes nach den Prinzipien der Wissenschaftslehre*. Hamburg: Felix Meiner Verlag, 1984.
– "Über Fichtes Lehrtätigkeit in Berlin von Mitte 1799 bis Anfang 1805 und seine Zuhörerschaft." In *Vernünftige Durchdringung der Wirklichkeit. Fichte und sein Umkreis*, 191–232. Neuried: Ars una, 1994.
– "Die zweite philosophische Auseinandersetzung zwischen Fichte und Schelling über die Naturphilosophie und die Transzendentalphilosophie und ihr Verhältnis zueinander (Herbst 1800 – Frühjahr 1801)." *Kant-Studien* 65 (1974): 397–435.
Léon, Xavier. *Fichte et son temps*. 3 vols. Paris: Colin, 1922.
Lessing, Ephraim Gotthold. *Gotthold Ephraim Lessing: Werke*. 8 vols. Darmstadt: Wissenschaftliche Buchgesellschaft, 1996.
Maimon, Salomon. *Kritische Untersuchungen über den menschlichen Geist*. Leipzig: Gerhard Fleischer, 1797.
Maréchal, Joseph. *Le Point de départ de la métaphysique, leçons sur le développement historique et théorique du problème de la connaissance*. 5 vols. Paris: Desclée de Brouwer, 1922–64.
Massolo, Arturo. *Fichte e la filosofia*. Florence: Sansoni, 1948.
McGrath, Sean. "The Tyranny of Consumer-Capitalism and the Third Age of Revelation." *Analecta Hermeneutica* 5 (2013): 1–14.
Medicus, Fritz. *Fichtes Leben*. Second edition. Leipzig: Meiner, 1922.
Müller, Matthias Müller. *Theologie im Transzensus: Die Wissenschaftslehre als Grundlagentheorie einer transzendentalen Fundamentaltheologie in Johann Gottlieb Fichtes Principien der Gottes- Sitten- und Rechtslehre von 1805*. Amsterdam: Brill-Rodopi, 2010.
Müller-Seidel, Walter. *Schiller und die Politik: "Nicht das Große, nur das Menschliche Geschehe."* Munich: C.H. Beck, 2014.
Nabert, Jean. "L'expérience interne chez Kant." *Revue de la métaphysique et de morale* 31 (1924): 205–68.
Orth, Ernst Wolfgang. "Der Terminus Phänomenologie bei Kant und Lambert und seine Verbindbarkeit mit Husserls Phänomenologiebegriff." *Archiv für Begriffsgeschichte* 26 (1982): 231–49.

Pareyson, Luigi. *Fichte: Il sistema della libertà*. Milan: Mursia, 1976.

Philonenko, Alexis. *La liberté humaine dans la philosophie de Fichte*. Paris: Vrin, 1966.

– "Vie et spéculation dans l'"Anweisung zum Seligen Leben."" *Archives de Philosophie* 55 (1992): 243–61.

Piché, Claude. "Der Phänomenologiebegriff bei Kant und Reinhold." *Archivio di Filosofia* 73 (2005): 59–72.

Radrizzani, Ives. "La Doctrine de la science et l'Aufklärung." *Revue de métaphysique et de morale* 49 (2006): 127–42.

– "La Doctrine de la Science et l'engagement historique." *Revue de Métaphyisque et de Morale* 101 (1996): 23–47.

– "Fichte's Philosophy of History." In *The Bloomsbury Handbook of Fichte*, edited by Marina F. Bykova, 277–91. New York and London: Bloomsbury Academic, 2020.

– *Vers la fondation de l'intersubjectivité chez Fichte. Des Principes à la Nova Methodo*. Paris: Vrin, 1993.

Rametta, Gaetano. "The Speculative Structures of Fichte's 1807 Wissenschaftslehre." Translated and annotated by Garth Green. *Idealistic Studies* 37 (2007): 121–42

– *Le strutture speculative della Dottrina della Scienza. Il pensiero di J.G. Fichte negli anni 1801–1807*. Genoa: Pantograf, 1995.

Redding, Paul. "The Role of Logic 'Commonly So Called' in Hegel's Science of Logic." *British Journal for the History of Philosophy* 22 (2014): 281–301.

Rousseau, Jean-Jacques. *The Discourses and Other Early Political Writings*. Edited and translated by Victor Gourevitch. Cambridge: Cambridge University Press, 1997.

– *Discours sur l'origine et les fondements de l'inégalité parmi les hommes*. Cork: Ligaran éditions, 2015.

Schelling, F.W.J. *System of Transcendental Idealism (1800)*. Translated Peter Heath. Introduction by Michael G. Vater. Charlottesville: University of Virginia Press, 1978.

– *Urfassung der Philosophie der Offenbarung*. Frankfurt: Felix Meiner Verlag, 2010.

Schiller, Friedrich. *Schillers Werke, Nationalausgabe*. Edited by Julius Petersen et al. 43 vols to date. Weimar: Hermann Böhlaus Nachfolger, 1943–.

Schlösser, Ulrich. *Das Erfassen des Einleuchtens: Fichtes Wissenschaftslehre*

von 1804 als Kritik der Annahme entzogener Voraussetzungen unseres Wissens und als Philosophie des Gewißenseins. Berlin: Philo, 2001.
Schmidt, Andreas. *Der Grund des Wissens: Fichtes Wissenschaftslehre in den Versionen von 1794/ 95, 1804/II und 1812*. Paderborn: Ferdinand Schöningh, 2004.
Schulze, Gottlob Ernst. *Aenesidemus oder über die Fundamente der von Herrn Professor Reinhold in Jena gelieferten Elementar-Philosophie: Nebst einer Verteidigung des Skeptizismus gegen die Anmassungen der Vernunft* (1792). Edited by Manfred Frank. Hamburg: Meiner Philosophische Bibliothek, 1996.
Schüz, Simon. *Transzendentale Argumente bei Hegel und Fichte: Das Problem objektiver Geltung und seine Auflösung im nachkantischen Idealismus*. Berlin: de Gruyter, 2022.
Seyler, Frédéric. *Fichtes « Anweisung zum Seligen Leben ». Ein Kommentar zur Religionslehre von 1806*. Freiburg and Munich: Karl Alber Verlag, 2014.
Siep, Ludwig. *Hegels Fichtekritik und die Wissenschaftslehre von 1804*. Freiburg and Munich: Alber, 1970.
Stolzenberg, Jürgen. *Fichtes Begriff der intellektuellen Anschauung: Die Entwicklung in den Wissenschaftslehre von 1793/94 bis 1801/02*. Stuttgart: Klett-Cotta, 1986.
Thomas-Fogiel, Isabelle. *Fichte: réflexion et argumentation*. Paris: Vrin, 2004.
Tilliette, Xavier. "Fichtes Erfindung der Wissenschaftslehre." *Fichte-Studien* 9 (1997): 1–16.
– *L'intuition intellectuelle de Kant à Hegel*. Paris: Vrin, 1995.
– "La Théorie de l'image chez Fichte." *Archives de Philosophie* 25 (1962): 541–54.
Tonelli, Giorgio. "L'origine della tavola dei giudizi e del problema della deduzione delle categorie in Kant." *Filosofia* 3 (1956): 129–38.
Traub, Hartmut. "Schellings Einfluß auf die Wissenschaftslehre 1804 Oder: 'Manche Bücher sind nur zu lang geratene Briefe.'" *Fichte-Studien* 18 (2000): 121–36.
Weissmahr, Belà. *Die Wirklichkeit des Geistes: eine philosophische Hinführung*. Stuttgart: Kohlhammer Verlag, 2006.
Widmann, Joachim. *Die Grundstruktur des transzendentalen Wissens nach Joh. Gottl. Fichtes Wissenschaftslehre 1804*. Hamburg: Felix Meiner Verlag, 1977.

Wood, David. *"Mathesis of the Mind": A Study of Fichte's* Wissenschaftslehre *and Geometry.* Fichte-Studien Supplementa 23. Amsterdam and New York: Rodopi, 2012.

Zanelotti, Kevin. "How Not to Read Fichte's *Anweisung zum Seligen Leben* (1806): Against the Mystical Reading." In *After Jena: New Essays on Fichte's Later Philosophy*, edited by Daniel Breazeale and Tom Rockmore, 131–50. Evanston: Northwestern University Press, 2008.

Zöller, Günter. "'Einsicht im Glauben': Der dunkle Grund des Wissens in der Wissenschaftslehre 1805." *Fichte-Studien* 34 (2009): 203–19.

– "'Das Element aller Gewissheit': Jacobi, Kant und Fichte über den Glauben." *Fichte-Studien* 14 (1998): 21–41.

– "'Life into Which an Eye is Inserted': Fichte on the Fusion of Vitality and Vision." *Revista di storia della filosofia* 69 (2014): 601–18.

– "A Philosophy of Freedom: Fichte's Philosophical Achievement." In *The Palgrave Handbook of German Idealism*, edited by Matthew C. Altman, 286–299. London: Palgrave MacMillan, 2014.

– "The Unpopularity of Transcendental Philosophy: Fichte's Controversy with Reinhold (1799–1801)." *PLI: The Warwick Journal of Philosophy* 10 (2000): 50–76.

INDEX